Quality Assurance in the Hospitality Industry

Stephen S. J. Hall

Quality Press
American Society for Quality Control
Milwaukee, Wisconsin

Quality Resources
A Division of The Kraus Organization Limited
White Plains, New York

Permission to reprint selections from *Effective Behavior in Organizations*, by Allan R. Cohen et al., granted by Richard D. Irwin, Inc., Homewood, Illinois.

Printed in the United States of America

94 93 92 91 90   10 9 8 7 6 5 4 3 2 1

ASQC Quality Press
310 West Wisconsin Avenue
Milwaukee, Wisconsin 53203

Quality Resources
A Division of The Kraus Organization Limited
One Water Street, White Plains, New York 10601

Library of Congress Cataloging-in-Publication Data
Hall, Stephen S. J.
    Quality assurance in the hospitality industry / Stephen S. J. Hall.
    p.   cm.
    ISBN 0-527-91653-6
    1. Hospitality industry—Quality control.   2. Quality assurance.
I. Title.
TX911.3.Q34H35   1990
847.94'068'5—dc20   90-30996
                                                                 CIP

ISBN 0-87389-093-0 (ASQC Quality Press)
ISBN 0-527-91653-6 (Quality Resources)

*This book is dedicated to my wife Marge
and to our children, Donna, Larry, Tom, and Peggy.
From "family" comes pride and from pride comes excellence.
Whether it's the home or the corporation—it works the same way.*

Contents

v

Foreword

By Doug Fontaine

Steve Hall is right when he says quality plus ethics equals excellence. Quality assurance is the most important element needed to succeed in the hospitality business. Quality has sometimes been perceived as a luxury item, but a Volkswagen or a Big Mac can also be excellent. A top-of-the-line hotel can offer quality, but so can a roadside inn.

My objective as president of the American Hotel and Motel Association in 1981 was to establish a program that we called "Quest for Quality." The program was adopted and the Association engaged Steve Hall as a resource person to help with the program's implementation.

Quality is something that most people and organizations believe they have, yet very few people can define what it is. People tend to think that the more expensive something is, the better its quality. If this were the case, it would be impossible to run a quality hotel or restaurant that charged average rates or catered to the average quest. Henry Ford proved years ago that the average American could afford a quality car. In recent year, Japanese and German manufacturers have shown that American companies were focusing too much on luxury automobiles and not enough on the economy market. French gourmet restaurants are wonderful; those who can afford them appreciate the excellent service, outstanding presentation, and exquisite food. The American hamburger, however, properly prepared and presented, can be just as pleasant a dining experience—*but the quality must be there!*

Quality is not a function of how much something costs, but rather how well the product consistently meets the expectations of those who purchase it. People always return to an establishment where the performance is consistent. People want their expectations met *every time* without surprises. If their expectations are not met and they have to argue to get what they expect, they simply do business with someone else the next time. *Quality means each person doing his or her job correctly each and every time.*

Doug Fontaine
Past President
American Hotel & Motel Association
Owner of Lafont Inn
Pascagoula, Mississippi

Foreword

By Everett M. Rogers

I first met Steve Hall back in 1965 at Michigan State University in a course that I taught on the diffusion of innovations. I still remember, 25 years later, certain applications he made of the diffusion theory to the hospitality industry (he was then an employee of Sheraton Hotels, on leave for graduate study at Michigan State). Steve started an interest on my part in hotel quality, a variable that I have often mulled over in the 40 to 50 days each year that I spend away from home. I lost contact with Steve for two decades, but his influence on my thinking continued.

So it is a special privilege today for me to read his book and to recommend it. Steve provides a very useful application of research-based thinking about the diffusion of innovations. This perspective helps us understand how an innovation (an idea perceived as new by an individual) spreads over time among the members of a system, such as (1) among employees in a hotel or (2) among hotels in the industry. For example, I have noted how the idea of an exclusive tower with extra security provisions has spread among many hotels in the past decade. Another innovation is the "frequent flyer"-type of bonus points system provided by several hotel chains. Many hotels today offer health spa facilities or exercise rooms, in keeping with the national trend toward healthy lifestyles. Less obvious, but more important, are the innovations in personnel selection, training, and management that lead to high-quality treatment of hotel guests: cleaner rooms, friendlier check-in people, and better food.

But the text is much more than just a neat application of diffusion theory to the hospitality industry. Steve integrates useful ideas from various management, cost-benefit, and other perspectives, and brings them to bear on the important pragmatic concerns of the hospitality industry. In my opinion, the text's strategic recommendations for hotelery also apply to many other organizations in the service industry, and beyond.

Here is a book written by an old pro in the hospitality industry, who draws on useful theory as well as wide experience. The result is interesting reading, relevant illustrations, and a useful framework for raising quality.

Everett M. Rogers
Los Angeles

Acknowledgments

Excellence is a way of life, a basic philosophy, an ongoing process, or, as Aristotle so aptly put it, a habit. For those who do not pursue excellence, or do so only with words, behavior modification is in order. Modifying behavior is, generally speaking, a long, slow process of learning and doing. That has been my own education in the subject—learning and doing, evaluating, revising, and doing again. Along the way there have been many teachers and advocates to whom I am indebted, beginning with the dedicated professors at the Cornell School of Hotel Administration, the Graduate Business School at Michigan State University, and the Harvard Divinity School. While at MSU, I had the honor of studying the communication of innovations (diffusion) under Dr. Everett M. Rogers, one of the foremost experts in the world. His expertise, plus his motivating teaching style, changed my life. My first official exposure to quality assurance came as QA Director for ITT-Sheraton Corporation in the late 1960s under Philip Crosby, who was then Director of Quality for ITT. Later, while serving as vice president of administration at Harvard University, it was President Derek Bok who supported and encouraged an administrative style that emphasized meaningful communications at all levels.

When I began consulting in 1980, Bob Richards, Executive Director of AH&MA, and Doug Fontaine, incoming President, saw the value of quality and initiated the "Quest for Quality" program. Ken Hine, who succeeded Bob Richards, continued the project. Pilot programs were initiated at the Boca Raton Resort & Club in Florida, the Sheraton Scottsdale Plaza Resort in Arizona, and the Ritz Carlton in Boston, which proved invaluable to me in putting into practice the concepts developed over the years. To Dean Robert Beck, who initiated the joint venture master's level hotel school in Cergy-Pon-

xi

toise, France between the Cornell School of Hotel Administration and ESSEC, a leading French business school, I am indebted because it was there that I began formally teaching quality assurance in 1984. Paul Beals and Gerard Guibilato, subsequent directors of the school, continued the emphasis on quality and added the study of ethics as well. In 1988, I had the opportunity to introduce both subjects to the International Hotel School at Glion, Switzerland and I am indebted to Bernard Gehri, President, for that opportunity. To Ronnie Hannaman, President of the Pennsylvania Travel Council, I owe the debt of having introduced me to Woodloch Pines, where I discovered the best example of excellence in action in more than 30 years of hospitality experience.

Finally, as the book came to realization, there was Barbara Talcott, Kanchan Pandit, and Shari Wasserman, who performed the word processing, and last but not least, my wife Marjorie and son Larry, an executive with ITT-Sheraton Corporation, who proofread the text and were most objective and helpful in their comments. There are many, many others who, in ways less obvious, made this book possible and to all who helped, my sincere appreciation.

Introduction

Hoteliers, perhaps more than others in the business world, like "magic buttons." Any product or process that seems to represent an easy solution to a problem attracts their attention. It probably stems from the fact that few businesses can compare with the hospitality industry for diversity, difficulty, frequency, and unpredictability of problems. It takes a special type of person to succeed in hospitality management and is therefore not at all surprising to discover that most managers develop a fondness, perhaps more of a hope, for an occasional "easy" solution. Quality assurance is a bit of a paradox. Quality assurance, in distilled form, is just simple basic management, but basic management, done well, is not really simple! Quality assurance is more than doing many small things consistently well; it is creating the behavior modification at all levels of the organization to motivate everyone to do a myriad of simple things consistently well.

The common approach of books dealing with quality assurance has seemed to me to be a somewhat traditional three-step, seven-step, five-step, etc., "do-it-yourself" approach. The attempt is to assure quality "by the numbers." Such a philosophy simply cannot work in service industries, especially in hospitality. The "numbers" approach assumes that for every standard stimulus there is a conditional response; that is, for every problem there is a finite solution. But the problems are too many, too complex, and too varied in form, and they don't always lend themselves to standard responses. It is somewhat like a chess game. The master who engages in chess totally committed to one tactic or strategy will be easy prey for the opponent who has the knowledge and ability to adjust his or her play based on what is developing on the board.

This book is not meant to be a "list" book, although, by necessity, there are some lists. It is not meant either to present the one right, unequivocally correct solution, for I do not believe that exists. Rather, this book is intended to discuss quality in such a way as to cause the reader to think about the problem and the process, and to formulate his or her own approach using the thinking contained herein, and the personal thinking developed during the process of interacting with the book. If discussion, debate, and even disagreement result from reading this book, my objective will have been achieved. Quality, or better yet, excellence, is something we should be thinking about and wrestling with constantly in our management process. We have talked about quality/excellence far too long, without great results. It's time now to make it happen!

1

In the Beginning

Introduction

Myth #1: QUALITY ASSURANCE CAN ONLY BE DONE EFFECTIVELY BY PROPERTIES WITH A LARGE STAFF AND A TRAINING DEPARTMENT.

I first heard of Woodloch Pines when I received a letter from Ronni Hannaman, president of the Pennsylvania Travel Council. "I've read all about Quality Assurance," the letter said, "and I have visited most of the big name properties mentioned. They can't compare to Woodloch Pines for Quality."

That's a strong statement when you consider the prominent resorts of America. Woodloch Pines? I have been to every major city in America since graduating from Cornell Hotel School in 1956, and to many of America's finest hotels. Where in the world was "Woodloch Pines?" I called to find out.

"Head west into Pennsylvania on Route 84 from Port Jervis, New York. Take Exit 10 and drive 20 miles northwest on Route 6 through the northwest Pennsylvania countryside. Turn right on 434 then left on 590 and go through Greeley and Lackawaxen, cross the river and drive west along it to Rowlands. Turn right in the middle of town, go five miles up the mountain to Woodloch Pines. Watch out for the deer."

Those were the directions I got from Harry Kliesendahl's secretary when I called to schedule a time to look at the property. "Just

1

get within 30 miles of Rowlands, and ask anyone where we are," she said. She was right.

Thirty-two years ago, Harry Kliesendahl, manager of five ice cream parlors on Long Island, and Donald Kranich, gas station owner, quit their jobs, packed up their families, and, together, bought a 12-room boarding house, renamed "Woodloch Pines," for $45,000. Harry cooked and Donald fixed things and for 32 years they have earned a profit each year. The property, with 2,700 feet on spring-fed Lake Teedyuskung, now has 160 rooms, all new. It has every activity imaginable except golf, and that is under construction in the form of an 18-hole standard course on site. Recently, Woodloch Pines was rated one of the top ten family resorts in America in a special Good Housekeeping nationwide survey. The recognition caused a real problem for Harry and Donald because, over the years, they have run almost 100 percent summer and winter without one word of advertising. They were not prepared for the hundreds of calls for reservations since they had no vacancies and had never dealt with travel agents. It's easy to think that that kind of popularity must have resulted from giving their product away. Nothing is further from the truth. Many families spend $5,000 to $6,000 per week for a suite. Woodloch Pines believes in earning a profit, and a good one at that, but emphasis is on "earning." They "earn" it by providing total quality in everything they do. From Steve who met me at the front desk, to Margaret and Chris who served us lunch, to every employee I met—chefs, secretaries, groundskeepers, and lifeguards—everyone acted like part of the family. Every hotelier in the world will tell you that the guest is a very important person but, at Woodloch Pines, you believe it because you feel it. Many are third-generation guests and already have reservations for next year. All this without a sales department or a training staff. "Everyone sells and everyone trains," according to Harry, "and everyone shares in our overall success." Harry and Donald just sold Woodloch Pines to their sons, John Kliesendahl and Russ Kranich, for $17 million. Harry and Donald will be engaging in some other projects now, secure in the knowledge that quality assurance, as they lived and breathed it, provided them with a good living and a compounded return on investment of 23.7 percent for 28 years. Who says that quality costs?

This book is not about Woodloch Pines, however. It's about the kind of quality assurance Woodloch Pines represents.

DISCOVERING THE OBVIOUS

The concept of quality assurance, as it has been promoted in the 1980s to the hospitality industry, is in danger of dying and becoming one more battered buzzword on the scrap pile of magic solutions. That is because it has been presented to hoteliers as a "new" concept, barely reaching adolescence—a revelation to the food and lodging industry, a lifeline by which the industry can save itself from impending disaster. The industry is being asked to adopt the idea of quality assurance as an innovation, when in fact it dates back to at least the sixth century B.C. and probably before. Hoteliers I have interviewed at all levels, throughout the U.S. and elsewhere, resent the implication that the ways they have been managing are wrong and must be replaced by a new concept called "quality assurance." Hoteliers don't deserve such accusations, and they know it. Hoteliers need help in prioritizing their efforts and in understanding the processes for more effective implementation. Telling the hospitality industry that it has a quality problem, followed by suggestions of "magic button" solutions, has created an understandable resistance to quality assurance. The entire question must be approached on the basis that quality in American hospitality is good but, in the American way, it can be made better. The emphasis has to be placed on substance rather than on form, and quality assurance must be viewed in terms of an integrated process rather than as the implementation of one or two isolated events. An excellent example of what I am saying can be found in the concept of "quality circles"—a concept that many American hoteliers instantly embraced. There is nothing inherently wrong with the concept of the quality circle, but a quality circle is only one part of a quality assurance program. The Japanese, given credit for perfecting the quality circle concept, say it is 15 percent or less of their quality assurance process. We like to say that a quality circle is to a quality assurance program what a huddle is to a football team. Huddles are important; many good things that are meaningful parts of the success of the team happen in the huddle. However, no team ever succeeded in the game of football solely because they have an outstanding huddle. Good players, with good plays properly executed, are also required. So too is determination and commitment.

We should also comment on the process of creating standards, which many experts today identify as the absolute heart of quality assurance. My mind immediately turns to Ellsworth Milton Statler (b1863–d1928), one of history's greatest hoteliers, who must be looking on in utter disbelief as we promote the value of standards and then invest our valuable time debating whether they are more effective written in two columns, three columns, or four. Enlightened managers know that written standards, in themselves, have never produced one ounce of improved quality. Standards, and good ones at that, have been in effect throughout history. Just look on the shelf of every chain manager's office and you will find the book or books of standards. There, for the most part, they sit, dusty reference books, probably outdated, whose presence alone by some magical power is meant to change the way people behave. It hasn't happened, and it won't happen, until we change our focus from the standards themselves to those who are meant to be guided by the standards. Management must adopt a different philosophy. They must change their focus from applying standards and/or writing them, to making those standards come alive for employees at every level.

That is the objective of this book. Quality assurance is pragmatic. If it works, it's good; and if it doesn't work, it's bad. And that is not a question of doing "a few things well"; it is a question of doing "all" things well. In the beginning, hoteliers understood quality assurance, and they understand it today! The issue is not that quality assurance is missing. That is not only untrue, it is blatantly unfair. The issue is that of helping hoteliers in a rapidly changing world to build upon their existing thirst for excellence to take it to new and exciting heights.

IF IT WEREN'T FOR "THOSE EMPLOYEES"

In 1981, following a speech in Hawaii by incoming president Doug Fontaine, the American Hotel and Motel Association initiated what has become known as "Quest for Quality." As part of that program I conducted a nationwide personal interview survey of 43 hotel and motel executives from chains to independent properties. Following the personal interviews, the perceived findings were confirmed by a survey mailed to 357 properties, which resulted in a 26 percent response. The many findings resulting from these two surveys are used when relevant throughout this book, but one finding deserves prime focus immediately. Interviewees were asked to name their greatest obstacle to delivering "quality." In more than 68 percent of the responses, blame was placed directly at the feet of "those employees." We were very careful not to include responses that referred to a lack of a proper labor pool, for that is a tangible factor in some parts of the country where the growth of the industry has outdistanced the awareness of opportunity on the part of potential employees. What we concentrated on were such comments as "lack of motivation," "improper attitude," "laziness," "insufficient education," or inadequate social awareness such as "poor grooming" and "inability to fit harmoniously into the organization." The response immediately brings to mind the question of who does the interviewing and hiring? Who provides the orientation, the training, the monitoring and measuring of performance? Who does the motivating and the evaluating? Who sets the leadership example? It is significant to note that the people who are complaining about "those employees" are the same people who are totally responsible for the performance of "those employees."

We must begin our understanding of quality with the acknowledgment that if the "followers aren't following," that is, if the employees aren't performing to expectation, one answer might be that the "leaders aren't leading." It's like saying that management has done its job but without good results, therefore, the players must be wrong. Managers of professional sports teams must look upon the hospitality industry with envy. When professional teams fail to get their acts together, it is the manager who goes, not the players. It's management's job, its responsibility, to build winning teams, and if certain members of the team are weak, they must first be helped to grow stronger or, failing that, they must be reassigned or replaced.

As hospitality management, we must stop pointing the finger of failure at our employees. It is a waste of our valuable time and energy and an exercise in total futility. The tradition within the industry that management rises to power through experience is aimed at preparing hospitality leaders for the task of managing human resources. Management cannot afford to have short memories. We have, by nature, employees with a wide variety of skill levels. It is our job to mold them into a professional team in which pride is the force that empowers a quality performance. If we find the task to be more difficult than we like, then we, as hospitality leaders, must examine our own skills and techniques, for the responsibility for success is ours and ours alone.

WHO WORKS FOR WHOM?

One way to place the human relations of hospitality in proper perspective is to explore the question of who works for whom. In terms of mental versus manual labor, paycheck, parking space and position on the organizational chart, there are no grounds whatever for the question. In terms of making the organization run properly, however, with an acceptable profit and a positive growth curve, the question is very relevant.

Let us focus on the position of maid. Few positions in the hotel or motel hierarchy are treated with less respect and esteem than that of maid. They are paid minimum wages with almost no supplemental income from gratuities. In 1986, I had the occasion to teach quality assurance at the University of Nevada, Las Vegas Hotel School, and while there, I was fascinated by a short piece in the monthly activities magazine put out by the hotel associates that offered suggestions for "acceptable tipping." Ten to twenty dollars was suggested for the maitre d' of a show. As far as I could see, the maitre d's job in Las Vegas was to stand at the door and assign seats as patrons arrived—good ones to those who tip well and less desirable ones to those who don't. He then tells an assistant to take you to your table, after which the waiter does the service work. If only 50 of the 800-plus guests tip an average of $10, and if this goes on for two shows per day, six days per week, the maitre d' picks up $312,000 per year. Allowing for some sharing with key subordinates, and discounting our math by two-thirds, the maitre d' still winds up with $100,000 or so, most of it tax free. Not bad for simply assigning tables!

The same article suggested 15–20 percent as acceptable tipping for waiters and waitresses. For cocktail waitresses it suggested $1 for every two drinks. For maids, however, it suggested $1 per room per day, depending upon the property and the contract if it is a union hotel. If every guest followed this guideline, and if a maid cleaned 14 rooms per day, 6 days per week, she would pick up an extra $4,368 per year in tips! The maids in Las Vegas and elsewhere don't seem to be held in great esteem! Yet, in 1986 when I conducted the "Consumer Perception Study of the American Hotel Industry" for AH&MA and Citicorp/Diners Club, of the 75 "most mentioned errors" in hospitality, "dirty guest room" ranked sixth. Within the 75 errors, we also found "inadequate linen in the room" (14th), "tired guest room" (18th), "poor housekeeping" (23rd), "poor condition of linen" (24th), "maids entering room early or late" (27th), and several more directly relating to the function of the maid. Needless to say, the guest room is very important, and we assign the full responsibility of keeping the room up to our standards to our maids. How does the maid perform the tasks of returning a used guest room to standards?

For starters, we assign each maid a cart on which we find linen, towels, soap, amenities, matches, glasses, trash bag, soiled linen bag, cleaning supplies—everything required to clean the room. We also supply the maid with a properly functioning vacuum cleaner, training in its use, and general training in making up the room, which is done according to a checklist. We provide the maid with the communicational process for room status, which is reported back to housekeeping and/or front desk.

In addition, we provide inspectors in many properties who supervise the maids and approve their work. The inspector reports to the executive housekeeper, who operates out of a well-organized storeroom/issue room/office somewhere in the basement. To complicate matters a bit, we require our executive housekeeper to flex (adjust) the maid staff in accordance to the room count. In other words, our lower seniority maids, low paid and poorly tipped, might not even get to work at all if occupancy is low.

Looking back over the scenario, we must agree that it takes a great deal of organization, motivation, coordination, supplies, and equipment for the maid to do the room-cleaning job effectively. Who supplies all of these tools? The answer is, of course, management.

The management role or function in the room-cleaning process is to provide the maids with everything required to perform the cleaning task to our standards. If management does its job well, the odds are in favor of the process succeeding. If management does its job poorly, there is no way whatever that the process can be satisfactory. To be sure, management has the authority to demand clean rooms. But management also has the responsibility to supply all the tools and systems required to assure clean rooms. Properly provided, the maids can clean the rooms without problems. Who works for whom?

The same applies to every employee in the organization. Before the waiter or waitress attends to the needs of the dining patron, someone has to develop the theme of the room, finance it, build it, market it, design menus, manage the food preparation process, store and prepare the food, maintain health and safety standards, account for all costs, collect all monies due, and clean up the dining room after the service takes place so that it can all happen again.

The transaction between a front desk clerk and a customer results from a wide variety of physical, systemic, and management functions that have already taken place—the extent to which they have taken place properly determining the effectiveness of the front desk event. Who works for whom?

The point is not that management, in fact, "works" for the maid, the waiter or waitress, and the front desk clerk. Despite the strong case that can be made, the concept requires too much of a philosophical adjustment to go from "they work for me" to "I work for them." But we can move to a position that is more integrative and helpful to our overall quest for quality. We can agree in the final analysis that both management and labor work together for the real boss, the customer. As we begin our discussion of quality assurance for the hospitality industry it is crucial that we understand and accept the fact that it is not "those employees" who are making it difficult to deliver quality, but it is "our team"—management and labor—who are not getting the job done.

I AGREE, BUT NOT FOR ME

During the national poll of hoteliers, and in every seminar/workshop that I have conducted since, in this country and outside, I have asked participants to rate themselves in terms of their deliverance of quality, on a scale of 0 to 10, with 10 as best. I have also asked them to rate their immediate competitors and, in most cases, I have asked them to rate the overall hospitality industry in their country. The precise form of the question is: "Using your definition of quality, how would you rate your property on a scale of 0 (low) and 10 (high)?"

The results are amazingly consistent regardless of the country from which the participants are polled. Respondents rate their properties at an average of 8.24. Respondents rate their competition at an average of 6.49. When asked, they rate their country's hospitality industry at an average of 6.50.

What does the data say? It says that virtually every manager rates his or her operation 26.7 percent above both the competition and the industry. What does the data mean? It means that hotel and motel managers are not being objective with their ratings because in almost every case, particularly in seminars and workshops, the survey group includes several competitors. Manager "A" is rating his or her property above competitors "B," "C," and "D," but they are doing likewise! Everyone seems to be saying, "Quality is a problem—but not for me."

One rationale for these results could be the tendency of individuals to define "quality" in their own terms rather than in terms of a universal definition. There is merit in this conclusion, and it is discussed in detail in Chapter 2. Another rationale, however, is the tendency of hospitality industry managers to sometimes allow ego to obscure fact!

KEEP YOUR EGO IN LINE

Ego is a good thing to have in the hospitality industry given the nature of the business. Few industries have anything near the management concerns found in hospitality. That is because few industries are beset with such a wide variety of events that must all take place properly in order for the guest to be satisfied. That, coupled with the divergent perceptions and expectations of guests themselves, complicates the management process further.

We do not mean to demean in any way the role of management in manufacturing. It takes great skill to bring together hundreds of raw materials in a cost-effective manner, to utilize efficient distribution channels, and to create a strong demand for the product. Competition is ever present and technology is always trying to render "what is" as obsolete so that it can be replaced by "what's new." And, on top of all of that, if you are in a highly vulnerable business like pharmaceuticals, some misguided and mentally unbalanced individual or individuals can tamper with 25 units of your product and cause you to recall all of it at a loss of millions of dollars. Manufacturing management is in no way easy, but still, in the final analysis, the product, with all of its complexities, is introduced to the consumer in the absence of those who produced it. If it works, and keeps on working for a reasonable time, the customer is pleased and the transaction is a success.

In hospitality as well as in the service industries in general, the product, be it tangible such as the food on the table, the elevator that takes guests to their rooms, or the TV set in the corner, or intangible, such as the many varied interactions with staff people at all levels, is always consumed or utilized in the presence of those who produced it. If the food isn't good, guests don't blame the distributor, they blame the chef. If the elevator is out of order, they don't blame the manufacturer, they blame the maintenance department, and if the TV fails, they blame management, and everyone they "blame" is within shouting distance! If any of the 20 or more employees guests see and interact with does anything to upset them, they often conclude that the whole operation is bad. And when they leave the hotel or motel, what they take with them is not a hard product but rather, a memory. The food that was prepared so well was consumed at the peak of its excellence and is but a memory. The service that was provided to perfection is but a memory. To be sure, it is the pleasant memories that cause satisfied guests to tell others and to come back again on their next visit to the area but, when they return, the entire process must be performed properly again or the memories are destroyed and our repeat guests become the guests of our competition.

Jim Bennett, long a respected general manager of fine hotels in America, says it best when he cautions his staff that "we are only as good as our last 30 minutes." With the exception of the seasonal operation, in the off-season, there is no opportunity for the hotel or motel manager to relax and catch his or her breath. In a 300-room property running 75 percent occupancy, with a 2.2 night average stay, it's 37,321 check-ins and the same number of check-outs, it's 73,125 rooms to clean each year, more than 150,000 meals to serve, and at least 40,000 morning wake-up calls that must be delivered precisely on time in a friendly, warm manner. It is also the caring for the guest that becomes unexpectedly ill and protecting those who insist, despite cautions, on smoking in bed. It is safety, security, health, and hospitality day after day after day.

I remember with great empathy the tale of the manager of a 300-

room motel inn on the outskirts of Washington, D.C. His house was full of professional people attending a convention on the week preceding the presidential inauguration. The group, scheduled to check out the day before the inauguration, decided to stay over and attend the festivities. A state law forbade management to eject a duly registered guest who was neither undesirable nor in arrears with his or her payments. Almost 300 rooms of guests with confirmed reservations thus arrived only to be told that they had no rooms and would be placed elsewhere, obviously at a far greater distance from Washington. The understandably irate guests who were "walked" did not blame the state legislature, they blamed the motor inn. Because the inn was part of a chain, they blamed the chain. Any one of us in their position would, at the time, have done likewise. Such is the life of the hospitality manager!

It's no wonder that a large ego is required in hospitality management. It is a very unusual person who can keep a firm hold on all the details of hospitality. Every minute is a new series of challenges, and "ego" is one way that management keeps themselves constantly pumped up for the task. But we let it get in the way, and when we do, it sometimes refocuses what is true and undesired into what is false but acceptable in our minds.

The question of quality falls into the realm of an issue that is refocused into acceptable terms by our ego. "Quality" in its basic word form, is something that is "desirable," and any insinuation whatever to the typical hotel and motel manager that quality is lacking causes a defensive reaction in most cases. The reasoning is that an admission that quality can be "improved" is tantamount to a confession that quality is "lacking." Therefore, since our egos will not permit us to be viewed as quality-deficient, we feel that we must defend against acknowledging potential improvement. As we discussed earlier, the situation is not helped by those who would drape the quality of the American hospitality industry in black crepe paper. American hotels and motels represent very acceptable and often high levels of quality. The issue is not in defending what we are but in becoming better regardless of what we are. The quality issue in American hospitality is to constantly improve in our deliverance of quality such that the next 30 minutes is better than the last and the 30 minutes after that better yet. To be successful we must step outside our egos and view our situation realistically through glasses that are free from all distortion. Instead of using our egos to convince us we are good, we should accept the fact as given and use our egos to assure us that we have the ability to solve any problem we can properly identify and to get better in the process. By not permitting our egos to distort the identification of problems and issues, therefore, we free ourselves to put all our energy into their solutions. As we shall see later on, a proper quality assurance program will result in a myriad of opportunities that require resolution. We must keep ourselves as ready as possible for that process, and that means not letting our egos dilute our efforts.

AN OVERVIEW

As we begin our quest for excellence, it is important to restate the process through this brief overview.

1. Quality/excellence is not a destination, it is a journey. Quality is an ongoing process that is without end. The decision to begin, therefore, should not be taken lightly.
2. Quality/excellence requires that behaviors be modified at every level of the organization. Quality is a new way of looking at one's self, one's work, and one's fellow workers. Behavior is not modified by dictate but by habit, thus the process takes time.
3. Like any new process, there are three stages. First, the tools and skills required by the process must be learned and understood; second, the tools must be put into use as effectively as possible; and third, the results of the process must be constantly monitored, measured, and revised until the process is working 100 percent properly.
4. We call the three stages *meshing, diffusing,* and *evaluating.* They follow somewhat in sequence, but they overlap. The quality assurance committee will always be working to achieve greater synergy, and the acquisition of new members means that there will always be some meshing even after the main meshing phase has taken place. Further, as long as there is evaluation, resulting in change, there will be diffusion to communicate that change.
5. The initial source of energy for a quality/excellence process is the perceived commitment of the most senior executive

and his immediate senior staff. A commitment that is unreal will be perceived as unreal, and the process will fail. Over time the energy shifts to all employees at all levels.

6. The ultimate measure of excellence is word of mouth, that is, customer satisfaction. Since quality/excellence is an ongoing process, it should never be promoted as present by the organization but rather by the end user, the guest.

7. The quality assurance committee is not the "doer" of quality but the director of quality. Exactly as in the training process, the quality committee becomes skilled at a task, teaches others to perform that task, and monitors the results to maintain compliance.

8. The major obstacle to quality/excellence is the belief on the part of top management that to seek quality/excellence is to admit to a deficiency in it. The facts are that "doing better" applies to every person and organization in existence. Striving for perfection is what leadership and winning are all about. Errors do not go away because they are ignored.

9. Quality/excellence does not cost, it pays! And not in intangible benefits alone but in real, hard cash, bottom-line profits. No one argues that doing things right the first time is *always* less costly. But some people believe that the process for doing things right the first time is expensive to implement and maintain. This is totally untrue. Quality/excellence, as presented herein, will save real dollars from the first moment of implementation.

10. The key words for an effective quality/excellence process are "slow" and "steady." The concept being presented argues for small but constant measures of improvement, because they are far more apt to last than are large dramatic steps that gain people's attention but not their commitment. The game plan is slow and steady. Stick to it!

2

When It's There, You'll Know

Defining Quality

Myth #2: QUALITY IS IN THE EYE OF THE BEHOLDER AND MUCH TOO NEBULOUS TO LEND ITSELF TO A PRECISE DEFINITION.

The Gallery of the Academy in Florence, Italy, holds the statue of David, carved out of white marble by Michelangelo in 1504. The statue is 14 feet high, weighs several tons, and is to exact scale and proportion in every detail, right down to the veins in the forearms.

It is said that Michelangelo learned anatomy by studying cadavers as they awaited the spring thaw that would permit proper burial. You have to be dedicated to gain knowledge that way! Before beginning a sculpture, he sketched the finished product in intimate detail from every angle, then personally selected the marble block to make sure that it had no cracks or faults. Only then did he begin the chipping process.

As we think of Michelangelo, we may think of "David," the ceiling of the Sistine Chapel, the Pietà in St. Peter's Cathedral in Rome, or many other works. But in virtually every instance of his work, we think of perfection; we think of quality. His work shouts "quality" without a word being spoken. Why is it, then, that although we know what quality is, the term defies easy definition?

QUALITY IS WHAT WE MAKE IT

Defining quality (more specifically, quality assurance, or QA) in the manufacturing industries isn't very difficult. Most simply, it is the absence of defects; that is, the product—whether it's an automobile or a disposable razor—performs as expected over its normal life-span.

Defining QA in the service industries is more difficult, although the outcome is much the same. To be sure, manufacturing and service industries deal with both product and human interaction, but the proportions vary. When we buy a new blender, for example, there is human interaction in the selling process, but the basic transaction is between product and consumer. We expect the blender to be reasonably priced and to blend properly the first time we turn it on and thereafter. The evaluation process is not very complex; either the blender works or it doesn't. That in turn implies that if every employee in the manufacturing process does his or her job properly, the blender will keep working for a reasonable period of time.

Not so with the service industry, at least not nearly to the same extent. True, the chef must prepare the food properly, the maids must make up the guest rooms according to certain specifications, and the engineers must maintain the pumps, fans, and boilers. But, unlike the purchase of a blender, the basic transaction is between people and people, not between people and products. In many hotels it begins with the door attendant and the front desk, and is carried on by maids, caretakers, waiters and waitresses, room service personnel, maintenance people, buspersons and cashiers. In each case, the interaction is interpreted—perhaps subconsciously—against expectations.

At some point, the guest will gather all those expectations and interpretations together into a judgment of the facility. Unless something dramatic has taken place—a rude employee, for example, or a bad meal—the guest will probably be unable to explain how he or she rated the facility. One thing is certain: if the experience was a pleasant one, the guest knows it. As with Michelangelo's "David," all the individual components blend harmoniously into near-total perfection. Although all the senses are employed in the assessment, what matters is how the senses are translated into a net perception—that is, whether the experience matched expectations.

Perhaps that's why it is so difficult for hoteliers to define "quality." But define it we must, for we are responsible for all the tangibles that make up the intangible perception. Without a proper working definition of "quality," it becomes anything we say it is—and therefore nothing at all.

I'M THE GREATEST

When Cassius Clay came out of Louisville, Kentucky, in the 1960s as a young heavyweight boxer, he filled the air with shouts of "I'm the greatest," "I'm the prettiest," and "I'm the meanest." As it turned out, the man who later became Mohammed Ali was all these things, and is considered to be one of the best fighters ever to step into a ring.

As brash as it seemed for Clay to make such outlandish claims, he had a unique advantage: he could prove it. Simply put two men of equal size and experience into a ring, then wait and see which one of them is still standing when the final bell sounds. Brutal as it may seem to many, the evaluation process is very simple.

For most hoteliers, defining quality is much more complex. That point became obvious with a 1982 survey of hoteliers, in which respondents were asked for their definitions. The results (which have often been confirmed since then) are exceptionally enlightening.

Approximately one-third of the respondents, for example, defined quality in superlatives—"outstanding service," "the finest food," or "the best accommodations." It made no difference whether the response came from a budget motel or a luxury hotel; quality meant "the best."

The interesting question is: "better," "finer," and "more outstanding" than what? Who can define what "best" really means? Even if money were not a factor, there would be little agreement on "best" in terms of guest room decor, or "finest" in terms of a Caesar salad. In fact, those terms imply that all consumers have the same levels of expectations, the same standards of taste and perception. As every hotelier knows, nothing could be further from the truth.

An illustration may help prove the point: one evening in 1957 when I, as a young Marine Corps lieutenant was assigned to the Officers' Club at the El Toro Marine Air Station in California, a party of eight other officers and their wives arrived at the lounge. One of the officers, a major, took me aside and explained that his wife was in a mood to drink heavily that evening; and he asked that the bartender leave out the gin and serve his wife only plain tonic. Having little choice but to deceive, I relayed the message to the bartender.

As the evening wore on the major was amazed to see his wife drifting further and further out of touch with reality. Worse yet, the major was giving serious thought to stripping the bartender and me of rank. He was convinced that his requests had been ignored. But in fact his wife had been served nothing more than ice, tonic, and a wedge of lime over the entire evening. Her intoxication was psychological. Nevertheless, she was convinced that the hapless bartender made the *"best"* gin-and-tonic in all of California!

Superlatives are too subjective to be useful in defining "quality." We have to be more objective.

THE PRICE IS RIGHT

According to the 1982 survey, one hotelier out of five believes that "quality" is defined in terms of a price–value relationship: quality is "a good value for the money," for example, or "getting your money's worth."

But the value of money varies from one person to another. For Imelda Marcos, wife of the deposed Philippines president, "money" apparently meant 3,000 pairs of shoes; for thousands of inner-city families around the country, however, "money" means just a single pair of new shoes, or a hot meal once a day.

As for "getting one's money's worth," consider the baseball game that is called after 16 innings with no score. Although the fans received 77.7 percent more baseball than they paid for, not everyone will be happy with the results. The few fans who appreciate good pitching will feel that they got their money's worth, but those who like base hits and home runs will probably be disappointed. And while the concessioners will be delighted to have sold more beer and hot dogs than usual, the players and umpires may feel that they gave more than they were paid to give.

There is some merit in the price–value approach to defining "quality." Certainly when quality is present—that is, when a person can say they received "quality"—customers generally feel that they received value for money spent. However, saying that one has received "value for money spent" does not necessarily imply that one has received "quality."

Nothing proves this more than in much of the food service industry in Las Vegas. The main business there, of course, is gambling; food is viewed by many casinos as a way to bring gamblers in and keep them there. Basically it is an amenity, a by-product of the main business. Patrons of the buffet that advertises "all you can eat for $3.50" undoubtedly get their money's worth, but the food and service are most often anything but "quality."

NO RING IN THE BATHTUB

About one in seven hoteliers polled in the survey had unique definitions of "quality" that undoubtedly were meaningful to them, but not necessarily meaningful to others.

In one example, "quality" meant "giving the guest a respite from home life." But others defined it as "treating the guest like he or she were a guest in your own home." One respondent said simply: "Quality is no ring in the bathtub." Although we have to struggle a bit as to whether it is better to make a guest feel at home or not at home, we can relate to the bathtub ring approach, which translates as "paying attention to details." A meaningful definition, however, must be universal. We must have a definition that all can accept, albeit with varying degrees of intensity.

WE COULD DO WITH FEWER LUMPS

A surprisingly large number of respondents (one in eight) felt that "quality" in the hospitality industry is simply "service." This is not quite true. If the mashed potatoes have lumps, no amount of great service will make them go away. Further, the word "service" is far too broad a term. We need to know what kind of service we are evaluating. If our coffee shop waitress came to our table with white gloves and a tuxedo, we would most likely look for the hidden candid camera. "Service" is certainly an important part of our industry, and it must be provided in a certain way in order for "quality" to be present. Used alone, however, "service" does not define quality.

YES, BUT WAIT 'TIL NEXT TIME

Above five percent of all hoteliers polled believed that "quality" is giving the guest *more* than he or she expects; that is, giving added value to the guest's purchase. While on the surface this is an appealing solution, a closer look renders it practically worthless.

To see why, consider a guest who indeed receives more than he expected on his first visit—a special amenity, for example, or complimentary cocktails. But isn't the guest then likely to expect even more such frills on subsequent visits? And doesn't that approach imply that the frills have to become more elegant (and more expensive) every month?

It's an easy trap to fall into, but we must remember that it must be paid for either out of our profits or through increased rates; from a purely philosophical standpoint, neither is a satisfactory solution. The decision to cut profits carries with it the understanding that a short-term reduction results in a medium-to-long-range increase; it may be perfectly acceptable, for example, for a new property to attract potential long-term business by offering reduced rates for its first 30 or 60 days. But trying to buy guests by giving "more and more" is a one-way trip to insolvency.

Meanwhile, there are only two valid reasons for raising rates: to recover uncontrollable expenses and because demand has increased, thus permitting higher rates without risking a loss of business. Financing a permanent "giveaway" policy is decidedly not an acceptable rationale for increasing rates.

In Figure 2.1, the results of a survey in which hoteliers were asked their definitions of "quality" and how important they felt it was to their operation, are demonstrated in the form of a pie graph.

WHAT QUALITY IS

Thus far our search for the universal definition of quality has led us to discover what quality is not. At this point, consider the following definition of "quality":

Quality is conformance to standards.

This concept is already in wide use outside the hospitality industry, and in fact is the essence of virtually every definition of qual-

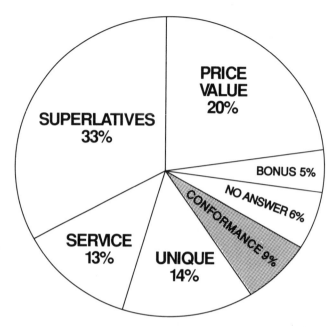

FIGURE 2.1 Definitions of quality, 1982 survey of American hoteliers.

ity. However, there are several relatively minor variations on the meaning of this term that should be noted.

For example, in 1982 the AH&MA Quality Assurance Committee defined quality as "the consistent delivery of *individual* standards." But despite the different wording, there is no appreciable difference between "conformance" and "consistent delivery"; thus, we can stay with the simpler term—conformance.

The addition of "individual" as a modifier of standards merely means that the goal of QA is not to homogenize hospitality by setting perfectly uniform standards across the industry. Because of guest expectations at various market levels, there cannot be one size of towels, one size of bars of soap, and one size of beds; in fact, individuality is what makes our industry so special. (When it comes to standards dealing with health and safety, of course, individualism must give way to the public good. Standards regarding exit stairways, emergency lighting, sanitation, and elevator safety cannot be individual standards, except when managers go beyond the basic requirements.) Thus, inclusion of the word "individual" in the AH&MA definition, though meritorious in concept, seems to make the definition of quality needlessly complicated and is quite unnecessary.

SO WHAT!

What's so important about "conformance to standards"? The answer is that virtually every business, including hospitality, functions within a preselected market segment. Each segment in turn is associated with certain customer needs and expectations. The reasonable goal of the proprietor is to keep his or her clients happy by meeting those needs and expectations as consistently as possible; in so doing, a sort of "covenant of trust" is established between the guest and the proprietor.

In the final analysis, it is this covenant that we call "quality." The agreement rests on a clear understanding by both parties—the hotel and the guest—as to what is expected. That, however, implies that the hotel's standards are observed each and every time.

Thus, "conformance to standards" is our basic definition of quality. It is simple, universal, and relevant.

WHO PACKED MY PARACHUTE?

If "quality" means conformance to standards, another question arises: what are standards? As with quality itself, the definition is a simple one:

Standards are "required levels of performance."

Many hoteliers will take exception to this definition, preferring to think of standards as "desired levels of performance"—targets that we "shoot" for even as we accept the fact that we'll probably miss them at least some of the time; in other words, standards are merely something we "would like" to attain. And herein lies a serious threat to the whole concept of QA.

The reason is that if standards become something we only desire, we implicitly accept the fact that they will often be unmet. The process then becomes little more than a wish list that reads well and sounds even better, but does little to build consensus between production and management and even less to provide consistency for the guest.

Standards that are only "desired," moreover, feed the basic belief among most hoteliers that "those employees" are the greatest obstacle to quality. All too often, management says "I know what I want, but my employees can't or won't give it to me." In reality, the manager doesn't really know what he or she wants—that is, what is to be insisted on—only what is desired; and if the manager isn't sure of what's really demanded, how can the employee be expected to know? We now have the makings of a vicious circle: as management becomes increasingly critical of production-level employees, the employees are less and less likely to measure up to expectations. That in turn gives more credence to management's "me-versus-them" policies.

We must put the concept of "desire" out of our QA vocabulary. If your son or daughter were in the Army Airborne division, you would almost surely want to know something about how parachutes are packed. Would you be satisfied to learn that the packmaster merely "desires" proper packing? Would you be comforted to learn that "when you pack so many parachutes every year, it is inevitable that some won't open properly"? Do you want to hear how difficult it is to pack parachutes given the kind of recruits you get in the Army these days? Or would you rather hear that every packer knows that a human life depends on his or her expertise, that packing standards are clear and concise, that every packer is thoroughly trained to those standards, and that the packmaster demands that it be done right every time, with no exceptions? Wouldn't you feel better if the packmaster told you that perfection in parachute packing was, is, and always will be an absolute requirement?

The basic philosophy is the same in QA. When we commit to provide certain services for our guests, we commit to do so with absolute consistency. The only way this can be done is through a well-defined and well-communicated system of standards.

THE BOTTLENECK IS ALWAYS AT THE TOP

Whenever standards aren't met, the result is an error, and as we'll see in Chapter 7, errors cost money. One of the basic problems within our industry, moreover, is the conviction that error is inevitable. There is no better example of a self-fulfilling prophecy: if we believe that errors are unavoidable, they will certainly be just that!

Errors aren't inevitable. They happen because of the following:

1. Employees have not been trained to know what standards are expected of them, or
2. They have been trained but have not been given the proper tools to meet the standards, or
3. They've been properly trained and equipped, but they just don't give a darn because no one seems to give a darn about them.

UNDERSTANDING "ZAP"

One major misconception about error must be addressed immediately. Virtually every survey I have conducted on quality/excellence around the world contains this question: "As a percentage, at what level of performance from your employees would you be happy— Housekeeping _____, Maintenance _____, Front Desk _____, Food Service _____, Morning Wake Up _____?" Although "morning wake up" generally ranks a bit higher (indicating that the respondents did give some thought to the question), the average response was between 85 and 90%. Translated, hoteliers believe that a 90% level of performance is satisfactory from "those employees." We call this percentage the "ZAP," i.e., the "Zone of Acceptable Performance." The fact is that any level of performance less than 100% *cannot be acceptable in quality assurance.* The argument that "I will never get 100% so 90% is pretty good" just won't fly. While we may never get 100%, we must make it our goal. To accept less is to guarantee getting less. Further, in the quality/excellence business 90% isn't always 90%; it could be 50%!

Let's take a somewhat general example. Let's say we have the five departments listed above, 20 guests to evaluate, and a target level of 90%. Thus, if we accept 10% error, we will have 2 of the 20 guests receiving an error in Housekeeping (20 guests × .10 error rate = 2 errors). We will also have 2 errors in maintenance, 2 in front desk, food service, and morning wake up, a total of 10 errors in all (20 guests × 10% error rate × 5 departments = 10 errors).

GUESTS	FUNCTIONS				
	HSKPG	MAINT	FRONT DESK	FOOD SERVICE	MORNING WAKE UP
1	● ●	● ●	● ●	● ●	● ●
2					
3					
4					
5					
6					
7					
8					
9					
10					
11					
12					
13					
14					
15					
16					
17					
18					
19					
20					

FIGURE 2.2   Distribution of errors: best distribution of 90% error rate (2 errors/function/20 guests)—one guest receives all errors.

With 10 errors to distribute over 20 guests, the absolute best thing we can do is to assign all 10 errors to 1 guest. That means that 95% of our guests (19) are error free and 5% (1) gets every error! That one guest will *never* return, *but* the 19 other guests have had an error-free stay, and they certainly will return. But, errors are errors—they can't be assigned—they happen indiscriminately. Thus, it is possible that 10 of our guests each have 1 error committed during their stay. If that happens, then figure 50% of our guests have had to deal with errors and 50% have not. Certainly not all of the 10 guests receiving errors will change hotel affiliations, but some will.

GUESTS	FUNCTIONS				
	HSKPG	MAINT	FRONT DESK	FOOD SERVICE	MORNING WAKE UP
1	●				
2	●				
3		●			
4		●			
5			●		
6			●		
7				●	
8				●	
9					●
10					●
11					
12					
13					
14					
15					
16					
17					
18					
19					
20					

FIGURE 2.3   Distribution of errors: worst distribution of 90% error rate—10 guests each receive one error.

However, what if 5 guests received 2 errors each, an error rate of 25%? Chances are that 2 or 3, maybe more, won't return. The point is this: if you can control the distribution of errors, make all you want! *But you cannot; therefore, the only way to succeed is to eliminate errors completely!* Figures 2.2 and 2.3 illustrate this point.

The primary message of this book is that errors can be eliminated, and profits generated, through a well-defined QA process. There are no magic buttons—just dedication, hard work, and perseverance.

But even more important, quality assurance requires a new commitment to human relations skills. Hospitality is still a people business, and it begins at the top of the hierarchy. When the human factor is set aside and too much emphasis is placed on the bottom line, the result is an erosion of quality and an increase in costs, particularly in areas like turnover. As costs become more crucial, more emphasis is placed on controlling them and even less is placed on people skills.

This is the dilemma of today's hospitality industry. We want quality, but we "can't afford it," and by not affording it, we drive costs even higher. To attain quality, to meet standards consistently and eliminate errors, managers must undergo a philosophical change. The spotlight must be turned around and focused on the production-level people and on the supervisors. They are the ones who carry our image and our success, and that is where the human relations skills must be applied.

3

Reaching Excellence

The Role of Ethics in Quality

Myth #3: WHEN YOU HAVE ACHIEVED QUALITY, YOU HAVE ASCENDED TO THE TOP OF YOUR CHOSEN PROFESSION.

When the reader has finished with this chapter, it will either be considered the most important chapter in the book . . . or the least important. It is highly unlikely that there will be much of a "middle road," for the following reasons:

1. When the subject of "ethics" is introduced to an organization or industry, the immediate reaction, in most cases, is one of defensiveness. The word itself, unfortunately, connotes a negative image to most hoteliers. They hear any discussion of ethics as saying, or implying, that they are deficient in ethical knowledge, thought, or action, and thus, the word suggests criticism. No one likes criticism.
2. Study and understanding of ethics and morality is just now becoming popular in American universities, and is only now being recognized as applying to every person in every facet of business and not just the specialized interest of the philosophy majors.

3. Many persons in business not only fail to see a connection between ethical behavior and profit, they see just the opposite—that ethical behavior produces an overhead cost and a reduction of profit.

However, without an understanding and application of ethics in hospitality, quality assurance cannot be fully understood, properly organized, or successfully implemented! It is precisely because of a lack of ethical understanding that quality assurance, since its formal introduction by AH&MA in 1981, has failed to gain effective momentum. The books being written and the programs being offered in quality assurance by and large are aimed at "correcting those employees" by establishing rigid rules and regulations aimed at control rather than by programs aimed at motivation.

ACHIEVING QUALITY IS ACHIEVING HALF A LOAF

Let us assume that a given hotel has achieved near perfect quality assurance. That is, the hotel has implemented programs and systems that eliminate error. The hotel has a fine program of standards, which are consistently met through an ongoing system of monitoring, measuring, reviewing, and redoing. Can the hotel be said to have "quality"? According to the definition that quality is conformance to standards, yes! But what if the standards are to rent rooms by the hour and to feature X-rated movies on a pay-for-view channel? What if the standards are to pour cheaper liquor than specified on the third and subsequent rounds? What if it were the standard of the hotel to do no employee orientation or training and to require no background health checks on new hires? What if it were the standard to reduce water temperatures below legally required temperatures in both dishwashing and in the laundry in order to conserve cost? Or to save the cost of testing fire alarm systems or of testing the chlorination in the swimming pool, or to stop worrying whether the fresh seafood is really delivered fresh? It becomes obvious that simply conforming to standards is not enough. It becomes crucial to develop the proper standards first, and then to conform. Standards, in turn, fall into three categories: those that deal with *market level*, those that deal with *health and safety*, and those that deal with *interpersonal relationships*.

Standards that deal with *market level* are easy to understand. There are market levels such as resort, commercial, convention, suburban, inter-city, etc., and there are market levels that are economic in nature. Budget and economy hotels, motels, and motor inns serve a most important function in our industry. The highway systems and the automobile have, throughout most of the civilized world, made travel economically feasible for virtually everyone. Providing lodging and food facilities to serve the various market levels of tourism is just good business. The Holiday Inns of the 1950s and 60s taught that valuable lesson. So, whether your market level standard involves valet parking, a door attendant, a bellhop, turn down service, or space for your guests' cars outside their rooms and a fast-food restaurant next door, your standards are a function of what market level you hope to penetrate.

Whatever the market level, however, *health and safety* standards are the same for all. Whether it's cordon bleu in your family dining room, or a chili dog in your fast-food snack bar, guests must be guaranteed complete and total standards of good sanitation. Whether you feature double king-size beds, two wash basins, and a phone in the bathroom, or a standard double, shower only, and a black and white TV, guests deserve the right to go to sleep at night with the confidence that if there should be a fire, the alarm systems will function, the employees will be well trained to protect every guest, and the fire department will be called immediately. And whether the swimming pool is Olympic size, or barely large enough to get wet and cooled down, it should be secure from the wanderings of adventurous small children who momentarily slip away, and it should receive all the chemicals required to prevent health problems. These are basic rights, afforded all guests.

Standards involving the marketplace, and health and safety, certainly require thought and good judgment. However, they are nonetheless easier to understand and accept than are standards that relate to *interpersonal relationships*. Yet, it is those standards relating to the interpersonal that cause us to move beyond our basic definition of quality and to suggest, for the first time in our industry, that perhaps our true quest is not quality alone, but quality plus ethics, and quality plus ethics equals excellence (see Figure 3.1).

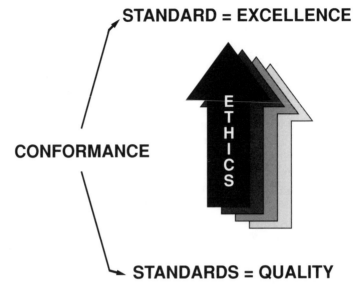

FIGURE 3.1   Role of applied ethics in quality excellence.

QUALITY PLUS ETHICS EQUALS EXCELLENCE

Although we often talk of ethics and morality, it is hard to differentiate the two. However, for our purposes in this discussion, it is unnecessary to draw a difference. We can use the terms interchangeably and define them both in the same manner. In suggesting a definition for ethics/morality, the author recognizes that hundreds of generations and the thinking of some of the greatest minds in history have attempted to produce the one great, unassailable, universal definition. Everyone seems to have a slightly different approach to the definition. One thing we do know, however, is that inherent in almost every definition of ethics/morality are the two words "ought" and "right," as in "doing what ought to be done" or "doing what is right." Let us begin with the basic statement that to be known as an ethical/moral person or as an ethical/moral organization, we, and the organization, "ought to do what is right." For purposes of our discussion, therefore, let us define ethics/morality as "knowing what we *ought* to do, and having the will to do it." Three possible conditions spring from this definition:

1. We do not know what we ought to do, and thus we do not (cannot) do it. (Education is required.)
2. We know what we ought to do but we do not do it. (A greater will is required.)
3. We know what we ought to do and we do it! (Excellence is the result.)

WHAT IS "RIGHT"

Defining "right" is the hardest task in ethics. Most people believe that ethics is situational, i.e., since situations vary infinitely, so do definitions of "right." Certainly situations vary, however, I would argue that if a given situation can be defined objectively, the vast majority of thinking people would arrive at the same or nearly the same ethical conclusions. The key, therefore, is to properly define the situation in question. Once the situation has been defined, the following tests should be applied to any conclusions regarding standards or actions:

1. Is the standard fair?
2. Is the standard legal?
3. Does the standard hurt anyone?
4. Have we been honest with those affected by the standard?
5. Can I personally live with a clear conscience with the standard or action taken?

Is the Standard Fair?

Can those for whom the standard is intended meet the standard consistently? What kind of management help or training is required to make consistent compliance possible? Can compliance be measured accurately such that reward and recognition or correction can be awarded objectively? It should be noted that "fair" does not mean or imply compromise, that is, simply setting a standard low enough such that everyone can comply. The key to standards is to set them such that everyone must reach somewhat to meet the standard. However, "reaching" is one thing; "out of reach" is another. For example, it's all well and good to set the standard that all room service breakfast orders will arrive at the guest's room in less than 30 minutes, but a standard like this is based on normal relationships, that is, normal occupancy, normal percentages of guests requesting room service, normal distribution of the time that orders are called in, etc. To set a high standard assuming normal conditions and then try to enforce it during abnormal conditions (full house, group check-out, high number of room service breakfast requests) simply is not fair. What is fair is to develop a standard for communicating properly to the guest when the abnormal situations arise, or, to establish a well-publicized program of pre-ordering the night before in order to take pressure off the morning orders, or both! The point is, make "fairness" one of the main tests for the validity of a standard.

Is the Standard Legal?

Most questions of legality are cut and dried; others are not. Standards that discriminate are simply illegal and cannot be allowed. But what about a standard, written or unwritten, of providing nice Christmas gifts to public officials who just happen to be involved in areas where approval decisions might be sought by the property? Is this just "good business practice" or is it compromising, or trying to compromise, in an illegal way, the performance of the official in question?

The whole area of truth in advertising has legal implications. Advertising "prime" and serving "choice" or advertising "fresh" and serving "frozen" are questionable practices. Promoting a property as air-conditioned when that is only partially true, or advertising special packages that are only provided in limited quantities, or hiring illegal aliens under the guise of "ignorance" are some examples of illegal standards. More to the point, there are probably not well-thought-out standards covering such actions—and there should be! By not creating finite, tangible standards, unwritten, intangible standards will prevail, and this is often a dangerous approach to the question of legality in that such philosophies simply teach employees that their employer is not above deceit; thus, why should they, the employees, behave differently. One manager I met in my travels went as far as to say he did not believe in written standards because he wanted to be able to decide issues at will without making any commitments whatever in writing. Fortunately such philosophies are uncommon to the hospitality industry, as they well should be.

Does the Standard Hurt Anyone?

This is a difficult test for the employment of ethics. Some decisions invariably hurt some that the many may not be hurt—for example, reducing staff in keeping with economic conditions. If, after alternatives are considered, it becomes necessary for 20 employees to be "laid off" in order that 120 may have their jobs preserved, then the decision must be made. Ethical considerations would argue, however, for fairness in the selection process, fairness in the severance policy, and fairness in the re-hire program when conditions change. Being ethical does not mean living one's life such that no one is ever hurt by your ethics. If that were the case, little would be accomplished. Being ethical means being totally conscious and sensitive to the hurts that can occur and doing everything possible to avoid or minimize them. If a standard is fair, and if, after proper training and support, the standard is still not being met, replacement of those charged with not meeting the standard is probably in order. The replacement will hurt, but it is based on objective information, comes as no surprise, and is carried out with a sense of compassion. But what if the property has the standard that a) no hourly employee can be on premises without having punched in on the time clock and b) employees may not punch in longer than 15 minutes before their appointed time to report for duty? Now, what if the available public transportation is such that some employees must arrive at the property one-half to three-quarters of an hour before the time required to report for work? The employees are disadvantaged because they must either stand around outside, or gather somewhere else and wait. That standard should be revised so as not to punish the employees whose situations cause them to be "hurt" by the process.

Have We Been Honest with Those Affected by the Standard?

If you cannot be honest about your standards, chances are you have an ethical problem. If your published standard is equal access and opportunity for all, but your unwritten policy is "no minorities will ever be hired for the front desk," you are being dishonest. Management may argue that it has to be this way; to honestly state "no minorities shall be hired for the front desk" would be totally illegal. That, of course, is true! But, to publish standards that you circumvent by not being honest in their enforcement is simply to say to all employees, "Our standards are not meaningful. We enforce them at will, at our discretion, thus, you, our employees, may do likewise." Of course, management holds all the cards, or almost all! Employees who don't meet standards can be terminated, but employees can't fire the boss! The one card management does not hold, however, is the one held by the guest who decides whether or not to stay at your facility. As excellence becomes more prevalent, as consumers come more and more to expect excellence, the operation built on dishonesty, occasional or blatant, will have difficulty surviving.

Can I Live with My Conscience?

Many hoteliers responding to the ethics survey cited the "Golden Rule" as the definition of ethics. It should be noted that the Golden Rule is not strictly the property of any one theology. Most religions have a variation on the theme that we should "do unto others as we would have others do unto us." It's not a bad definition of ethics at all in its purest form; that is, we are all meant to treat each other fairly, honestly, and with compassion and understanding. Interpreted in any form that suggests "doing unto others *so that* they will do likewise unto you" or, "doing unto other *only if* they do likewise unto you," is not proper and not the intent of those who suggest using the rule. More to the point, most hoteliers have a sense of justice and fairness inherent in their basic make-up and philosophy. At times, our basic sense of justice and fair play becomes shaped or shaded by our situation or environment. Our owners put intense pressure on us to make a certain profit. They don't specifically say "be unethical," but when those gray areas of ethics arise, we may tend to lean on the side of profitability and give up a bit of our ethics! Don't be misled by this point. Being ethical does not mean giving up profit. But, at times there can be a conflict. Sometimes we, as managers, put pressure on our employees in the same manner, saying such things as, "Don't tell me how you did it, just get it done!" Using conscience as a test for ethics is where that part of our definition stating "having the will to do it" comes in. We generally know what is right to do, but we often lack the will to do it, and generally the reasons fall into one or more of the categories listed below:

1. It's not really "very wrong."
2. We're in business to make a profit and that's the bottom line.
3. It really doesn't hurt anyone.
4. If I don't do it, I will suffer or lose my job.
5. Everybody else is doing it.
6. If I don't do it, I'll have far greater problems than if I do!
7. Who will ever know?

Yet everyone complains that ethics and morality are eroding in America! Who can turn the situation around? Only we as individuals. We have to be proud of ourselves, take a stand, and have the will to see it through. We will not always succeed, any more than the greatest baseball hitter gets a hit each time up, or the greatest salesman closes every deal. But, we will do darn well and . . . the industry will benefit because of us.

ETHICS AND THE HOSPITALITY INDUSTRY

In 1988, I conducted what I believe to be the first comprehensive survey of ethics in hospitality in America. I use the term "comprehensive" loosely because, while the questions covered a relatively wide area, the survey was sent only to those AH&MA member hotels, motels, and motor inns in the United States of over 300 rooms. I readily acknowledge that a very large part of the heart of the hospitality industry in America are those facilities of less than 300 rooms, and that not all hospitality properties belong to AH&MA. Time, cost constraints, and the belief that those managers completing the survey in hotels above 300 rooms had, in all probability, some experience working in properties of less than that number all contributed to my decision. Regardless, the results indicated that considerably more work in the area of ethics, for the entire industry, is called for. In all, 800 surveys were sent out and 104 received back; not a bad response. The following are some of the more prominent conclusions:

1. Hoteliers believe themselves to be highly ethical. Hoteliers were asked to rate 18 industries, including news media, retail clothiers, funeral directors, government officials, investment counselors, etc. in terms of "being ethical"; the top four were (1) hotel industry, (2) medical profession, (3) motel industry, and (4) restaurant industry. (A consumer-side survey asking the same question would be most enlightening.)

2. Respondents believed:
   - A greater knowledge of ethics is highly desirable.
   - Ethics can be taught.
   - The application of ethics improves profitability.
   - Teaching schools are doing a fair to inadequate job of teaching ethics.

3. There is ambivalence between what is a "business decision" and what is an "ethical/moral decision."

4. Ethical decisions are made most often *after* a situation arises and *if* the situation poses a potential problem or threat to the establishment.

5. The foundation for ethical/moral judgment comes from parents and not from school, church, work, self, or other sources.

I have taught ethics and quality at the Cornell-ESSEC graduate level school (IMHI) in Cergy-Pontoise, France, and at the International Center at Glion, Switzerland, and have also given seminars in many parts of the world. The United States is not unique in its approach to ethics in hospitality.

When you ask business people, including, of course, hoteliers, to describe their world, you get responses like "It's a jungle," "dog eat dog," "every man for himself," "kill or be killed," "all's fair in love and war," "unions are destroying America," "nobody wants to work anymore," etc., etc., etc. An outsider would think there was no hope for American business, but that simply is not true. Most of the managers in the survey had a good sense of the definitions of ethics and morality. Conclusions based on such a small sample size are always dangerous; however, the following conclusions seem to come through:

1. Hoteliers have a good sense of ethics.
2. Hoteliers appreciate the value of ethics.
3. Hoteliers are not applying enough ethics because
   - There is not enough encouragement to do so.
   - There are not good processes to do so.
   - The rewards for doing so are not fully understood.
4. Standards are affected by the application of ethics.

ETHICS AND THE BOTTOM LINE

If we revert to our basic definition of quality as conformance to standards, that is, consistency, we conclude that it is important in that it builds trust on the part of the guest. And trust builds repeat business. This being so, it follows that the more ethical the standards, i.e., the more that the guest perceives the standards to be as they "ought" to be, the stronger yet will be the trust. Thus, the stronger the trust on the part of the guest, the stronger the bond. When there is a strong bond between guest and hospitality operation, guests will not only return as guests, they will be willing to pay more for their service. People pay willingly when they know they will receive what is right every single time! Quality always pays. Quality based on a strong ethical foundation always pays more! Ethical quality, i.e., excellence, is just plain good business!

THE ETHICS OF INTERPERSONAL RELATIONSHIPS

Market level and *health and safety* ethics are, as we noted, quite tangible. *Interpersonal relationships,* on the other hand, are not. Thus the application of ethics in the area of interpersonal relationships requires considerable thought, and this is where the process falls down, because if the general manager does not have sufficient time to wrestle with all of the ethical questions, chances are it won't happen. Further, ethics, like quality, is basically a frame of mind, a way of life throughout the organization. It is crucial that a strong commitment to quality and ethics be present in the most senior executive (or failure must result); yet, such commitment alone does not insure success. The whole organization must be committed. In this regard, the quality assurance director and the Quality Assurance Committee, to be discussed in Chapters 4 and 5, are the logical people to carry the banner for ethics.

Interpersonal ethics fall into several categories as follows:

1. Hierarchical—up and down the organizational chart.
2. Promotional—how we project our image.
3. Transactional—between employee and guest.
4. Contractual—between the organization and non-guest outsiders, in written or informal form.

Let us look at each in turn.

Hierarchical Ethics

In every organization, management has the responsibility to care for its employees. In return, employees have the responsibility to perform properly in their work and in their relationships with the organization. In other cultures, Japan most notably, this is done better than in the United States, where the management/labor relationship is, more often than not, antagonistic in nature. Employees in America are often viewed as "uncooperative," "unskilled," "unmotivated" individuals who don't want to work and must be managed constantly if any productive effort is to be gained from them. It simply isn't true. Managers who become overly impressed with their own importance should remember one of the basic rules in interpersonal relationships: "Before I care how much you know, I have to know how much you care!" Managers, of course, are employees too. They have owners or, if fortunate enough to be owners, they more likely than not have a board of directors or a bank or other lending institution involved. Given none of the above, managers, particularly in the service industry, have the consuming public to please. Regardless, managers need to be appreciated just as much as do other employees and, thus, it is quite a mystery why the hospitality industry, in particular, seems to filter out of those who reach the top, the great interpersonal skills that got them there!

The ethics of the hierarchy has to do with the interpersonal relationships at every level. Relationships are cross-cultural in that this industry, perhaps more than any other, employs persons of varying cultures. They are cross-racial for the same reasons. Few industries have as wide a spread of employees with traditional values and those with modern values as does the hospitality industry. (Hospitals are an example of a social order with an even higher spread, but other examples are rare.) The several qualities that differentiate between a traditional-thinking person and a modern-thinking person are discussed later on. But, as a general statement, in hospitality, entry-level and production-level employees tend to be traditional in nature, and management tends to be modern in nature, referring primarily to the cultural background from which each comes. What this traditional–modern continuum means is simply that the greater the spread along the line, the more difficult will become the diffusion of ideas. Hospitality management must not only be aware of the varying needs along the traditional–modern continuum, but it must work hard at communicating and interacting appropriately at each level. Management must ask these questions. Are my employees well trained? Do they have the proper tools to do their jobs? Are they compensated fairly for their work? Have I provided proper leadership at every level—leadership that is knowledgeable, professional, and skillful in dealing with those for whom it is responsible? Do my employees have a proper working environment? Are my employees known as individuals, or as names and number only? Do I truly care about my employees, or am I too caught up in the bureaucracy of success to worry about them? Sincerity and honesty are the key words in this discussion because human relations gimmicks, somewhat prevalent in business today, just aren't convincing to employees. I used to have a boss who would come out of his office, pat me on the back, and say, "You're doing a good job, Steve!" I often wondered what would happen if I said, "What is it, exactly, that I am doing that is so pleasing?" Fact is, he had no real idea of what I was doing, and his compliments were hollow and meaningless. Management gamesmanship!

Many standards apply specifically within the hierarchy between employees—standards of dress, grooming, conduct, conditions of employment, *health and safety*, attitude, expected levels of performance, etc. Ask yourself for every standard within the hierarchy, "Is this right? Is it what I ought to be doing?"

Promotional Ethics

One of the biggest areas of ethical discussion centers around advertising and promotion. I shall never forget a tour I once took of a chemical factory that made oleo, among other products, for commercial private labelling. Out of one large vat came 34 "different" oleo brands. Some brands were in quarter-pound sticks, others in full-pound packs, yet others in plastic "tubs." Every brand was differentiated. This one was "fortified," that one "smoother," or "richer," or "creamier." Some claimed to be "better for your health," others "tasted better," and still others were "easier to spread." Advertisers can do wonders with words and pictures. They can make genies come out of bottles of liquid soap, whole kitchens shake when degreaser is poured in the drain, and housewives float across kitchen floors on a magic carpet, and we accept it. We accept it because we know it is exaggeration and part of the game. In hospitality we exaggerate as well, but the stakes are higher. Whereas margarine doesn't cost a lot and it is just as good as 33 other brands, hotel rooms aren't cheap, and because they are so people-oriented, no two are really alike. While we certainly want to put our best foot forward in our promotions, we must be ethical, for to be otherwise might have short-run gains but will always have long-run losses. It's not just portraying our property that needs our ethical input, it is the specials we run as well. In our survey on ethics, we presented the following case:

> We have been promoting a special weekend package for several weeks. A couple arrives for the weekend with a confirmed reservation for our standard rate, and are not aware of our special reduced price weekend. Do we charge them the normal rate per their reservation, or do we tell them of the special rate package?

Frankly, I was surprised to discover that more than half of the respondents would charge the regular rates. In my opinion it is unethical to deny a guest something you are making available to everyone else, simply because the guest in question failed to see or hear your ads. *Denying the guest* results in the possibility that the guest will discover your deception and tell several others about your business ethics and policies. *Telling the guest* and reducing the rate guarantees that he/she will tell others and hold you up as an example of trust. Thus, besides doing what is "right" in this case, there is a long-run economic gain as a result. We end this discussion on this note. If you are going to put words like "quality," "excellence," "fine food," "efficient service," "comfortable rooms," "friendly employees," "great atmosphere," "management that cares," and on and on and on in your promotion, then read this book carefully. It will help to keep you an honest person in the eyes of the public!

Transactional Ethics

All relationships between the physical property and the guest, and the employees and the guest, come under the heading "transactional ethics." Within this category fall all of the health and safety considerations, the service considerations, considerations of comfort, and all of the communicational interactions between guest and staff. If we have promoted our operation and facility properly, the expectation of the guest will match what we provide. If we provide what we promised with consistency, we have a good transaction. A quality assurance program itself is an ethical response to the guest. Given that "Guest A" has a reservation for our hotel, we ask ourselves, "What ought we to be doing for 'Guest A'?" The answer has to be, "Give 'Guest A' all that we have promised to give with total consistency." If you are ethical, you will keep your word. To keep your word, you will need a program.

What are some examples of transactional ethics? It doesn't seem very ethical to include a phone in every guest room and not tell the guest until check-out time that you charge $1.00 for every call. It doesn't seem ethical to have the valet deliver the dry cleaning and, 10 minutes later, have the bellman deliver the shirts! It doesn't seem ethical to ignore telling the guest on check-in that you're having a problem with your air conditioning and it will be out of order for two days. Guests might question the ethics of starting demolition of guest rooms on the next floor, at 8:00 in the morning, without telling them beforehand that you have a renovation program underway! One front desk manager had a real brainstorm. Whenever tours would book, invariably some couples would ask to have rooms close by each other. He would intentionally room the two couples as far apart as possible. When they complained, he would apologize, say that he tried his best, and then offer a compromise. It just so happens that there is a suite available where both couples can stay together for only a slight bit more money. Being such a good deal, the guests accepted. The hotel sold a suite that would otherwise be vacant and picked up two needed prepaid rooms, to be sold again. Is this clever management or is it unethical management? Many to whom I have posed the question say, "It's clever management if you don't get caught!" That's a good definition of unethical!

Contractual Ethics

Is it ethical to ask vendors to contribute free food and beverage for the annual hotel outing? Most hoteliers believe it is all right to do so. However, what does that do for competition? Is the vendor making a contribution out of the goodness of his heart? Or, does the vendor expect something in return? If the same vendor offers free steaks to the purchasing agent, is this acceptable? Why should the purchasing agent say no to a free gift when the hotel does not?

Any interaction between the hotel and outsiders doing business with or providing services for the property are considered contractual ethics, even though there are not always actual contracts. Obviously vendors qualify. But, so do municipal inspectors who must pass on health and safety questions. If you try to "buy" their approval (assuming they are willing to sell) for something you are not providing, what about your ethical relationship with the guest to whom you are now not providing what he or she is paying for? For example, say you are improperly storing flammable and/or hazardous materials but the inspector is not being pushy because you have developed a strong relationship. Are you being ethical to your guests, who put their trust in you to provide them safety?

What about the age-old question of a well-groomed lady of the night working your cocktail lounge? We asked the question in our survey. Most hoteliers do not believe this is an ethical/moral issue. It is not their job, they say, to legislate the morality of their guests. What the guest does is the guest's own business as long as no one is hurt or disturbed by the process. There is some truth in what they say. It is most difficult to legislate the morality of guests, and it's downright dangerous as well to make any accusations that could open you up for a lawsuit. Yet, most managers face this issue at one time or another in their careers. Left unchecked, the situation can only grow worse. One such person in the lounge leads to two or more. That leads to more blatant solicitation, perhaps to drug use and/or the ripping off of guests. Most guests don't complain because they don't want the publicity. When the situation is bad enough, the hotelier calls for help from those whose job it is to police such activities. Yet, the management had it in their power to prevent the problem from the start by taking a firm stand with all who might be aware of the problem that it simply will not be allowed.

HOW CAN THE QA COMMITTEE HELP?

Other than applying an ethical test to every standard, how can the committee act to resolve ethical issues? Perhaps this true case will illustrate a way. The case was brought up by a student in my class on ethics at the Institute de Management, Hoteliere International, the joint Cornell-ESSEC masters level Hotel School in Cergy-Pontoise, France. All names have been changed.

Vanessa from Germany was a beautiful 21-year-old college graduate, with a degree in hotel administration, when she was hired by the accounting department of a prominent London hotel. The comptroller personally interviewed her and took a strong interest in her development, spending considerable time helping her to better understand her job. She considered Mr. Harvey to be her mentor and not only appreciated his help, but liked him as a person. Over a period of weeks, Mr. Harvey found reason to spend more and more time during the day discussing Vanessa's job. She learned among other things that he was 46 years old, lived 38 miles from London, commuted by train, and was married to a woman he described as "very understanding and tolerant of his difficult job, long hours, and occasional needs to stay overnight in London." As time went on, Mr. Harvey and Vanessa began discussing business over lunch in the hotel. One afternoon he suggested dinner away from the property, and it was then that Vanessa, somewhat naive to be sure, began to sense a somewhat different agenda than one purely work related. She went to dinner. The conversation was largely social and ended with a blatant suggestion that even a closer relationship was possible! Vanessa liked Mr. Harvey as a friend but had no interest in a physical relationship, however casually or formally he presented it. She told him, but he persisted. The night ended amicably, but in the days ahead, Mr. Harvey kept up his steady pressure, suggesting that he could help Vanessa's career because he "knew so many important people." Vanessa told him she was not interested; he didn't seem to hear her! She told him she had no experience in such matters; he offered to "teach" her! In short order, Vanessa faced showdown time. What to do? The following are suggestions:

1. She could tell the general manager, whom she knew. She also knew, however, that he was also "involved" with someone in the hotel. She could not talk with him.
2. She could put Mr. Harvey in his place decisively and abruptly by telling him "No" in no uncertain terms, by avoiding personal contact with him, and by threatening stronger action if he did not leave her alone. She would just lose her job and probably her reputation as well. How would anyone believe one so beautiful who obviously had developed a close relationship with the boss?
3. She could tell her peers. Would they sympathize with her? Probably not.
4. She could submit to his desires. This was out of the question for Vanessa; on that she was clear.
5. She could go to personnel, but the personnel director had been at the hotel two years. Mr. Harvey had been there 17 years and was on the executive committee as well. Whose version of the problem would prevail?
6. Or, she could do what she did do—quit! She simply resigned, and later, entered IMHI.

There could have been another option open for Vanessa had there been a meaningful QA program and a capable QA director. She could have gone to him or her and discussed her situation. The committee could have scheduled (without her presence) a discussion on the overall issue of sexual harassment, without pointing fingers or naming names. The committee could have developed a code of ethics covering such issues, and then published it. By keeping the discussion general and impersonal, Vanessa's problem would have been solved and the hotel's standards raised. Certainly there is no guarantee that the solution would be successful. The general manager might not have permitted the QA committee to deal in this area, or the comptroller might have reasoned that Vanessa should go regardless. However, the QA committee approach to the resolution of ethical issues like this is an excellent approach because of the diversity of committee membership and the general nature of the committee's overall objective, that of achieving excellence throughout the entire organization.

The issue with ethics is that of looking beyond the short range. Reputation is like a tree. It takes a long time to grow and, if cared for properly, will result in a magnificent thing of beauty. But, if not cared for, the tree is damaged or destroyed and never will be the same again. The proper application of ethics will result in the long-range success we need in order to prosper. *Quality* plus *ethics* equals *excellence*. And the place to begin is with the quality assurance director and the committee—right from the start.

4

Picking The Team

The Quality Assurance Director and Committee

Myth #4: PROGRAMS ARE ALL RIGHT, BUT QUALITY WILL REALLY ONLY START WHEN THE GENERAL MANAGER DEMANDS IT.

I AM QUALITY

A few years ago we were called in to put in place a quality assurance program at a prominent resort hotel on the island of Nassau. Whereas ownership desired a program, the general manager was less enthusiastic. Following our first visit and introduction of the program, the general manager took us on a tour of the property and, during that tour, announced that he thought quality assurance programs were a waste of time. "I am the quality program," he said. "Quality is whatever I decide it is!"

In point of fact, the employees had no clear understanding of what management desired, and frankly, no motivation to find out. Check-in, check-out lines were horrendous, turnover was high, employee grievances were numerous, there was no rapport between the guest and the hotel staff, rooms were not particularly well maintained, and the food service, in a word, was bad. There was a tremendous lack of consistency and, as a matter of fact, after several months of implementation, the program was shelved. The reason for the lack of success was purely a lack of commitment on the part of management resulting in a subtle undermining of a program sought by the owners. More to the point, the manager failed to understand that in hospitality, quality is the sum total of a myriad of small tasks done to perfection. The manager's role is that of an orchestra leader, organizing all of the participants into a motivated, well-trained team. Behind most successful orchestra leaders, however, is a key individual who performs the logistical tasks of schedules, facilities, administrative relationships, and handling of the many brushfires before they get out of control. Such an individual is to the orchestra leader just as the quality assurance director is to the general manager. The role of management is support, motivation, reward, and recognition. The quality assurance director runs the program.

WHO SHOULD BE THE QUALITY ASSURANCE DIRECTOR?

The quality assurance director (QAD) should be someone in the organization with the following characteristics:

Someone Who Wants the Position and the Responsibility

Putting someone in the position of QAD simply as a "make busy" activity, or as a way to express cooperation to higher ups while rendering the actual program toothless, is obviously not a positive step toward success. Picking a QAD who is not interested and/or is unwilling to accept the responsibility will result in absolute failure. Good management is choosing the best possible person for every job and then supporting that person's performance.

Someone Who Is Able to Devote at Least One Day Per Week to Quality Assurance Alone

It is a misconception that quality assurance requires the total time of the quality assurance director. Perhaps the program will grow to that level in time, but initially the role of the QAD is that of mobilizing others to help diffuse the concept of quality. By the same token, if a QAD begins thinking quality 10 minutes before the Quality Assurance Committee meeting, it will be obvious to all concerned, and that doesn't work either. Begin slowly. Require at least one day of concentration and build from there as success warrants.

Someone Who Has the Respect of His or Her Peers

People follow those whom they respect. They don't always agree with the decisions of leadership, but if they are convinced that the leader has made a decision based on sound logic and consideration of all points of view, they will accept the leadership willingly. Putting someone in charge of the quality program who bases his or her leadership on power and not on respect is the wrong choice.

Someone Who Is Upwardly Mobile

Upward mobility means that the selected QAD is looking forward to a future in hospitality, not back on a career that has topped out. We expect the QAD to have vision, to see possibilities, to desire to produce a better environment for everyone. Further, the role of QAD is a training ground par excellence because the QAD is involved with every single area of the hospitality operation. Someone on the move upward will produce the best results in quality assurance.

Someone Who Is Politically Astute

Hospitality in general is a political environment in that, where people are involved, politics is the basis on which most social systems function. There are, however, areas of operations that are off limits for the Quality Assurance Committee. For example, addressing the underlying causes of a grievance to ascertain if proper standards could have prevented the situation is a proper function of the committee. To become embroiled in grievances of compensation or corporate policy in which the issue of unmet standards is not the question, are areas to be avoided. The QAD must have a sense for such pitfalls and must have the skill to direct the committee's attention away from those areas and back into areas of standards and compliance.

Someone with Administrative Skills

Lastly, the QAD must have some administrative skill. It would be difficult to find an upwardly mobile, committed person with political acumen who does not have administrative skills; however, administration skills can always be improved and thus it would be wrong to assume more than is visible. If the relationship with the general manager is a close one, as it must be for success, then the general manager can be most helpful in guiding the QAD toward better skills of administration.

The perfect QAD candidate may not have all of the characteristics listed above, but the list is an excellent start for success. It cannot be overemphasized that along with a committed management, selecting the right leader is crucial.

DEPARTMENT HEADS ARE IMPORTANT

The Quality Index ©* is an evaluation tool used to ascertain trouble areas, i.e., areas of potential improvement, in an overall quality assurance program. One of America's finest hotels instituted a quality assurance program on their own and, on the surface, quite correctly. They selected as a quality assurance director, a bright, upwardly mobile, experienced young woman who began the program and, in just three months, determined that it was not working and did not show promise of success. To her credit, she encouraged management to survey the property using the Quality Index ©. The results indicated, among other things, that the program had lip service support from department heads, but, beneath the surface, they were apathetic despite the quality of the QAD selected. The selection had been done by the general manager without any discussion whatever with department heads. Since the QAD came from the ranks of the supervisors, she naturally viewed the world from that perspective

---

*Quality Index © is a copyrighted evaluation tool created by Stephen Hall Associates.

and began the program by concentrating on the production level employees. Without the support of the department heads, she was ineffective because the program was viewed simply as "one more management program aimed at correcting the production level." Try as she might, the QAD could not move the program forward, and in her frustration she wisely called for help. The Quality Index © survey was performed, and it revealed the problem. Management, with the concurrence of the QAD, replaced her with a department head, putting her on the committee as a valued member. The program then began to pick up the speed it had lost. QADs do not have to be department heads necessarily, but department heads must buy into the quality program for it to succeed. There is merit therefore in looking to the department head or assistant department head ranks for your QAD.

CAN THE GENERAL MANAGER BE THE QAD?

The general manager who insists upon taking the role of quality assurance director might not destroy the program, but the odds that it will be unsuccessful are very high! As I have stated previously, the absolute total commitment of the general manager is crucial, but, in the role of QAD, the manager's presence is viewed more as autocratic than democratic. Even the most popular of managers will have difficulty because the members of the committee will tend to be reserved in their participation. A large aspect of successful QA in service industries is the covenant of trust between management and employee. The general manager who makes himself or herself the director of quality assurance is doing little to enhance the spirit of trust.

WHY NOT MAKE THE TRAINING DIRECTOR
THE QAD?

There is a strong temptation in larger properties to look to the training director as QAD because "their business is primarily people-oriented." Training directors often seek the position as a natural choice. I would argue strongly against using the training director as the QAD because training is a critical part of the quality process. Directing proper training to areas of greatest need is a major function of an active quality assurance program. The quality assurance director is responsible for determining, with the QA Committee, where training is needed, and whether or not it is effective. If the training director is also the QA director, he or she is both judge and jury of training, and this is not a good situation. This suggestion in no way is intended to be critical of training directors. On the contrary, they are essential. Professional training directors will welcome outside support and validation of their work. I strongly recommend against the selection of the training director as the QAD.

ESTABLISHING THE QUALITY ASSURANCE COMMITTEE (QAC)

The first question in choosing the Quality Assurance Committee is, "How many members are enough?" Obviously it depends on the size of the property. It would be fair to say, however, that less than three is no longer a committee and more than seven begins to produce diminishing returns. In both extremes, the QAD is considered one of the members. Keep in mind that the committee should constantly invite relevant outsiders to help in their work. If, for example, the topic is standards for the buspersons in the main dining room, having the dining room host or hostess, a key waiter(ess), and a busperson sitting in on the discussion is most valuable. Not only do they bring relevant and specific expertise, but their presence says to all who eventually live by these standards that management cares enough to include the input of those faced with the tasks at hand. Building a sense of equity is the key to successful quality assurance. But we can never lose sight of the fact that it is management's ultimate responsibility to set the standards that define the operation's position in the competitive marketplace.

CHOOSING QUALITY ASSURANCE COMMITTEE MEMBERS

As in the case of the QAD, committee members should have certain characteristics.

Select Only Department Heads or Assistant Department Heads

Many managers who grasp the full spirit of quality assurance immediately want to constitute a committee made up of representatives from all levels. They push, therefore, for a committee made up of production-level employees, supervisors, and department heads, believing that such a committee will portray the program as democratically involving everyone. This approach, idealistic as it is, does not work. As previously stated, quality assurance is a top down program. Employees expect leaders to lead, and one crucial characteristic of leadership is "example." If department heads are viewed as willing to work hard on a program perceived as new, before this program is imposed on the production and supervisory levels, they will adopt it far more readily. Add to this the situation in which communication and persuasion is required from management persons not on the committee and it becomes obvious that production-level employees and supervisors are placed in a very difficult spot as members of the committee. In time, as success is earned, subcommittees and quality circles can be formed, but by then, the entire concept has been accepted. Managers must resist the temptation to move outside the department head and assistant department head ranks for their quality assurance committee members.

Select Members Who Are Willing and Have Time

Managers can destroy a quality assurance effort by placing on the committee persons who do not want to be there. The committee must never be used as a place to punish or as a place to keep people busy who otherwise might not be. The QAD must be a crucial part of the selection process and should spend time with all department heads, ascertaining their interests and desires, before the committee is selected by the manager.

Select Members Who Can Accept Constructive Criticism and Productive Change

If errors did not occur, there would be no need for a quality assurance program, therefore, identifying errors, resolving them, and then working to prevent them from reoccurring is the key. It is human nature not to want to be associated with errors, but, associated or not, errors exist. The proper attitude for a committee member is one that seeks out errors with the self-confidence that only by identifying them can they be corrected. A committee member who cannot accept criticism, i.e., will not admit to an error, and is unwilling to accept a change aimed at preventing errors, will add only negative energy to the committee. It is said that quality assurance is "to err, and err, and err, but, less, and less, and less." The proper attitude focuses on "less, and less, and less" and not on "err, and err, and err." I am certain that this discussion sounds self-evident, but do not be surprised to find even the most proficient and dynamic of department heads unwilling to allow any outsiders to see their errors or even suggest that they exist. We are only human. We don't like to be criticized, but hiding errors under the rug will defeat the quality assurance effort. Identifying them, resolving them, preventing them—that is the stuff of true leaders!

Select Members Having Diverse Skills

A good quality assurance committee is not necessarily a strong social environment. It is not important that members have common interest and common goals except in their desire to improve quality. The committee should get along, to be sure, but the more diversity, the better. It is never necessary or desirable to have more than one member from the same department, i.e., the chef, the food and beverage director, and the catering manager. A large part of the value of serving on the committee is the education that takes place as everyone begins to understand and appreciate the other persons' jobs. If a seven-person committee is in order, try the chief engineer, the executive chef, the executive housekeeper, the sales manager, the front office manager, the chief of security, and the assistant manager. This is not an exclusive list to be sure but, as a starting point, a committee such as this, with their vast knowledge and experience, can solve and prevent any error they can identify. That is the kind of powerful committee you need to guarantee success.

FOREVER IS A LONG TIME

I have seen many cases in which quality assurance committee members join the process with some degree of skepticism, not being sure whether they want to serve on the committee for an extended period. After a year or two, when it comes time to put new members on the committee, those same skeptics resist strongly any attempt to replace them and tend to view such a move as a personal criticism of their work. It is best, therefore, if members are picked for the committee with the full knowledge beforehand that they will only serve one to two years before they are replaced to permit others to participate. This, of course, does not apply to the quality assurance director. He or she serves at the will of the general manager, assuming continued desire to perform. At the end of the first year, in month 14, one member could be replaced. In month 16 a second member would be replaced, and so on until the committee is recycled.

Under committee selection, we discussed the fact that members should be department heads. Depending upon the size and organization of the operation, there probably won't be enough department heads to recycle the committee. Once established, therefore, management personnel below the ranks of department head should be considered. This does not lessen our requirement that committee members should be from management and not from the production level.

A committee member who moves off it is eligible to come back on at any time.

THE ROLE OF THE MANAGER

The QAD and the committee members constitute the Board of Directors of the quality assurance program. In this analogy, the general manager is the owner. The board is selected and put in place by the manager and works to serve the manager. The manager must make a strong commitment to the process and work closely with the

QAD at all times. The manager must read the minutes of the meetings and, upon occasion, sit in on a meeting or part of one. But, the manager must let the committee do its work with full trust and confidence.

STRUCTURING A QA POLICY

We have talked about managerial commitment and its importance to successful QA. Now that the quality assurance director and the committee have been chosen, and the program is officially underway, it is time for management to put its commitment into writing and publish it for all to see. In terms of timing, the first meeting of the committee would be most appropriate, as the general manager officially initiates the formal QA process. There are many forms for the QA policy, but I recommend that the best policy is the one that recognizes the following points:

1. Complete standards in writing at every level.
2. Total training for all in the implementation of standards.
3. Total commitment to measuring performance.
4. Commitment of time and money to the QA program.
5. Total support for the QAD and the committee.

The policy should be as short as possible and should be direct without any reservations. It must be signed by the general manager or the most senior executive on site, by whatever title he or she is called. Finally, the policy must be given to every employee, posted for all to see, and communicated at the Executive Committee meeting, in the house organ, and, of course, at the kick-off meeting of the QA Committee. I would call your attention to the policy published by Walter J. Hickel, Jr., executive vice president of the Hickel Corporation and most senior executive of the Hotel Captain Cook in Anchorage, Alaska. The Hotel Captain Cook is, by far, one of the finest, if not *the* finest, hotel in all of Alaska, and certainly one of the most successful. It is the kind of property that exudes quality from the minute you drive up to the front entrance. It's interesting to note that when Walter Hickel Senior, ex-governor of Alaska and former secretary of the interior, who conceived of and built the Hotel Captain Cook, does his inspection, he starts deep within the en-

HOTEL CAPTAIN COOK

QUALITY ASSURANCE POLICY

The management of the Hotel Captain Cook is 100% committed to the consistent delivery of our published standards at every level of our operation. We are 100% committed to provide, at every level, a trained staff that has a full understanding of all of the standards relevant to their performance. We are 100% committed to the constant measurement of our standards and strongly encourage employee communication and participation at every level in the ongoing measurement review process. Management is 100% committed to the budgeting of time and financial resource required for our Quality Assurance Program and further commits to total support to the Quality Assurance Committee charged with the responsibility for directing the QA Program.

Walter J. Hickel, Jr.
Executive Vice President

FIGURE 4.1 Quality assurance policy of the Hotel Captain Cook.

gine room. His theory is very simple; if quality can be achieved in the remote corners of the property, it will be present everywhere. He is right, at least at the Hotel Captain Cook, and Walter Junior, continuing the management, has not only continued the high quality but raised it to new heights. Figure 4.1 shows the quality assurance policy of the Hotel Captain Cook.

THE IMPORTANCE OF EARLY COMMUNICATION

There are three groups who should be informed early that a quality assurance program is underway. They are the following:

1. Executive Committee
2. Department heads
3. Union(s)

Unless care is taken, all three groups will view quality assurance with suspicion. The Executive Committee will view the program as one more project to worry about when the real worry is tightening up control to maximize profits. The department heads will view QA as more work for them, a possible erosion of their power, and perhaps even the exposure of some of their failings. The union will view QA as one more productivity scheme that will result in fewer jobs or more work for less pay.

These are, of course, generalities that are often not true and, with proper sensitivity, need never be true. Quality assurance is a better way of life for everyone at every level of the organization, and certainly for guests who pay the salaries, wages, and benefits of the entire organization.

Executive Committee

Let the committee in on the discussion from the start. Tell them that quality is aimed at modifying the behavior of people at every level by doing a much better job of communicating standards and measuring performances. Make certain the committee understands the basic process for implementation and secure their total commitment to the process. Do this before selecting the quality director or the quality committee members. It is crucial to have the executive committee completely on board *before* the program is discussed with anyone else in the organization.

Department Heads

The most senior executive should go to the department heads with the commitment for QA and the quality assurance director selected. In fact, the quality assurance director should play an important part in this meeting by participating in the discussion and basically selling himself/herself and the program along with the general manager. Understand the natural anxieties of the department heads. Make sure they know that a) it is their program, b) some of them will be on the committee initially, and c) each of them will be on the committee eventually. Do not present the program in any way as something to be decided. Management has made the decision. Department heads are being asked not to decide to do the program, but to accept it. What they say is important, to be sure, but this must be the most senior executive's program—his or her responsibility. Management should come across as willing to shoulder the problems and eager to credit others for success. Having the quality policy in final form will be helpful when the meeting takes place.

The Union(s)

Unions should be approached in the same way as are the department heads. The philosophy of management is that a program will take place. Management wants the support of the union, but that support is not the deciding factor whether to go forward or not. That decision has been made by management. On the other hand, unions have a reason to be sensitive. If there were no tensions between management and labor, there would be no unions. When something is not understood by a person, or an organization, the only decision possible, particularly if there is any suspicion of motive at all, is "No." So, don't ask the union for a decision, that is not the purpose. Tell them about the program and that it starts at the top and that there will be good communication throughout the process. Keep an open door for the union representation. Require a close communication between QA director and union leadership. Make certain that the union understands the improved communication inherent in the program. And do this very early in the process, after the QA director and before the QA committee is selected. In this way, your actions will communicate positively your desire to work cooperatively and also your commitment to success. Again, the quality policy will confirm your dedication.

5

Building the Foundation for QA

The Team Begins Its Work

Myth #5: *THE ONLY ROLE OF THE QUALITY ASSURANCE COMMITTEE IS TO SOLVE PROBLEMS THAT ARE PRESENTED TO IT.*

READY, SET, GO

As we begin the formal quality assurance process, there are three areas of concerns, as follows:

1. The when and why of meetings.
2. The elements of good control.
3. Developing high energy.

The Quality Assurance Committee must meet at a regularly scheduled time every week of the year. This becomes the first standard for the program. By maintaining a scheduled time and place, members form the habit of making themselves available in the proper frame of mind to concentrate on the subject at hand. Meetings must start promptly on time and should not last more than one hour. The one hour limit must be rigidly maintained. Because hospitality is a

59

people business and because there is no limit to the amount of time spent talking about people problems, meetings in the hospitality business generally are more frequent than necessary, last longer than required, and tend to ramble on without structure. Among the most frequent complaints from management personnel is that fact that there are "too many meetings that last too long and don't accomplish much." If the quality assurance meeting falls into that category, the program will be severely handicapped. Given one hour to do its business, the committee will tend to better focus its energies. Members will be confident that they will not be trapped for hours but will be able to schedule their time with confidence and, as the process begins to gather momentum, the meetings will always seem to end with interesting topics still ahead. This is helpful for maintaining interest.

As the program proceeds, a large measure of the work of quality assurance will be done by non-committee members outside of the committee meeting. The work of the committee thus becomes that of directing and coordinating the efforts of others. If the program does not develop in this manner, it should be reviewed and redirected. Quality assurance must never be viewed as the sole responsibility of the quality assurance director and/or the committee, but rather, as the work of all who are members of the organization.

AGENDAS AND MINUTES

The problem with most meetings is that they have no structure. Members are called together, with little more than a general idea of the topic and, by and large, are required to do their thinking as the meeting progresses. This encourages long meetings, and there is little relationship between the length of the meeting and its productivity. Yet, when agendas and minutes are introduced, they often tend to become a burden. Such need not be the case. On the other hand, the concept of minutes, particularly, is so misunderstood that they often fail to be effective. More often than not, minutes are viewed as complete records of meetings to the extent that they become almost verbatim records of who said what and why. Thus, they become burdensome—burdensome to prepare, burdensome to read, and burdensome to use as records.

While serving as vice president for administration of Harvard

University, I attended the monthly meetings of the Harvard Corporation, a small body of elected individuals charged with the overall administration of the university. Decisions made by the corporation were major in scope, covering expenditures of hundreds of millions of dollars as well as major policy decisions such as investment strategy. In those days, the Harvard endowment exceeded a billion dollars, a fact that gives some idea of the magnitude of the corporation's work. Yet the minutes of the meetings basically consisted of records of corporation votes. The philosophy was that the result of all the rhetoric pro and con on any issue was the actual vote that ultimately resolved the issue, and that was all that mattered. The town meeting tradition in New England town government works in the same fashion. Whereas discussion on any issue might go on for hours, the only meaningful conclusion is that reached when the motion is acted upon. When we speak of minutes for a quality assurance committee, therefore, we should think in terms of the following three basic areas:

1. Items of information
2. Items of action
3. Items of decision

The minutes of a quality assurance committee should rarely exceed one page. Items discussed as informational should be so noted as one- or two-line records.

Information

1. John Smith, Purchasing, discussed the process for receiving and storing fresh vegetables.
2. Joe Jones, Front Desk Manager, described the process for credit card verification.
3. Mary Martin, Personnel, described the new employee orientation process.
4. Ideas to improve dish handling were received from Don Brown, assigned number 127.

When action is required, it must be noted, again in brief form.

Action

1. John Smith was asked to draft standards for receiving and storing fresh vegetables. DUE 9/26.
2. Joe Jones will poll other properties to provide more input. DUE 9/26.
3. Mary Martin will provide a list of all employees who have taken the new orientation program. DUE 10/3.

Finally, all decisions must be noted.

Decision

1. Minutes of meeting 9/12 were accepted.
2. Standard was approved by G. M. for room service task—"recovering servicing carts"—9/14.
3. G. M. approved standards for Bellhops dated 9/14.
4. Standards for task—valet—deliver vehicle approved by QAC 9/19 and sent to G. M.

As you can see, a complete record of the hour-long quality assurance meeting can be contained on one page if only the relevant data are recorded.

MAKING IT SIMPLE

One solution to producing effective minutes and agendas is to have the quality assurance director spend 15 minutes following a meeting with the designated clerk, during which time the minutes are written and the agenda for the next meeting is placed at the end of the same page. Doing both while the information is still fresh saves time and energy, and it results in minutes going out quickly so as to be more effective. Figure 5.1 shows how a typical minutes and agenda form should look.

QUALITY ASSURANCE COMMITTEE MINUTES

_____

MEETING DATE: _____   PLACE _____

START: _____   FINISH: _____

MEMBERS ABSENT: _____

OTHERS PRESENT: _____

DECISION

ACTION

INFORMATION

NEXT MEETING DATE: _____ TIME: _____ PLACE: _____

AGENDA:

DISTRIBUTION: ☐ Normal   Plus:

FIGURE 5.1   Quality assurance committee minutes form.

PASS THE WORD

The minutes of the Quality Assurance Committee are valuable over and above simply serving as a record of information, action, and decision. They can add energy to the QA program.

In many organizations, committees often take on a somewhat secretive cast. That is to say, committees are formed, they meet, decide issues, and hardly anyone except the committee even knows that they exist. Yet, everyone likes to be recognized for contributing to the betterment of the organization. Furthermore, everyone likes to believe that his work on the committee is important. Finally, when people not on a committee see and hear of the committee's good work, they become more enthused that things are actually happening and less anxious about how the committee's actions affect them directly. For these reasons, it's a good idea to distribute minutes to all department heads and above who are not on the committee. Also, the normal human resistance to change, and anxieties relative to job security and future, which will be present to varying extents in production- and supervisory-level employees, can be greatly diffused by making all minutes accessible to them. This is achieved by keeping a three-ring notebook, up-to-date with all minutes, in a place where it is accessible for all to read, if interested. For example, the employees' cafeteria and/or time clock area are places where most employees are present at one time or another. As an alternative to the book idea, a place could be created on the employees' bulletin board and labelled "QAC Minutes." Each week the new minutes could be posted.

WHAT ABOUT "TOP SECRET?"

QA committee members may argue that their work will often deal with personalities and, therefore, general distribution of the minutes is dangerous. This raises a crucial point that must be resolved before the committee can begin serious work. The work of the QA committee is to discuss standards, not personalities. The concern of the committee is *not* how a particular person is performing but rather, what is the task to be performed. The Quality Assurance Committee should leave consideration regarding how a particular person performs in a given job to that person's supervisor or department head, and deal with the basic question of whether or not standards are being met. If the committee deals specifically in terms of developing standards, measuring conformance, and reporting results in a totally objective manner, the committee will slowly and surely gain the respect of all employees at all levels, and the QA program will be successful.

DEVELOPING HIGH ENERGY

People become enthused when they are permitted to participate in a process in which they truly believe their participation is appreciated and meaningful. By limiting the size of the Quality Assurance Committee, every member is assured of an active role. By the use of minutes and agendas, each member is kept well informed and is able to properly prepare when called upon. By limiting meetings to one hour, members do not have time to become disinterested or bored. Nonetheless, until the program is up and running full speed, there will be some question from members as to direction. The quality assurance director, therefore, must be very conscious of the first few meetings, because it is during these meetings that the tempo and tenor of the program is established. We refer to this initial phase as the "meshing" phase, because it is then that members of the Quality Assurance Committee begin to structure their interrelationships and commit to a course of action. To facilitate that process, the first 8–12 meetings should complete the following tasks:

1. Discuss in general the concept of "quality," the basic definitions, and the committee process re: times, schedules, agendas, minutes, overall philosophy, etc. (one meeting).
2. Perform a needs analysis on quality (1–2 meetings) (see Chapter 13).
3. Discuss and try to identify the top 10 areas in the property where specific improvement could be made (one meeting).
4. Using the cost of error process, cost out together three or four of the top ten errors and then ask each member to cost out one of the remaining errors individually. Discuss each cost of error calculation (1–2 meetings).

5. Collect and review, as much as possible, whatever is available as existing standards (1–2 meetings).
6. Review existing orientation programs (one meeting).
7. Collect all job titles and organize in outline form (done outside of meeting by QAD).
8. Select one job title that the committee believes will make the greatest progress in standards. (2–3 meetings).
   - Call in the relevant department head and someone with that job title.
   - Discuss that particular job title.
   - With the department head and job title representative, identify the job tasks for that job title.
   - With the department head and job title representative, write standards for the most crucial tasks within the job title.
9. Invite the general manager to review progress on the above in order to
   - Demonstrate the direction of the committee.
   - Illustrate the value of the process.
   - Solicit the approval of the general manager for the process. (one meeting)

No precise timetable exists for the preceding. Guidelines for the number of meetings devoted to each task are given, but they are only suggestions. Each step must be done well, whether it takes one meeting or three. When completed, the members will have developed a sense of understanding of the main elements of the quality assurance process. They will begin to see the importance of their work. They will also begin to understand that quality assurance is an ongoing process for as long as there is commitment from the general manager. And, they will begin to understand each other and come together as a team.

PRE-PLANNING IS CRUCIAL

It is said that in any speech, the first three minutes are crucial. In that time period, the audience decides, consciously or subconsciously, whether or not they are interested in the presentation. For that reason, successful speakers, be they lecturers, teachers, ministers, committee chairpersons, or whatever, carefully plan their presentations, giving emphasis to the first 3–5 minutes. On a broader scale, the same holds true for the QA program. No matter how enthusiastic committee members may sound, they still arrive at the first QA meeting with some apprehension. The term "meshing" is used to describe the first 8 to 12 weeks of the QA program, because that is exactly what happens if done correctly. The members "mesh" together, form a team, bond together with one common goal—to improve quality. It is absolutely crucial, therefore, that the quality assurance director carefully plan each and every meeting during this phase. Many of the tasks performed during that time, such as reviewing existing standards, require preparation beforehand. Someone has to collect the existing standards and have them ready for review or much valuable time and energy is lost. Thus, the collection of existing standards is a critical part of the process. The same holds true for reviewing orientation, working on cost of error (requiring proper forms, flip chart, and overhead viewer with transparencies), and for other functions such as a needs analysis for which data must be collected. The quality assurance director is also concerned at this point with how he or she is being viewed. If the meshing phase is well organized, and committee members have the sense that the QAD is truly and sincerely committed to making the program a success and has worked hard to that end, they will solidify the QAD's position, and the entire process will work more successfully. PLAN, PLAN, PLAN—every critical event of every meeting of the meshing phase.

THE GM AND THE QAC

The general manager should not, as previously discussed, be a member of the Quality Assurance Committee. Neither should the GM attend meetings on any regular basis or even spontaneously without first telling the quality assurance director. The reasons are twofold and basic: First, quality is best achieved by the organization performing under free will to achieve a goal to which they are personally and freely committed. The desired relationship between management and the organization is one of mutual respect and faith. Management believes in the ability of the organization to succeed, and the organization believes that the management is acting in a fair and equitable manner, recognizing the contributions of employees at all levels and rewarding when earned. Quality results. Therefore, the general manager should trust the committee to do its work. Secondly, whenever the general manager is present, employees tend naturally to become what they believe management wants them to be. This phenomenon only lasts as long as the interaction, but it is a real phenomenon. Thus, when the GM is present at the QAC meetings, the committee members will act differently, usually resulting in decisions being deferred to the manager. This is counterproductive to the committee goals.

This does not say, or even imply, that the general manager should not attend committee meetings. Rather, attendance should be infrequent, with a specific purpose in mind, and with the quality assurance director's knowledge beforehand. Hopefully, the "specific purpose" will fall into two categories: a) to compliment the committee on its performance, or b) to ask that the committee address a specific concern of the general manager. Both reasons present the kind of positive image needed in the program.

There is one time when it is important for the general manager to attend the QAC meeting. That is at the opening of the first meeting. The general manager should make the following points:

1. I (the GM) believe in quality and give total support to the committee. (Presenting the Quality Assurance Policy of the property at this point is a real plus!)
2. I (the GM) have total faith in ————————, the QA director, and in the committee, and the QAD has access to me whenever needed.
3. I (the GM) am sincerely appreciative of the willingness of the committee members to take on the quality responsibility.

The general manager should control the urge to make a long speech and especially to dwell on the need for quality. In short order, following the needs analysis, the committee will understand, better than anyone, the need for quality. The GM should talk for 10 or 15 minutes and then excuse himself or herself and let the committee get to work.

REPLACING A MEMBER

Members of the Quality Assurance Committee will occasionally need to be replaced because a) they are not performing, b) they have lost interest, or c) time constraints prevent full participation.

The work of the Quality Assurance Committee is far too important to be left in the hands of someone who has lost interest or will not carry his or her share of the responsibilities. The quality assurance director must be up front with the committee members at the start. All must agree to participate fully or they must resign from the committee. The quality assurance director, in communication with the general manager, should discuss any member who is weak in participation, and, without delay or fanfare, the general manager should discuss the situation with the particular committee members in question and, if warranted, ask him or her to step down. Remember, quality assurance is a new process for most. It is not productive to view a weak member as either inadequate or a failure. It takes a while for some people to become fully enthused about the program; thus, patience and understanding are in order. The relevant member should be asked to step down without loss of self-esteem. It is not uncommon for people to fight the program initially and then become supportive as they begin to understand. Thus, if a change in membership is called for, make it quickly and quietly, without prejudice.

6

Camels and Horses

Understanding Group Dynamics

Myth #6: GROUPS ARE INEFFECTIVE VEHICLES FOR ACHIEVING ORGANIZATIONAL OBJECTIVES.

DESERVED OR UNDESERVED?

Groups and committees have traditionally been subjected to charges of incompetence. It has been said, for example, "a camel is a horse put together by a committee." It is generally believed in the hospitality industry that the way to get something done is to assign it to a selected individual. Assigning it to a committee will only result in lost time, indecisive answers, and incompetent implementation. The reputation is not completely undeserved because we have certain expectations from our group or committee and one's expectations are not always met. However, we should not have expectations per se because there is nothing in the definition of group or committee that suggests anything by way of credible results. A "group," according to Webster, is "an assemblage of persons or things forming a separate unit," and a "committee" is "a body of persons appointed or elected to take action upon some matter or business." Contrasted with, for example, a board of directors whose raison d'être is "to direct," both groups and committees are not mandated to action. A group or committee, therefore, bears the same relationship to the output of positive action as a battery bears to the output of

70

positive power. Until the battery is energized, or empowered, it remains a battery, incapable of producing power. Until the group or committee is energized or empowered, it remains a body of people incapable of producing positive results. What is required of a group or committee is that it be molded into a team. The word "team" carries with it the implication of a body of individuals organized around a specific function for purposes of winning, that is, performing the function better than others can perform it. Thus, when we speak of group dynamics, we are discussing those elements both positive and negative that impact the molding of the group (or committee) into a team. If we now ask the question of whether or not a team is more effective in meeting assigned objectives than is an individual, we are left with the further question of defining the objective to be met. If it is one requiring rapid decision making (the Drill Sergeant Model), a team would be less effective. The fire captain, in performing his command duties during the fire, has little time for consensus decision making. Or, if the decision objective requires unique creativity (as in the Einstein Model), it is unlikely that a team could improve the result. Imagine Monet seeking consensus before each stroke of brush to canvas. There are a whole range of decision objectives in which teams of varying sizes and levels of expertise are beneficial to differing degrees. And generally we do not think about them. Lawyers, for example, discuss cases that are particularly complex, as do doctors. From such discussions often come innovative solutions. Business leaders belong to associations in which there are teams of specialists advising in such areas as benefits, insurance, legislation, distribution, investments, and so forth. Some basic studies that I have done regarding personality types among hospitality managers indicates a trend away from the extrovertive style once thought to be a requirement, towards the introvertive style emphasizing a more introspective, consensus type approach. On the other end of the decision spectrum are objectives that require time and in-depth analysis in order to both reach correct conclusions and to insure adoption of those conclusions by those affected. Human resource development, long-range planning, marketing strategies, and diversification are examples in which the input from a team is essential. These are long-range commitments in which attention to detail is crucial to the company's success. Achieving excellence is such a commitment. The proper application of quality and ethics is no longer just a short-term objective of successful management, it is now a required way of life. Today's enlightened managers know that excellence must permeate the entire organization from top to bottom, and they know that this state can only be achieved by the diligent work of a professional and dedicated quality assurance team.

SHOW ME A GOOD TEAM

There are some inherent differences between groups and teams, that is, individuals collected into a body versus individuals homogenized to a common objective. Individuals in groups or committees tend to bring to those organizations their own objectives and agendas. Team members focus on the organization objectives and agenda. Group members carry a basic apprehension and distrust into the group because they do not sense a cohesion to a common goal. Team members learn to depend upon others for their success and others depend upon them. Groups are often formed by others to carry out assigned tasks, whereas teams are cast more in the role of being assembled by others to work through means and systems to achieve an organizational objective. Groups tend to develop in members a basic unwillingness to take a risk, because the return for such risk is unclear, whereas teams encourage risk taking and risk taking is rewarded if it furthers the success of the team. The key element in contrasting groups and teams seems to come down to the issue of consensus. Groups tend to operate on the philosophy of majority rule; thus decisions tend to be unanimous as members defer to the group leader, or simple majority as votes are called. In a team approach, more emphasis is placed on discussion and analysis until the team reaches consensus agreement. Consensus recognizes and encourages the input of all members and operates on the philosophy that for every issue, there is a "one right solution" that time and active participation and analysis will identify. Teams, therefore, will take longer to arrive at decisions, but the decisions will be correct decisions a much higher percentage of the time. I have conducted test cases throughout North America, and in South America and Europe, comparing consensus decisions with non-consensus decision making, and the consensus approach always produces better decisions. H. L. Mencken had a famous quote as follows: "For every problem there is a solution which is simple, direct and wrong." This does not conflict with the management corollary that says, "When the right solution is found it will be simple." Rather, Mencken recognizes that often the quick, simple, direct solution, produced by quick, simple, direct managers, will be wrong. Consensus changes "quick, simple, direct, and wrong" into "considered, thorough, analytical, and correct!"

The bottom line of the discussion to this point is summed up in the following:

1. Quality assurance committees need time to develop into a team.
2. Quality assurance committees need to operate on the basis of total consensus decision making.
3. The quality assurance director's role is that of team building and not group directing.
4. Forced adoption is to be avoided at all cost.
5. Feedback is a crucial element in all communication.
6. Relevant employee input is essential throughout the quality assurance decision making process.
7. The fastest way to achieve meaningful excellence is to establish a slow, steady, thorough pace and be diligent in its execution.

COROLLARIES THAT BUILD TEAMS

In 1976, Richard D. Irwin, Inc. of Homewood, Illinois, published a book by Cohen, Gadon, Fink, and Willits, entitled *Effective Behavior in Organizations.* In it, they identified several generalizations of group dynamics. Attention to these generalizations will help to understand the dynamics affecting the molding of groups and committees into teams. As I discuss each, I will relate it to the principles we have already noted as germane to the quality assurance process, specifically the role of the Quality Assurance Committee and the quality assurance director.

The effectiveness of a group cannot be one-dimensional. Functionality depends upon productivity, satisfaction, and development.

Once constituted, the Quality Assurance Committee will quickly become ineffective if there is no real sense of involvement and achievement on the part of the members. One-hour meetings, once each week, will assure attendance and participation. Approaching standards in small but meaningful steps will build satisfaction, and bringing outsiders in from time to time to discuss or present related issues or processes will help the committee to develop its individual and collective expertise. The general manager is essential in his or her role as overseer of the process. The manager should be visible but not intrusive, present but not predominant, approving but not dictatorial, and, most importantly, patient. The meshing phase of implementation is the time when the basic dynamics of productivity, satisfaction, and development are sorted out. Time and effort expended at this basic beginning stage means solid performance as the program develops.

A crucial emergent factor in any group is the degree to which members turn out to like each other and the group.

If misunderstood, this corollary can be counterproductive. Groups have a tendency to discuss and become involved in almost any subject except the task at hand. Under ideal conditions, keeping the group focussed on the main task or objective is the constant role of the leader. There is a tendency among some managers to believe that staffing the committee with members who are highly socially compatible, or permitting members to be selected on the basis of friendship as the main criteria, results in greatest productivity. Of more importance than friendship in the initial selection is diversity and expertise, assuming, of course, that willingness and commitment are present. The idea is to formulate the strongest quality assurance committee possible from among department heads and assistant department heads, after which concerted effort is expended in building an environment of respect among the members. While "liking" and "respecting" are not necessarily mutually inclusive, generally it is easier to like someone you respect, more so than respecting someone you don't like. "Liking" can neither be legislated nor forced. It occurs naturally in a proper environment. The level of interaction of the group is important, as attested by the following three corollaries:

The greater the interaction among people, the greater the likelihood of developing positive feelings for one another.

The greater the positive feelings among people, the more frequently they will interact.

The greater the interaction required by the job (task) the more likely that social relationships and behavior will develop along with the task relationship and behavior.

The key, thus, is for the general manager and the quality assurance director to avoid any semblance of domination and, further, to be astutely aware of domination by any member of the Quality Assurance Committee, or attempted influence by someone outside the committee such as an owner, resident manager or a powerful department head. Interaction must be sincere.

The more attractive the group, the more cohesive will be its members.

1. The more cohesive the group, the more eager individuals will be for membership and, thus, the more likely they will be to conform to the group norms.

2. The more cohesive the group, the more influence it has on its members.

3. The less certain and clear a group's norms and standards are, the less control it will have over its members.

We speak now of the larger and expanding group, that is, the diffusion of quality/excellence to the property at large. The Quality Assurance Committee must be perceived as working together, cohesively, towards well-defined standards presented in basic, simple, understandable terms. There is a direct relationship between the perceived strength, dedication, commitment, and effectiveness of the Quality Assurance Committee and the strength, dedication, commitment, and effectiveness of the overall program. That is why "slower is faster." Time spent building the firm foundation is time well spent.

Group cohesion will be increased by acceptance of a superordinate goal subscribed to by most members.

Group cohesion will be increased by the perceived existence of a common enemy.

At the start of World War II, in both Europe and the Far East, America was totally unprepared for war. A massive effort was put forth and, in just a few years, America had developed the strongest land, air, and naval forces in all of recorded history. Credit was given to the expertise of American management, which could go from making cars to making tanks, from toy soldiers to bullets, and from bicycles to bombs because of the application of the skills of scientific management. Yet the true heroes and heroines of WWII were the people on the production lines. Almost every one of America's workers had a personal involvement in the war; husbands, wives, sons and daughters, aunts, uncles, friends and neighbors, were in the uniform of their country. A common enemy and a superordinate goal resulted in production unique in history. Management was important to the process, to be sure, but in the final analysis it was a management-labor team that produced results. The common enemy in quality assurance is error. The superordinate goal is to eliminate *all* error. What is left is to have the goal of eliminating errors subscribed to by all employees at all levels. The penalty for trying to force all employees to adopt quality assurance philosophy will be excessive turnover. The reward for patience and steady progress will be excellence.

Group cohesion will be increased when there are low numbers of external required interactions.

Stated more directly, management must resist the temptation to jump in and direct the quality assurance effort, especially when it begins to succeed. One of the hardest tasks of management is refraining from intervening when you have given an assignment to others and they are completing it differently from the way you would have done it. This is true even when the objective is being attained better than you might have done. Yet, progress requires change. Let the committee do its work!

The greater the cohesion of the group, the higher the productivity will be, if the group supports the organization's goals; and the lower the productivity will be if the group resents the organization's goals.

The key phrase in this corollary is "if the group supports the organization's goals." This is true throughout the organization—for

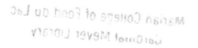

every employee. As the quality assurance program grows, from general manager commitment, to Quality Assurance Committee, to departmental heads, supervisors, and production level people, commitment to the overall goal is crucial to success. It cannot be legislated, to be truly effective. Commitment is earned by good communications, sincerity, hard work, and patience. In a capsule, this is why, later on, we will present the dynamic "on-line" approach to writing standards. By building on small successes, commitment increases, which encourages more success, etc.

Here are some corollaries that affect members within the group:

Members who contribute most to task accomplishment are accorded the most respect of the group; while members who contribute most to social accomplishment (developing of relationships) are accorded the most liking in the group.

When asked, most managers would rather be respected than liked, given that a choice need be made. In practice, the urge to be liked is very strong. The tendency for groups is to be overly social and, in the process, sacrifice some productivity. One-hour meetings with specific agendas will focus attention on the accomplishment of tasks. Nonetheless, the productivity of the Quality Assurance Committee must be monitored periodically. Ideally, the social aspects of the committee will focus around the task requirement and the resulting team will enjoy both friendship and respect.

The higher the background of external status, the higher the emergent internal status of a group member. Lower status members defer to higher status members, allowing higher status members to initiate interactions, make statements without being challenged, and administer informal rewards and punishments. Higher status members will usually "talk for the group" in public situations, make more contact with outsiders, and usually have the widest number of connections with the group. The lower one ranks in a group, the more one defers to others.

The above is the basis for excluding the general manager and those below assistant department head level from the Quality Assurance Committee. A secondary reason for not appointing those below assistant department head is that management must "put their money where their mouth is," that is, lead by example. Quality assurance is a top down process. By the time the program reaches the production-level people, the commitment of supervisors, department heads, and the general manager will be highly visible and creditable, essential elements for success.

The more one individual group member fails to conform to the group norms, the more frequently negative sentiments will be expressed towards him or her. The less a member conforms to a group's norms, the greater will be the interaction directed at him/her for some time. Should the interaction fail to bring the member into conformity with the norms, interaction will sharply decrease. The greater a member conforms to the group's norms, the greater the group's liking for the member.

Management and the Quality Assurance Committee commit to excellence. A process of developing standards is set up and slowly standards are reviewed and revised. Relevant production-level and supervisory-level employees are included in the discussions. People are trained in the new standard and the performance results are monitored. Compliance is recognized and rewarded. This is the basic form of the quality assurance program and becomes the norm of the program. The task is to gain acceptance and compliance to this norm. However, every organization has those who, for whatever reason or reasons, do not act according to the norms. At times it is courageous and correct to go against the norms, such as in the case of speaking out against prejudice. For the most part, members are expected to conform to the norm. Like a nail that sticks up above the wooden deck, employees who do not conform will be hammered down. If they persist in nonconformance, they will eventually be pulled out and replaced. We now have a real Catch-22, because the introduction of quality assurance requires a change from the norm. The point is that social systems resist change and deal harshly with those who visibly and vocally and vehemently resist the norms. The quality assurance director, especially, must be aware of this dynamic and, when a member is strongly resisting the norm, action must be taken to bring the situation under control before the member is cut off from group acceptance. This does not mean or imply that the resisting member is always wrong. It does mean that a red flag is waving and that it should be attended to without delay.

The members who conform most closely to a group's norms have the highest probability of emerging as informal leaders of the group. Informal group leaders may occasionally violate norms without punishment, provided that they have earned their leadership by general conformity to the group's norms.

The person most able to make changes is the person most perceived to conform to the existing norms. It seems like a contradiction, but it is not. A new manager, if he or she is enlightened, will take time to evaluate the existing system before changing it. This is exactly why the approach to excellence set forth in this book urges patience and establishes a process: a slow, steady path to excellence rather than the traditional approach of rewriting all operation manuals, establishing hundreds of new job standards, initiating massive training, and then demanding compliance, following which, measurement becomes impossible and the program fails. Including relevant employees in discussion of standards indicates a true desire to understand the present before making a fatal leap into the future.

A GROUP TO BE AVOIDED

Groups consist of individuals, and, before groups become teams, the individual personalities must be recognized and addressed. Five negative roles that people can play in groups should be identified and understood. Before the group shuts the door on such individuals, or before the individual playing a negative role can destroy the group, action should be taken. A good place to start is for the committee to discuss these roles and to agree as a committee that they are counterproductive to the success of quality assurance. In extreme cases, a committee will have to be replaced if the negative role persists.

Negative Roles

1. The *dominator* tries to run the show, asserting real or alleged authority, demanding attention, interrupting others, making arbitrary decisions, and insisting upon having the last

word. "Now I've had some experience at this sort of thing, and let me tell you what to do . . ."

2. The *blocker* is often a frustrated dominator. When he finds his authority is not conceded, or when the majority is moving in another direction, he becomes stubborn and resists the group on every count. "That idea will never work; you might just as well throw it out . . ."

3. The *cynic* sometimes succeeds the blocker. Thwarted in his isolated position, he scoffs at the group process, deliberately provokes conflict, or becomes painfully nonchalant. "It's obvious that you people will never agree; let's call it quits."

4. The *security seeker* may want sympathy, or just personal recognition. In one case he becomes self-deprecatory about his own plight, in the other, he continually calls attention to his own apparently unique experiences and accomplishments. "I had worse than that happen to me once . . . and I wish you'd tell me what I should have done."

5. The *lobbyist* is continually plugging his own pet theories, or pleading the special interests of other groups to which he may belong, although he is seldom willing to register as a lobbyist. "Now you understand this makes no difference to me, but don't you think we're being unfair to . . .?"

In summary, the identification of roles is a far easier task than the task of handling the various roles in an actual group interaction. Our objective is not to oversimplify but rather to lend some structure to the study of group dynamics. By understanding that group dynamics is a process of taking what comes, charting a course, and molding disparate personalities into a unified team whose prime focus is to solve the group's objectives, the quality assurance director will have a substantially better probability for success. Put another way: viewing the quality assurance director's role as simply "chairing the meeting" is a sure-fire way to invite disaster. If this chapter has heightened the awareness of management and the quality assurance director to the responsibilities of quality leadership, it will have achieved its goal. On the other hand, if the reader, as a result of this chapter, perceived his or her level of expertise to be more than just a basic awareness of the elements of group dynamics, then we have gone too far. We have simply thrown the reader a ball, shown him or her the playing field, and named the positions of the players. Understanding the intricacies of the game will require much more effort. But, in terms of ultimate success, it will be effort very well spent.

THE PROBLEM OF BURNOUT

The hospitality industry is notorious for burnout! Hours are long, and the dynamic nature of always being in the presence of the public becomes at times very stressful. There is a lingering philosophy among older members of hospitality management that those entering should work long hours for low pay in the beginning "just as I did when I was starting out!" The pace, of course, is faster today, the hotels much bigger, the services offered are often greater in scope, and entrance-level employees have far less pride in their vocation than had those 50 years prior. Turnover is greater. Burnout is frequent but, instead of recognizing it and working to overcome it, many managers consider burnout, like dealing with errors, as an inevitable part of the business. "If you can't stand the heat, get out of the kitchen!" Turnover, however, is costly, not only in hard dollars relating to hires, but also in terms of the negative impact on a well-trained staff continually integrating new employees. There are several causes of burnout, as follows:

1. *The boss who is never satisfied:* There are some managers and supervisors who never seem to be satisfied no matter what is done. All the employee hears is what is wrong, never what is right. The employee's motivation to do anything more than basically required is destroyed. This exacerbates the situation, causing more criticism and slowly but surely destroying the employee's effectiveness.
2. *The boss who never gives recognition:* Everyone needs to be appreciated. We want to be appreciated by our boss but if that is not to be, we will seek someone else to provide our "warm fuzzies." But, if there is no one available, if there is no recognition, we will go elsewhere to find it.
3. *The boss who does not give clear directions:* It's very hard to perform to the expectations of a boss who is not capable of communicating those expectations effectively. Ambiguity breeds anxiety, and anxiety, left unresolved, results in burnout.

4. *The boss who demands more than can be accomplished:* A superordinate task is a motivator assuming there is consensus that it can be accomplished. But, an impossible task is a guarantee of failure, and failure leads to burnout.

Two other factors that contribute to burnout are stress and fatigue. Stress is brought on by our need to respond physically to our environment, which requires us to change and, in changing, invest time and energy. The environment of the air controller, for example, requires constant and total concentration on a variety of concurrent situations, each of which is potentially life threatening. This is not a normal environment. Although less critical, a busy front desk can also require constant and total concentration on a variety of concurrent situations. When the changed environment is prolonged, the tremendous expenditure of energy results in fatigue and thus burnout. Fatigue can also result simply from working too hard for too long. The end result is the same—burnout.

The True Culprit

The real culprit behind all of these situations, however, is *hopelessness.* If, in any or all of the above situations, we have before us hope that we can change the situation and thus remove ourselves from the pathway to burnout, then it is unlikely that burnout will occur. If, however, we become convinced that nothing we can do will alter our situation, then we quickly burn out and become yet another turnover statistic, or worse, we lose touch with reality and become emotionally impaired.

Quality Assurance to the Rescue

Assume now a well-defined and communicated set of standards governing our work. Assume that we are trained to those standards, and are measured against them. When the standards are met, we are recognized and rewarded and when they are not, we are given help. We have just eliminated the boss who 1) is never satisfied, 2) never gives recognition, 3) does not give clear directions, and 4) demands the impossible. We have not solved stress and physical fatigue; however, constant awareness as to the level of performance against standards will certainly red flag this problem, as both stress and fatigue will cause a fall-off in performance. And, when the quality assurance program matures to the point where employees at all levels feel comfortable discussing their jobs and the related problems, and when supervisors and managers become willing to listen and take seriously the feedback they receive, there will be a sensitivity that will replace hopelessness. We must remember that quality assurance is an ongoing process that recognizes and values the worth of the individual as part of an overall team. Done properly, that is, as a sincere philosophy of management rather than a manipulative scheme, quality assurance will eliminate burnout and, as a result, save thousands of dollars otherwise lost.

7

Making Quality Pay

The Cost of Error

Myth #7: IT IS IMPOSSIBLE TO CALCULATE THE COST OF AN ERROR IN HOSPITALITY; THE INDUSTRY IS TOO LABOR-INTENSIVE AND ERRORS ARE TOO COMPLICATED TO BE ANALYZED.

SCRAP, REWORK, AND WARRANTY

We all know that errors cost money. The question is: how much money, and how can we prove it?

In manufacturing, the basic components of cost resulting from error are scrap, rework, and warranty (or service). Scrap can be weighed, rework counted, and the costs of servicing warranties added up. Although we don't have scrap barrels for plastic, metal, and broken pieces, hoteliers do have similar measurements. Only the labels are different.

We have barrels for waste food, for example, and they can tell us many things. Discarded food might suggest that meals are poorly prepared, or served in excessive amounts; it could also tell us that we are not receiving the quality of food we are ordering or that we are not ordering food of high enough standards. Perhaps our food quality is eroding through improper storage. The laundry "scrap barrel" could tell us that the guest towels are being used to wipe up floors, while the engineering barrel indicates how many motors have been replaced because they ran too long with dirty filters. The glass in the kitchen tells how many glasses have been thrown out because of careless handling—and how many dishes get broken through accident or careless handling. Barrels tell us much more than we have noted above; that's not the point. That they have something to tell us is. It pays to know what is in the scrap barrels!

We have rework costs too—expenditures that arise because a job wasn't done right the first time. How many maid trips are made to deliver the towels that should have been left during room makeup? How many banquet change memos are written because someone failed to get all the information the first time? How many guests are kept waiting while we search frantically for a missing car—all because of a misplaced valet slip?

And we have "warranty" and "service" costs, although we call them "amenities" or "customer relations expense." Not all amenities result from service errors. Baskets of soap, sewing kits, and shampoo are not only nice touches, but are also expected in many hotels. But the bottle of wine sent to the table of the dissatisfied guest, or the basket of fruit delivered to a guest who didn't receive the promised type of room are unnecessary expenses resulting from error.

If everything goes as planned, in fact, there is no need for a customer relations department, and no need to send apologetic letters. And whereas repair and maintenance calls sometimes result from unforeseeable equipment failure, any competent chief engineer in the industry will admit that many such calls could have been avoided by better engineering management and preventive maintenance.

Thus far we have talked about some of the hard costs of hospitality error: costs relating to "scrap," "rework," and "warranty." However, although these costs represent a major segment of the error cost of manufacturing, they are a lesser percentage of the total error costs in the services industry, in which the product is far less tangible. Thus, a system to measure error costs in hospitality had to be developed. In 1981, the author introduced a cost of error process for the hospitality industry that, for the first time, properly identifies both the components of cost and the magnitude. The system makes use of probability and segments costs and consists of three major components. They are the following:

1. *Hard costs*—money that must be expensed at the time of the error and as a direct result of it. Examples would be ameni-

ties, rebates, transportation (as in the case of transporting a "walked" guest to another hotel), letters written, phone charges, and such costs as replacing a guest's shirt or jacket lost in the cleaning process.

2. *Soft costs*—costs relating to events required as a result of an error in lieu of the normal manner in which the money is spent. For example, we pay a maid to make up rooms, but when the maid is spending 15% of her time correcting errors, then her productivity is decreased by 15% and that is a soft cost of error. The same applies to the front-desk personnel, bellhops, waitresses, assistant managers, and others. There's a saying in quality assurance, "Why is there always enough time to do things over but never enough time to do things right the first time?"

3. *Opportunity costs*—future sales lost as a direct result of the error. For example, statistics developed from a nationwide study by the author in 1985, in conjunction with AH&MA and Citicorp/Diners Club, indicated that some 20% of frequent male and female travelers "float," that is, change lodging accommodations because of errors encountered. Whenever a guest does not return because of an error, it is an opportunity cost.

Opportunity costs can be questioned on the basis that they represent sales and, as such, some hoteliers say that a sale "not made" only "costs" that amount represented by the profit from the sale. The profit, of course, varies with the department, higher for rooms, lower for food, etc. Precision, however, is difficult at best. If we work only with net departmental profit, in rooms, for example, we null out any advantages we have regarding fixed cost, because we are working with overall averages. If our break-even occupancy percentage is 65%, a lost room sale at 55% hurts more than does a lost room sale at 90%, even though the profit in the room sold at 90% occupancy is greater. This is true because of the importance of selling enough rooms to underwrite our fixed costs. What all of this means is that there are many ways to analyze cost of error, especially in the opportunity costs area. Thus, we will talk in terms of gross sales lost when we develop opportunity costs. The reader may alter those costs to fit his or her overall objectives of the cost of error process. Our point is only that the cost of error calculation is not precise, nor is it meant to be. It requires thought. Nonetheless, it will identify the order of magnitude of error cost.

When we speak of "cost of error," therefore, we are speaking of the sum total of hard costs, soft costs, and opportunity costs. In the process of developing that figure, however, we will segregate the cost components into the three parts for easier evaluation and decision.

The fact is that we all too often accept error costs—waste, inefficiency, inattention to detail, and poor attitude—as inevitable, i.e., as "part of the business." If we knew what these errors really cost, we would pay more attention to eliminating them.

That's what this chapter is all about—calculating the cost of error, or COE. Although specific numbers may vary from one property to another, it's important to go through the 11 steps that follow. Only in that way can we see how much those nagging little errors really cost us every year.

HIDDEN GOLD

Regardless of the kind of industry, errors cost more than many of us think. And because of the nature of the hospitality industry, the cost of a single mishandled situation can often be prohibitive.

One of the questions in our 1981 survey of AH&MA members was: "How much do you think errors cost each year as a percentage of total revenues?" The answers ranged widely, of course, but the average response was 1.2 percent. Respondents were then asked to cost errors using the standard "cost of error" form.

The results were astonishing. By asking managers to cost 50 common errors—"lost reservation," for example, or "room not ready at check in"—we determined that the average cost was more like 5% of total revenues. Given that one prominent resort identified 379 errors as part of their quality assurance program, we can assume that errors probably cost more than 10% of total revenues. That means that a 300-room property with a 70% occupancy rate, an average room rate of $80.00, and a ratio of room revenue to total revenue of .65, could be talking about as much as $943,000 if those errors could be eliminated. Remember, we are talking about the total of hard costs, soft costs, and opportunity costs.

True, those numbers don't apply to each and every case. We

probably would not lose one guest because our engineer doesn't keep our boiler clean and efficient, even though that could cost us 10% in fuel costs alone. And, the cost of error process does not take into account, for example, the cumulative effect of errors. A single error, for example, probably wouldn't cost us a guest's future business, although several errors might be more than enough. Also, our simplistic analysis ignores the problem of stress-related turnover, which will almost certainly be high in an operation with excessive errors. The cost to replace a front desk clerk, for example, can be as high as $5,000, including search, orientation, training, and break-in. And since not every new hire will work out, it might be necessary to repeat the process two or three times.

Errors cost money—much more than we realize. Eliminating them will recover the hidden gold buried in every property that does not have a good quality assurance program.

The Bellhop as Manager

It's important to understand that few errors are "site-specific"; that is, an error in one department usually sets off shock waves in at least one other department. The result is that what seems to be a fairly minor mistake very often costs us several times over.

Consider a bellhop who arrives with a guest at the room only to find the room not ready. Understandably, the guest is upset, with perhaps a bit of anxiety setting in. He or she is probably tired. Is another room available? Will it be the type requested? How long will it take? Is the unready room a sign of other deficiencies?

At this point, the bellhop becomes the pivotal person. The error has placed the bellhop in the role of assistant manager, in fact, since he or she is on the spot and must solve the guest's problem. Will the bellhop be able to set the guest's mind at ease and handle the situation professionally? Perhaps, if he or she is experienced or quick-witted enough. But the bellhop depends on customer tips, and that means rooming as many guests as possible. Instead, he or she must now correct someone else's mistake. As a result, the bellhop may be as upset as the guest.

The Domino Effect

The bellhop now phones the front desk clerk, who must then take the time to reassign the guest; that means sending another bellhop or the assistant manager to the floor with a new key. The clerk must also call housekeeping to place the original room in the "unmade" category, so housekeeping must now get the room cleaned. So . . . we have the bellhop angry at the front desk clerk, who's angry at housekeeping, who's angry at the inspector, who's angry at the maid; everyone is angry at someone else. Attitudes go downhill, and so perhaps do guest relationships.

But the chain reaction doesn't stop there. If the general manager learns of the incident, he or she may try to save the day by sending an apology with a basket of fruit or cheeseboard. Chances are that management will not be notified, however, because no one wants to tell him or her, and it is unusual for a hotel to require that such events be communicated.

Result: The guest eventually checks out with a negative image of the property that probably could have been assuaged. Just as bad, management, because of not being aware of the problem, loses an opportunity to evaluate the cause, which is somewhere in the room-status communication process. And assuming that the bellhop and others did a good job of making a bad situation acceptable, management, because it is not informed, also loses the opportunity to recognize their performance. No wonder most hotel employees complain that the only time they hear from management is when things go wrong!

The point is that most errors have multiple or domino effects; a problem in one area almost always causes problems in one or more other areas. And when employees are frustrated by errors, they slowly lose their pride and, in turn, their energies. What we have, in other words, is a perfect setting for more errors!

Before we get into the details of COE analysis, it's important to note that the employees themselves, at every level, must become involved in the cost of error process. Only then can they see firsthand the damage that errors create. That's much more effective than having management try to make the point through communication alone.

But errors are not solved simply by analyzing them; they're solved by reviewing and writing standards and requiring compliance. Use the COE analysis as an informational and awareness tool that fosters understanding. Management's attitude should be, "Don't tell me about the errors you have identified, tell me about the ones you have eliminated." In short, don't emphasize what is going to happen—emphasize what has been done.

Figure 7.1 shows a typical cost of error calculation form.

COST OF ERROR ANALYSIS

Before beginning an actual analysis, we should spend a moment on the heading of the form, self-explanatory except for the section labeled "ID." Each error has a discreet identification. The system that I use is in three parts. First, an alpha designation of the department within which the error occurs is used. In our example, that would be housekeeping. I use the designation "HSKP." Second, a running total of errors within that department is kept. Let's assume that our example is the 10th error analyzed in the housekeeping department. Thus, HSKP-10. Third, we would want to designate a running total of all errors, regardless of department. Assume our example represents the 32nd error analyzed overall. Our "ID" designation would be HSKP-10-32. There are many ways to identify errors. Pick a method that best suits you and your needs. Now let us look at the cost of error process.

There are 11 steps to the cost of error calculation process. Initially they may seem complex and confusing. Considered more carefully, however, they flow in a very logical process. The 11 steps, in general terms, are the following:

1. Define the error.
2. Determine the consequences.
3. Establish a cost for each consequence.
4. Establish the frequency (profitability) of consequence per error.
5. Calculate the expected cost for each consequence.   Post expected cost in appropriate column.
6. Total the expected consequence costs by category.
7. Calculate the total possible chances for error to occur/year.
8. Estimate the frequency (probability) of error occurring/year.

COST OF ERROR CALCULATION

Property _____

Department _____

Date _____ ID _____

Done By _____

1	ERROR

2	CONSEQUENCES
A	
B	
C	
D	
E	
F	
G	
H	

3	COST OF CONSEQUENCES

4	PR

5	EXPECTED CONSEQUENCE COST		
	HARD	SOFT	OPPORTUNITY

6	TOTALS

7	POSSIBLE ERRORS/YEAR	8	PR

9	ERRORS/ YEAR

10	ERROR COST BY TYPE

11	TOTAL COST OF ERROR

Stephen Hall Associates
SPECIALISTS IN QUALITY ASSURANCE

FIGURE 7.1   Cost of Error calculation form.

91

9. Calculate the number of times error occurs per year.
10. Calculate the error cost per year by categories.
11. Calculate the total cost of error per year.

Now let us look at each step in more detail.

Step One: Defining the Error

The first step in analyzing error cost is to define the error as inclusively as possible. That point isn't as obvious as it may seem. For example, stating the error as "Guest taken to room; room not ready" is too general. The room could not be ready because it hadn't been cleaned; there could have been a mechanical problem, or perhaps the previous guest's baggage were still in the room. All these factors could render a room "not ready," but they occur with different frequency and are resolved in different ways. Be specific with your definition: "Guest room not ready; not made up," for example, or "Guest room not ready; still occupied."

In this connection, note also that specific employee functions should be included in the analysis whenever appropriate. If the room is not ready because there are missing towels or washcloths, that indicates a problem with the performance of the room maid and also the process by which the room is inspected prior to the guests' arrival. The error should thus be identified as "Guest room not ready; not properly made up." This places the error in the housekeeping department, and, although we do not yet know the root cause, we do know that it is specifically the housekeeping function that must be evaluated. Properly defining the error is a crucial first step.

Figure 7.2 shows the first section of a cost of error form.

Step Two: Determining the Consequences

Having defined the error, ask the question, "When this error occurs, what are the possible consequences?" This may be the most important step in COE analysis, because it demonstrates how errors cut across departmental or positional lines. Done properly, the domino effect of an error is made clear to everyone.

Whereas most errors have more than one consequence, the first

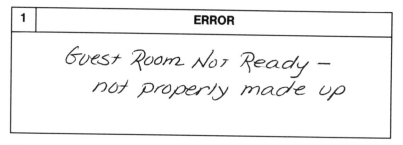

FIGURE 7.2   Section 1 of COE form—error is defined.

and most important is, "Guest will not return." Studies performed by Stephen Hall Associates with AH&MA and Diners Club/Carte Blanc resulted in a list of the 10 most costly errors and determined that on average, at least one of the 10 errors occurs every time a guest stays in a hotel or motel (see Table 7.1). The same study revealed that an alarming 20% of all guests will not return if they encounter even one of these errors. That means that the possibility of permanently losing a guest is very real—and, of course, very costly.

For each of the 10 errors listed in Table 7.1, the word "freq" refers to "frequency" and indicates the percent of times the error occurs. For example, under "unfriendly employees," male frequent travelers encounter "unfriendly employees" 12% of the time (approximately once each 8 trips). "Disc" means "discontinuance" and refers to the probability that the guest won't return if the error occurs. For male frequent travelers, the discontinuance" rate for the error "unfriendly employees" is 32% (approximately every 3 times the error occurs), and for female frequent travelers it is 48% (approximately once every 2 times the error occurs). Combining frequency and discontinuance, in simple terms, for male frequent travelers, unfriendly employees will cause the typical hotel to lose a customer 3.84% of the time, or 3.84% of the guests will not come back because of unfriendly employees.

One out of eight male guests encounters "unfriendly employees" (12%), and approximately one out of three guests encountering the problem won't return (32%)
(.12 × .32 = .0384).

For female frequent travelers, the percent of guests lost due to "un-friendly employees" is 4.32%.

($.09 \times .48 = .0432$)

Combining all of the data for all 10 areas, we learn that male frequent travelers encounter at least 1 of the 10 errors every 1.036 trips, i.e., every single trip! Female frequent travelers encounter at least 1 of the 10 errors every .909 trips (again, almost one per trip!). Twenty-four percent of males and 31 percent of females won't re-turn, when 1 of the 10 errors is encountered.

Most hoteliers find this data hard to accept because, as dis-cussed in Chapter 1, most hoteliers do not believe that errors occur frequently "in their hotel." (They all occur with the competitor.) However, the enlightened manager, the one who says, "What if, . . ." "What if this data is real? . . ." that manager, with quality assurance, is sitting on a gold mine!

TABLE 7.1   Ten Most Costly Hotel Errors, their Frequency of Commission, and Resulting Discontinuance (by percentage).

	MALE		FEMALE	
	FREQ (%)	DISC (%)	FREQ (%)	DISC (%)
1. UNSATISFACTORY FOOD SERVICE	19	20	13	18
2. POOR FACILITY MAINTENANCE	18	27	13	35
3. SLOW CHECK-IN/CHECK-OUT	18	15	18	31
4. UNFRIENDLY EMPLOYEES	12	32	9	48
5. ROOM NOT READY ON ARRIVAL	10	11	13	15
6. POOR OVERALL SERVICE	9	48	10	58
7. REQUESTED ROOM TYPE NOT AVAILABLE	7	14	7	16
8. MORNING WAKE-UP CALL NOT MADE	5	14	3	19
9. NO RECORD OF RESERVATION	4	31	5	27
10. OVERBOOKED; GUEST WALKED	2	59	1	81

Returning to our illustration, "Guest room not ready; not made up," we can identify at least six possible consequences:

	Type Cost
1. Guest will not return	Opportunity
2. Bellhop loses 15 minutes	Soft
3. Housekeeper loses 10 minutes	Soft
4. Assistant manager loses 15 minutes	Soft
5. Amenity is given	Hard
6. Manager letter is written	Hard

Let's consider the consequences of lost employee time, a soft cost. Some managers will argue that there is no lost time; the employees are there anyway. True enough, but if the bellhop were not occupied solving the guest's problem with the unmade room, he or she might be in the lobby assisting a guest, thus making a friend for the property rather than, upstairs, trying to keep one. Or he might be delivering guest messages or picking up guest laundry rather than trying to explain why the front desk doesn't know what rooms are ready.

Meanwhile, the housekeeper is busy enough without having to spend time figuring out what happened and how to remedy it. One such event might not be too damaging, but how often do such events eat into the housekeeper's time and prevent the accomplishment of such tasks as scheduling, reorganizing the linen room, or evaluating performance? And wouldn't it be better if the assistant manager could greet guests and visit departments rather than handle guest complaints?

Don't underestimate the value of lost time—it's the archenemy of good management. And until we consider lost time a consequence of error, we will never be able to properly analyze it.

There is one other aspect of "lost time." It would appear logical that the elimination of lost time would result in higher productivity, which seems to translate into reduced staff. Put another way, management views the reduction of lost time as "reduced overhead through reduced staff." Employees view the reduction of lost time as lost jobs! Both management and labor are wrong. In point of fact, the reduction of lost time results from the reduction (elimination) of error. When errors are eliminated, guest satisfaction goes up. Higher guest satisfaction means more business and more business means either more staff or more efficient staff. Since our staff is already more efficient, we do not need more staff. Thus, reducing lost time

2
CONSEQUENCES

A	Guest will not return.
B	Bellman loses 15 minutes.
C	Housekeeper loses 10 minutes
D	Asst. MGR. loses 15 minutes
E	Amenity is given.
F	Manager writes letter to guest.
G	
H	

FIGURE 7.3   Section 2 of COE form—error consequences are defined.

by eliminating error doesn't cost jobs; quite the contrary, it builds job security.

One final note. We have provided eight spaces (see Figure 7.3) for consequences. Some errors have more consequences, most have less. The idea is to identify the obvious consequences, not necessarily to find eight. However, experience has taught us that more than eight is probably not a good investment of our time.

Step Three: Establishing the Consequence Cost

We know that consequences cost money. We can now figure out just how much money.

Some consequences are fairly straightforward. When a bellhop loses 15 minutes (soft cost), we enter 25 percent of the wage rate, plus benefits. Other consequences, such as "guest won't return" (opportunity cost), are more difficult. If the error is great enough (walking a guest with a confirmed reservation, for example), there's a good chance that the guest not only won't return but will also change chain affiliation.

Try to be conservative in calculating COE. If the guest does not return, we haven't lost him or her for just one night, but for the entire stay—2.2 days (assuming 2.2 days to be the average length of guest stay. This, of course, varies with the property). What's more, we've lost more than the price of the room; we also sacrifice the other sales (restaurants, lounge, phone calls, newsstand purchases, etc.). Let's reflect that figure by assigning a room revenue to total revenue ratio of 0.65. (The ratio of room revenue to total revenue also varies with each property.)

Now we can see the revenue losses incurred by a non-returning guest:

$$\frac{2.2 \text{ nights average stay} \times \$70.00 \text{ room rate/night}}{.65 \text{ (rooms revenue to total revenue)}} = \$236.92$$

Note that this is simply lost revenues; it does not include lost tips or employee flexing that takes place when occupancy is low. Neither does it consider the effect of negative word-of-mouth (which is usually assumed to reach 10 other potential guests). The result is that a revenue loss of $236.92 for "walking" a guest is probably very conservative, but will serve for illustration purposes.

Now let's continue by estimating the cost of lost time (soft costs). Assuming that the bellhop makes $4.00 an hour in wages and benefits, the housekeeper $9.00, and the assistant manager $12.00, the total cost is as shown below:

	Time Lost	Wage and Benefit Per Hour ($)	Cost ($)
Bellhop	$\frac{1}{4}$ hour	4.00	1.00
Housekeeper	$\frac{1}{6}$ hour	9.00	1.50
Assistant Manager	$\frac{1}{4}$ hour	12.00	3.00
			$ 5.50

The cost of a special guest amenity—a fruit basket, for example, or a bottle of wine—is easily measured; let's assume an average price of $12.00. The cost of writing a brief business letter is generally estimated at about $10.00.

Now we can estimate the total economic cost of "guest room not ready; not made up" in the following list:

Step Two: Consequence	Step Three: Cost ($)
1. Guest will not return	236.92
2. Bellhop loses 15 minutes	1.00
3. Housekeeper loses 10 minutes	1.50
4. Assistant manager loses 15 minutes	3.00
5. Amenity is given	12.00
6. Manager letter is written	10.00

Step Four: Establishing the Consequence Probability

Not all the consequences listed in the previous sections will occur each and every time an error is made, of course. To get the true cost of error, we introduce the use of probability theory to determine how often these consequences are likely to result.

Starting with the first consequence—"guest will not return"— we know that not every disappointed guest will stay away. If we're lucky, some will give us another chance; others conduct business nearby, and will return because of the convenience. It is reasonable to assume that 10 percent of the guests who are taken to an unmade room will try another property next time; the probability for that consequence is thus 0.1, or 10 percent. (If, however, you feel more comfortable with 8 percent, or 15 percent, or some other percent, use those numbers.)

On the other hand, we can be pretty sure that the bellhop and the housekeeper will each lose time whenever the error of "unmade room" occurs. But, to be conservative, let's assign a 90 percent probability for consequences 2 and 3. The assistant manager may or may not become involved, however; so let's use 40 percent as a probability for consequence 4.

Consequence 5—giving an amenity—is a management decision, and the type and cost of the amenity vary with each managerial philosophy. Most hoteliers feel that their recognition of responsibility for the error goes a long way in bringing unhappy guests back to the property. What we don't know, of course, is how many would return even if the property hadn't acknowledged its error. At any rate, let us assume that for this type of error, an amenity is provided about three-quarters of the time. The probability of consequence 5 is thus 75 percent.

The same probability figure can be assigned to a letter of apology by management. To be sure, the letter should be written in every case; to be conservative, however, assume that management is aware of only three out of four errors, or that the manager is convinced that the error was satisfactorily resolved on the spot.

Our worksheet now looks like this:

Consequence	*Gross Cost ($)*	*Consequence Probability*
1. Guest will not return	236.92	.10
2. Bellhop loses 15 min.	1.00	.90
3. Housekeeper loses 10 min.	1.50	.90
4. Asst. mgr. loses 15 min.	3.00	.40
5. Amenity is given	12.00	.75
6. Mgr. letter is written	10.00	.75

Step Five: Calculating the Expected Consequence Cost by Category

If we now multiply the gross consequence cost by the probability, we have the expected cost of each consequence. Place the expected cost in the appropriate column depending upon type, as shown in Table 7.2.

TABLE 7.2   Expected Costs of Consequences.

CONSEQUENCE	GROSS CONSE-QUENCE COST ($)	CONSE-QUENCE PROB-ABILITY	EXPECTED CONSEQUENCE COST ($)		
			HARD	SOFT	OPPORT.
1. GUEST WILL NOT RETURN	236.92	.10			23.69
2. BELLMAN LOSES 15 MIN.	1.00	.90		.90	

TABLE 7.2   (Continued).

CONSEQUENCE	GROSS CONSE- QUENCE COST ($)	CONSE- QUENCE PROB- ABILITY	EXPECTED CONSEQUENCE COST ($)		
			HARD	SOFT	OPPORT.
3. HOUSEKEEPER LOSES 10 MIN.	1.50	.90			1.35
4. ASST. MGR. LOSES 15 MIN.	3.00	.40			1.20
5. AMENITY IS GIVEN	12.00	.75	9.00		
6. MGR. LETTER IS WRITTEN	10.00	.75	7.50		

Step Six: Totalling the Expected Cost per Error by Category

Having calculated the expected cost of each consequence and posted it by category, we now add the costs to obtain the expected cost of each error by category—that is, the expected cost each and every time a guest is taken to a room that isn't properly made up.

	Hard	Soft	Opportunity
Total cost per error:	$16.50	$3.45	$23.69

Step Seven: Calculating the Annual Potential for Error

The next question is, "How many times could this error occur every year?" In the case of the room not being made up at check-in, it could conceivably happen with every check-in. That's unlikely, of course, but the step is an important one for purposes of making everyone aware of the processes involved with the error.

In our example, consider a 300-room hotel with an average occupancy of .75 with a 2.2-night average stay. The number of check-ins per year is thus:

$$\frac{300 \text{ rooms} \times .75 \text{ occupancy} \times 365 \text{ nights}}{2.2 \text{ nights average stay}} = 37,329 \text{ check-ins/yr}$$

Nothing helps people to understand hotel operations more than numbers like these. Suddenly everyone appreciates the front desk, not to mention the maids and bellhops. Each year, 37,329 guests expect to walk into an assigned room and find it totally in order. Each year, a bellhop has 37,329 opportunities to tell a guest about the hotel and its services, thus reinforcing the guest's decision.

Possible errors/year = 37,329

Step Eight: Estimating the Error Probability

We've just seen that every year, 37,329 guests check into our 300-room property. What are the chances that upon reaching the assigned room, the guest will find the room isn't ready?

Ask the bell staff; they'll have a good idea as to how often they find rooms unmade. Confirm with the housekeeper. Ask the assistant managers and check your list of amenities and what they were for. Look over your manager's letters. If all of these fail to provide you with a reasonable estimate of probability, use your experience and intuition.

Whatever you do, don't kid yourself by assuming away the problem. Do one out of every 100 guests reach an unmade room? If so, the probability is .01. Let's be conservative and assume it happens only once per 200 check-ins, for a probability of .005:

Probability = .005

Step Nine: Calculating Number of Errors per Year

Errors per year is obtained by multiplying the potential for error by the probability; that is, 37,329 × .005 = 186. Every year, in other words, 186 guests arrive at their room to find it unmade.

Errors per year = 186

Step Ten: Calculating the Annual Cost of Error
by Categories

We now know how often this error occurs and how much it costs. Calculating the annual cost of the error by categories is a simple process of multiplication.

Total hard cost for the error (6)	$ 16.50
Errors per year (9)	× 186
Subtotal hard cost of error (10)	$ 3,069.00
Total soft cost for the error (6)	$ 3.45
Errors per year (9)	× 186
Subtotal soft cost of error (10)	$ 641.70
Total opportunity cost for the error (6)	$ 23.69
Errors per year (9)	× 186
Subtotal opportunity cost of error (10)	$ 4,406.34

Step Eleven: Calculating the Overall Annual
Cost of Error

Now that we know the cost of the error by categories, figuring the overall cost of error is a simple case of adding the subtotals in step ten.

Subtotal hard cost of error (10)	$ 3,069.00
Subtotal soft cost of error (10)	641.70
Subtotal opportunity cost of error (10)	4,406.34
Total cost of error	$ 8,117.04

Figure 7.4 demonstrates the completed cost of error calculation.

A WORD OF CAUTION

Granted, not everyone agrees with this COE analysis. Some argue that errors are an inherent part of the hospitality industry and can-

COST OF ERROR CALCULATION

Property	BIG BUCKS INN
Department	HOUSEKEEPING
Date	9/20/89 ID HSKPG-10-32
Done By	SSJH

1 ERROR

Guest Room Not Ready – not properly made up

2 CONSEQUENCES	3 COST OF CONSEQUENCES	4 PR	5 EXPECTED CONSEQUENCE COST		
			HARD	SOFT	OPPORTUNITY
A	Guest will not return.	236.92	.1			23.69
B	Bellman loses 15 minutes.	1.00	.9		.90	
C	Housekeeper loses 10 minutes	1.50	.9		1.35	
D	Asst. Mgr. loses 15 minutes	3.00	.4		1.20	
E	Amenity is given.	12.00	.75	9.0		
F	Manager writes letter to guest.	10.00	.75	7.50		
G						
H						

6 TOTALS			16.50	3.45	23.69
9 ERRORS/YEAR					186
10 ERROR COST BY TYPE			3069.00	641.70	4406.34
11 TOTAL COST OF ERROR			8,117.04		

7 POSSIBLE ERRORS/YEAR	8	PR
37,329		.005

Stephen Hall Associates
SPECIALISTS IN QUALITY ASSURANCE

FIGURE 7.4 Completed COE form.

not be completely eliminated; some question the accuracy of the calculations. Still others look at the total cost for the error and aren't impressed. These attitudes are dangerous for effective quality assurance.

In the first place, errors are not inevitable. They can be eliminated, and in later chapters we'll see just how they can be eliminated to reduce costs and boost profits.

For those who question specific calculations, please remember that the analysis allows for individual objectivity; if you disagree with these costs or probabilities, by all means use your own. The important thing isn't the specific numbers, but to go through the exercise in the order provided.

For those who minimize the impact of the cost of one error, I suggest they give considerable thought to the total possible errors that can impact guests in the hospitality industry. If, for example, $8,000 is not impressive, consider that there could be 50 other errors, some with less impact, some with more. Consider then whether $400,000 is an impressive figure!

Remember too that such objections to the cost-of-error analysis are often ego-centered; management is reluctant to acknowledge that errors cost, and often fear that the COE calculation reflects on their reputation and ability. As a result, they tend to downplay COE. Such was the case at the Boca Raton Resort and Club, a five-star property in Southern Florida. When management reached the cost of error analysis point in its quality assurance program, the whole process seemed to stop. Department heads were unwilling to identify and cost errors, thinking it would reflect on their abilities.

Hoping to solve the problem, Scott Morrison, who was then the general manager, told the QA Committee members about a costly error he himself had made: It seemed that guests often ordered a large glass of fresh squeezed orange juice at breakfast, only to be unable to finish it because they didn't realize what the resort meant by "large." Scott's solution was to serve a small glass of juice and, upon finishing it, if the guest wanted more, a second glass was served. If the guest was satisfied with the small glass, however, he or she was charged only for that size and juice was not wasted.

That seemed like a fine solution, except that many guests thought that the waiter had made a mistake or that the hotel was overcharging for its juice. Waiters and waitresses became embroiled in far too many discussions in trying to explain the policy. Although the idea was to help the guest, it came off just the opposite, and the policy was finally scrapped.

The effect of Scott's "true confession" was that department heads realized that everyone makes errors, and that the sin is not in making an error but in failing to acknowledge it, correct it, and prevent it from recurring. Because the manager took the lead in acknowledging and analyzing one of his own errors, the rest joined in and the COE process was off and running.

Closing our eyes to errors doesn't make them go away. Whether or not you agree with the logic and assumptions of the COE, the fact remains that errors do cost money and thus must be eliminated. Finding fault with the process and using that as a reason to ignore cost of error is a most foolhardy decision on the part of management.

Let us close this discussion of cost of error by reemphasizing its true value. In order for employees at all levels to get excited about quality assurance, i.e., excellence, they must understand and believe that a) errors cost money, and b) errors make everybody's work that much harder. The precise cost of error is important not as a finite number *but* as an order of magnitude—a way of establishing that errors are *very* expensive. And the process of calculating cost of error is most educational in helping everyone to understand the domino effect of an error and to begin to appreciate the immensity of the various functions in hospitality operations. For instance, in our example of the "Room not ready—not made up," it will come as a most impressive surprise to all except the front office manager (and perhaps to him or her as well!) to learn that the property goes through the check-in process 37,329 times each year (and is expected to do it each time without error!). We should not become slaves to the cost of error process nor should we brag too much about the money we have "saved" or will save. On the other hand, ignoring the value of cost of error is to severely handicap the quality assurance program. So, use it, recognize it for what it is—a working tool—and go forward to eliminate errors.

8

Why? Why? Why?

Getting to the Root Cause

Myth #8 *QUALITY OCCURS WHEN THE GUESTS, OUR CUSTOMERS, COMPLETE THEIR INTERACTIONS WITH US WITHOUT ERROR HAVING OCCURRED.*

Current thinking among most of America's service companies actively engaged in quality assurance is that quality is "customer driven." This approach can be a Catch-22 for hoteliers. Carried to its extreme, "customer driven" means "giving the customer what he/she wants when he/she wants it." If this means designing product to meet customer needs and delivering product and service according to commitment, then the philosophy is sound. It relates more, however, to a manufacturing operation. In the service industry, the extreme wide variance in customer needs and the different perceptions of time make the "customer drive" philosophy more difficult unless careful thought is given to its meaning. The key in hospitality is to establish the market level you wish to promote and then develop, around that market target, a set of standards that are consistently met. However, in the area of human interaction, consistency is not always appreciated. For example, I was recently involved in a discussion of measuring standards with a large group of service-related executives. We were discussing the number one error in hospitality as determined by a national hotelier survey that we conducted: "Employees who don't know the services or facilities offered." The issue was: "How do you measure whether or not the bellhop does a correct job in building an interpersonal relationship with the guest, promoting the property, and communicating the features and function of the guest room during the rooming process?" A senior executive interjected that "the last thing he wants after a long travel day is a verbose bellhop!" Thus, do you create precise standards, rigidly enforced, or do you keep the whole process loose and free? Or, do you create the standards but train the bell staff to "read" the guest and adjust the interaction accordingly? Obviously, the latter is the most desirable, but it requires considerable training, and employee attitude is the key to everything. And, certainly, such an approach is "customer driven." However, to adopt a view that effective quality assurance occurs when the quality control is placed immediately before the guest receives the product and/or service is very counterproductive to the quality process. There are four problems with carrying the "customer driven" philosophy to the point of focusing solely on the final product or service delivered to the guest.

1. Quality assurance is *not* an event, it is a process requiring the active, willing, proficient participation of internal human resources, as well as of external suppliers. The key to this participation is attitude. Focusing too strongly on the end product at the exclusion of focusing on the process will result in even more focus on the "end" because, without proper process, the end product can never be successful.
2. Providing a perfect end product can often mean accepting considerable waste if focus is placed too strongly on final inspection and interim inspection is ignored.
3. Many elements of the service equation have no direct relationship to the customer. For example, proper engineering management in the production of heat and hot water can reduce costs 10–20%. If we focus totally on delivering hot water and not at all on the efficient transfer of heat in our boiler, guests will be happy but we will be wasting financial resources.
4. Many elements of hospitality service are areas in which gratuities play a major role in employee compensation. Ethically, every guest deserves the same treatment whether he/she is a large tipper or a non-tipper. If the philosophy of end user

satisfaction is overstated, it could become the *raison d'être* for preferential treatment.

We can summarize the discussion thus far by agreeing that quality is customer driven in that guest or customer satisfaction is the ultimate measure of our success, but it takes a fine-tuned process based on well conceived and developed standards in a total environment of positive attitude at all levels to achieve true quality.

There is one further potential pitfall in concentrating too heavily on the end user's satisfaction. It is possible with such concentration to focus more on symptoms than on causes when it comes to eliminating error.

THE ROOT CAUSE

Case 1   A guest was served stale orange juice at breakfast. He complained and was responded to in a most satisfactory manner. The next morning, in fact, the maitre d'hotel proudly told him that the solution to the problem of a guest receiving stale juice was the hotel's new requirement that waiters and waitresses smell every glass of juice before leaving the pantry to be certain it is fresh.

Case 2   The restocking carts for the "in room" mini bars at a prominent southern resort caused the corridor carpet to ripple during travel, and the carts were also hard to turn, resulting in extensive damage to corridor corners. The resort put metal angle guards on the corners and reduced the loading on the carts, thus requiring more trips to restock carts and subsequently more labor cost.

Case 3   Arriving at a $250.00/day resort hotel at midnight, I gave my car to the valet. There was no bellhop visible so I took my bag and walked across the expansive lobby only to stand at the reception desk for 10 minutes waiting for someone to notice me and check me in. When the desk clerk finally came out of her "office," she told me that she has to work at the computer after 10 P.M. and can't always see or hear someone at the desk. It had been that way for a long time but since few guests checked in late it didn't seem to be a problem.

Let's look at the process for resolution.

Case 1—the stale orange juice caper. Management solved the symptom. A guest should not get stale juice in the future. But smelling the juice before serving it does not answer the question of why the juice is stale in the first place. Is it opened too soon? Iced down too late? Is it taken off the receiving dock in reasonably short time? Is it refrigerated properly? Is it turned over regularly? These are the right questions to ask. In point of fact, the solution was found in the answer to the most basic question: "Was it already stale when we received it?" The fault lay with the supplier and the solution lay with better purchasing control.

Case 2—The mini bar cart caper. Putting metal angles on the corners did prevent damage but were unsightly. Further, they did not solve the problem. Lightening the load helped but did not solve the problem and required more restock time. Solutions varied from larger wheels to restretching the carpet to putting bumpers on the carts, to restocking with hand-carried baskets, to firing the employee and getting someone who was better able to push the cart. The ultimate cause of the problem was that the wrong cart was being used, but it didn't stop there. When asked "why" was the cart purchased, it developed that purchasing, asked to get a cart, called their normal supplier and ordered simply "a cart." No attempt was made to determine use and fitness for use. Thus, the process of getting to the root cause ultimately resulted in a better, more effective job of purchasing.

Case 3—The missing night clerk. When followed through to conclusion, it was determined that no additional desk staffing was warranted. The one bellhop on duty at that hour often was busy elsewhere. However, since there was always a valet runner available at the front door, he or she could very well announce the late arrival of a guest. The Quality Assurance Committee figured out that if a bell could be installed at the front desk, with a button at the front door, the valet or door attendant could announce the arrival by pushing the button as the guest crossed the lobby. To be sure, the valet or bellhop should take every guest's baggage to the desk and, once there, ring a bell on the desk if the clerk was not available. In my case, there was no bellhop and I had only one small bag and carried it myself. In the course of the quality assurance conversation the 40-year veteran chief bellhop, whom we had asked to join us in the discussion, told us that such a button was already in place at the entrance and had been used until just a few years ago. Why wasn't it used now? The battery was dead! Further, the ivy had covered it and the new valets did not know it existed. But there is more to the story. What about the guest who arrives at the desk from inside the hotel? The valet at the entrance could use the bell to alert the clerk. Could the clerk do the input work at the desk instead of in a room virtually out of sight? Not with the present equipment, but with the modern equipment available, remote input is easily feasible. The net final result of the root cause exploration was a solution to the problem and a heightened awareness of guest needs in the process.

As simplistic as it sounds, the path to the root cause of error is asking the basic question "why" until all the elements of the process are identified and justified.

"I Didn't Know"

The most classic example of the root cause process occurred for me in a prominent hotel in Bermuda. All department heads, plus selected supervisors and production-level people, some 25 in all, were assembled to discuss the process of identifying and resolving errors. As a simple example, I asked the dining room waiter present what his biggest problem was. He responded that often during the meal hours, he would run out of tablecloths.

Feeling quite comfortable with the process, I then asked the linen supply girl why she did not leave enough tablecloths at each station in the dining room. She responded by telling the group that the laundry did not issue her enough to cover the full need. The laundry manager then informed me that the large ironer had a defective part and would only run on one-half speed, thus production in all flatgood areas was poor. I then asked the obvious question to the chief engineer. "Why don't you fix the ironer?"

The chief said that the particular part that broke came from the States and required a three-week wait every time it broke.

"You mean," I asked, "that the part in question fails often?" The answer was yes. When asked why he did not order two or three parts so as to have a spare, he said that he tried but purchasing would not permit it.

Purchasing then interjected that they would have ordered two parts, but management had a general policy that only one repair part could be ordered at a time. In other words, there was no inventory of repair parts.

When we asked the general manager why it did not make sense

to order two parts if they are critical, he replied that it made excellent sense and that he would have approved the purchase immediately had he only known of the critical nature of the problem.

The problem was solved, but it took a chain of six people to solve it. And, in the final analysis, the problem was simply one of communication. Imagine all the frustration that had taken place over the past few years because of a relatively inexpensive part not permitted to be in inventory, not by specific decision, but by general policy.

Further related to the subject of root cause is the question of cost. The inability to appoint the dining room tables according to standards will certainly cause at least some guests not to return, albeit a very small percentage, to that property on their next trip to the island. And it may not be tablecloths alone! The waiter is certainly frustrated by being prevented from doing his job well. It's sometimes difficult to hide negative attitude from the guests. Further along, the working relationship between laundry manager, head housekeeping, chief engineer, and purchasing agent can't be helped by the situation. It is very difficult to measure the cost of reduced cooperation, yet it is obvious that teams perform better when there is a high level of mutual respect than when there is even slight animosity. Managers tend to look at these dynamics as inevitable parts of the business, but they need not be so. There is also a cost involved in expediting our order that should be routine. Costs that are visibly hard, out-of-pocket costs are easy to understand, but the intangible cost resulting from the tension and frustration of the human element is not so easy to measure. It is, however, the foundation of quality and the most damaging cost of all. For when people are under duress and stress, they tend to make errors. It's a downward spiral to mediocrity, which only the general manager can stop. And he can stop it by committing to a quality assurance program.

We should note, as we conclude this discussion, that the cost of rectifying and/or preventing this error was simply the interest lost on the money spent to stock the second part—a small price to pay in view of the return. An axiom of management says, "The solution, when found, will be simple." That statement is the cornerstone of quality assurance.

Bring in the Expert

Whenever problems are being analyzed to determine root, or basic cause, the discussion should include the most knowledgeable people possible. And the most knowledgeable people on any problem are those involved with the process. Production-level employees may not have the solution to the problem, but they have, more than anyone else, a grasp of the process. If the process can be adequately defined, the solution is usually obvious and inexpensive. Including someone involved with the process has another dimension. It says to all employees, "You are important! We're concerned with your job and we want you to help us find ways to make it easier and better." Invite employees to the quality assurance meetings whenever their presence can aid the process. Make the Quality Assurance Committee the place where goodwill abounds and solutions are found. And don't forget to bring the relevant department head if he or she is not already a member of the Quality Assurance Committee. Done properly, the root cause process of tracking down and eliminating causes becomes a game, after which it becomes a way of life. Imagine the power in an organization in which every employee believes in the process of eliminating errors and their causes, at every level, and assumes the responsibility to do so as an integral part of their basic job. Awesome!

9

Spreading the Word

Communication of Innovation

Myth # 9: IN THE SERVICE INDUSTRIES, QUALITY
ASSURANCE IS SIMPLY A MATTER OF HAVING
EMPLOYEES FOLLOW THE RULES SET DOWN BY
MANAGEMENT.

As we begin our discussion of "diffusion," or the communication of ideas, it is important to do so on a firm base of understanding. A quick review of the basic communication model is in order.

Without the effective transmission of information, quality assurance is impossible. Yet, in the face of such a positive statement, there remain many who believe that effective communications is part and parcel of simply "being." After all, we have been communicating since birth, and could not, we believe, have reached our present position without being effective communicators. Sadly, this is not true. "Communicating" is something we all do and, for the most part, do with success. Communicating *effectively*, however, is the province of but a few.

Our approach will, by necessity, be in the basic form of an outline. Volumes have been dedicated to the process of communicating, which, of course, is space we do not have. Therefore, we make the basic assumption that the reader has already had considerable exposure to proper communication techniques and/or he or she is intelligent enough to grasp the concepts set forth and embellish them

113

correctly. We feel comfortable with these assumptions. Further, quality assurance tends to focus on the human behavioral elements of communication—"What did I really hear?" . . . "What was really said?" . . . "Why was it said and what does it mean?"

As we begin, let us keep in mind that we have a built-in obstacle—the obstacle of ego, brought about by our familiarity with "communications." We are too close to it, having communicated most of our lives, and we believe there is little to be learned. This tends to be a self-fulfilling prophecy and limits our absorptive capacities. The maximum benefit will be gained from what follows if it can be approached with a totally open mind.

DEFINITION

The definition of "communications" is even more difficult than that of "quality." To a great extent, "communications" means something different to each defining perspective. For example, many people define "communications" as "the transmission of information, ideas, emotions and skills by the use of symbols, pictures, words, figures and graphs." Others view "communications" as "the vehicle by which power is exerted." They focus more on the impact of communications than on the process.

Behaviorists define communications as "the eliciting of a response from the listener through verbal symbols." Still others focus on the criteria for success; for instance, "communications" occur whenever there is a meeting of meanings between persons.

Yet another approach to the definition states, "an act of communication occurs any time certain attributes of one person are capable of altering the future behavior of another."

And then there is always the approach that covers everything. For example: "Communication is virtually any behavior performed in the presence of another."

In short, the definition depends upon perspective. It is, at the same time, a process, a power builder, a response elicitor, and a means to mutual understanding. All of these perspectives are found in quality assurance; thus, we conclude that a single definition of communications is not appropriate for our needs. It is either that conclusion or a definition that is far too long to be practical.

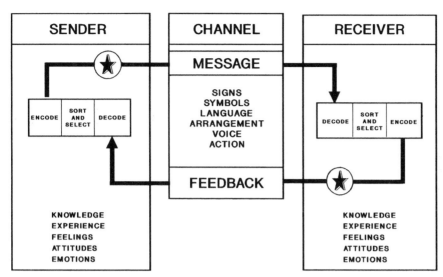

FIGURE 9.1   The communications model.

THE COMMUNICATIONS MODEL

What is helpful to our objective is to begin to understand the various elements that go into the communications model (see Figure 9.1). Those elements are listed below:

Sender—the originator of the communications.

Channel—the means by which the communications are transmitted.

Receiver—the person or persons who receive the communications.

Message—what is communicated. It may or may not be the same for the sender and the receiver.

Feedback—the sender's perception of the effectiveness of the transmission.

Environment—the combination of elements that establish the attitude of the sender. The receiver is also affected by the combination of elements that surround him or her. The environments of sender and receiver are often different and, at times, even in conflict.

Both the sender and the receiver(s) are involved in three additional activities as follows:

Decoding—The process of perceiving the message in the case of the receiver or the feedback in the case of the sender.

Sorting and selecting—The act of analyzing the output of the decoding process.

Encoding—The process of structuring the message in the case of the sender and the feedback in the case of the receiver.

Before leaving the communications model, we should point out the significance of the circled stars on the sender and feedback channels. If the message is structured and sent correctly, it should be received as sent and the feedback should, thus, be exactly as sent. Sending the image of a five-pointed star of a certain size and a certain orientation should result in a feedback that is an exact duplicate!

UNDERSTANDING THE "FILTERS"

For anyone who wears glasses, the process of determining the exact lens requirements is well known. The patient is asked to view a chart by looking through a device that permits the examiner to offer various combinations of lenses by simply turning knobs and pressing levers. Objects can be made to come into better and better focus until the "one right combination" of lenses is achieved. The examiner then reads the codes from the applicable lens in use, and, from those codes, glasses or contact lenses can be ground or produced.

It will be helpful to keep that process in mind as we discuss the communications model because, in order to be considered truly effective communicators, the lenses must be perfectly in focus at all points in the process.

For example, let us discuss the situation where the general manager of a hotel observes a busperson in the dining room talking with another busperson during the dining period, something that the manager has, on numerous occasions, said was not to happen. What lenses are involved?

First, the "owner" of the rule apparently violated is the general manager. Has he or she, thus, observed a blatant infraction or, because of past emphasis on the process, does it simply *seem* blatant at that time? The manager saw an event, to be sure, but did not see, nor could not see, the motivation behind the event. Perhaps the busperson was transmitting a message at the request of a waitress. Perhaps a guest had requested service and the guest was in another busperson's area. Perhaps someone had forgotten to properly instruct the busperson. In other words, rule or no rule, there could be valid reasons why it was not maintained in that instance. The manager's lenses need to be in focus to properly define the problem before addressing it. Without proper focus by the sender, a proper message cannot be structured.

Assume that the general manager now calls the dining room manager to the table and expresses his displeasure with what he has seen. Is this the time and/or place for such communication to take place? Is the "problem" one that requires immediate action? Has the manager used the correct form of communication? Has the manager put the corrective action in proper focus?

How does the room manager perceive the communication? Is the communication an indictment of the room manager's ability? Is the room manager threatened? What action is the general manager requesting? If it is direct action, what does this say about the room manager's authority? The room manager must have the general manager's message in clear focus.

Now a message is sent by the dining room manager to the busperson. Is it done by first trying to ascertain why the infraction took place (which may result in no infraction at all!)? Will the communication to the busperson be perceived as an embarrassment, a put-down, a help, or a harassment? Did the busperson understand the rule? Was he or she properly trained? How does he or she view what was done? What effect will the communication have on future performance? Is the room manager trying to be helpful or trying to impress the general manager?

The busperson now reacts on the basis of how he or she views the communication, and this reaction becomes feedback to the general manager. The reaction can take many forms, depending upon whether the busperson understood the message, accepted the message and/or is motivated to change as a result of the message. It could well develop that we have created a whole new cycle of communication as a result of the interpretation of the feedback.

An astute leader is aware of the various lenses that need to be in focus during effective communications and plans the communications to take place when all points of focus are at their highest point of clarity. The astute leader understands that it is not the communication per se that is important but the *results* of the communication. To be sure, there are times when direct and strong communications are called for and the results justify the risks. Generally, however, these occur far less frequently than most of us believe.

Before we leave our analogy of "lenses" we should consider the subject of "selectivity." It is possible for a sender to have all the parts of the communication process in proper focus and still not be an effective communicator because of selectivity. Selectivity occurs in the feedback element in the case of senders but it is also a major problem in the ability of the receiver to properly understand the message being sent.

Selectivity is characterized by "seeing, hearing and/or feeling only what we want to see, hear or feel . . ." and is called "selective perception." It is also characterized by remembering only those parts of the communication we wish to remember . . . called "selective retention." (See Everett M. Rogers' *Diffusion of Innovations,* 3rd ed., NY: Free Press, 1983, p. 166.) In effect, although the lenses may be aligned, that is, the communication is proper, we have inserted a filter that permits only parts of the communication to come through. For example, let's consider the department head who, prior to coming to work, has the typical recurring discussion with his or her teenage son regarding "responsibility," "maturity," and the "elimination of excuses." Now consider that the very first interaction of the day concerns a young employee who is offering excuses for a task that went wrong. Is the manager in the proper frame of mind to discuss the problem rationally or is there a possibility that a "no excuses" filter might be in place, a filter that refuses to accept from the employee what might be a very plausible explanation of what caused the error? Selectivity is particularly prevalent when major decisions have been made. Consider the decision to create a new theme restaurant. Is the decision maker likely to accept any changes or criticism of that decision, even if properly founded? Probably not. What about the socioeconomic filters that are placed between management and the production employee? How many managers *really* believe that a dishwasher can make a logical, valid suggestion? It's an American tragedy that such filters are utilized because, in general, *no one* knows a task as well as the person doing it. Many good suggestions—cost-reducing suggestions—are lost because we have installed filters and are guilty of selective perception and retention.

The objective of this discussion will have been met if the reader will simply accept the idea that communication—*effective* communication—is not simply "casting a message in the general direction of a receiver," but, rather, is a more complex process of understanding the various points at which the process can get out of focus and working to make such points have the least possible total negative impact.

Perhaps the following classic quote will help you to remember the importance of proper focus!

> . . . I know that you believe you understand what you think I said, but, I am not certain you realize that what you heard is not really what I meant to say!

FORMS OF COMMUNICATIONS

The various forms of communications relate to the communications model. Let us assume that we are the sender and consider the element of feedback.

One-way communications are those in which there is no instant feedback capability. Examples would be such obvious forms as newspapers, magazines, radio, television, film, and noninteractive video. In these forms, information is passed to others with feedback coming only after a passage of time. It is possible, however, to utilize a one-way model even in a direct person-to-person relationship. Often managers view the communicational process as a "send to" process only and are blind and deaf to the receipt of feedback. Such approaches are effective for purposes of forced adoption, that is, direct order type of objectives, but do little to build the kind of trusting relationship required for long-term effectiveness. In the area of training, one-way communicators are notoriously ineffective. The onus is on the sender to be complete in every detail of the message because of the inability of the receiver to respond and, thus, indicate total understanding or lack thereof. Often, egos interfere with what should be interactive communications, converting them to the one-way form. Management-by-memo is a good example. Many managers in the hospitality industry feel that all that is required for compliance to management's demands is to put out a memorandum on the subject. This is a common approach in the military, where instant, non-compromised compliance is the object of the order. This form works only as long as management is willing to direct every action and as long as the actions require little by way of judgment on the part of the receivers. We do not mean to imply that there is no role for interpersonal one-way communications for, in some instances, they are effective. "All employees must use the employee's entrance," for example, is quite acceptable. In that instance, there is little room for debate or confusion as to meaning. The fact remains, however, that one-way communications should be used sparingly and with discretion if lasting results and long-term trust are required elements of the relationship.

Two-way communications generally take more time but are significantly more effective. In this form, the receivers have a chance to provide instant feedback, allowing the sender to make changes in subsequent messages to achieve total understanding. By allowing receivers to be part of the process, they more readily comply because they feel that they are part of the process, not merely the objective of the process. Feedback, of course, does not have to be only verbal. Every good public speaker has learned to "read" the audience and, thus, to respond with additional explanation to puzzled looks. (It also helps to speak louder and become more animated when heads nod and eyes droop!) An obvious question might be, "How can I, as a general manager, conduct two-way communications with a staff four levels removed?" The answer is that "most probably you cannot!" Your staff, however, can. If the two-way model is as effective as we believe it to be, then management should practice it with those in the organization with whom the form is possible and insist that the form be used by all levels throughout the organization. Nothing is sacrificed by way of power with the two-way approach if power is considered "getting the job done effectively and correctly with consistency" (the definition of "quality"). In fact, the two-way form builds a team power that is virtually always more effective than is individual power.

In terms of the receivers, the forms of communication are the following:

Interpersonal—between two people (dyadic) or between a person and a small group or between a small group and another small group. The interpersonal form permits the most effective feedback of all forms.

A-personal communications—between one person and a large group of receivers such as in a speech or between one person and a mass audience, as in a media approach such as newspaper or television. The speech will allow feedback, albeit difficult at times, but the use of media, as already discussed, makes feedback very difficult.

The greatest variety of communications occurs in terms of the channel selected. To list a few, we have direct verbal, memo, articles, manuals, radio, television, film, video, telephone, signs, symbols, arrangement, nonverbal actions, etc. Each channel can be broken into "one-way" or "two-way," interpersonal or A-personal. Each has its particular "best" use, but all are forms of communication.

Thus far, our discussion of forms has been purely objective and, therefore, easily internalized. When we look at the message component of the communications model, we become more subjective.

What we have to understand thoroughly to be effective communicators is that messages are sent in both verbal and nonverbal forms. And, in terms of nonverbal, they are sent in written and nonwritten forms. It is the nonverbal, nonwritten forms of communication that can often be the most crucial and damaging ones. Such communications go on continuously. We send messages by how we look—our appearance—by how our office looks. We send them by how we act, by expression, and by body language. In terms of quality assurance, we send messages by how effective we are in setting and maintaining our personal standards. A manager who is always neat in appearance, punctual in practice, and efficient in handling problems will inspire others to be likewise. To demand compliance with others while permitting noncompliance in our own lives will not result in high quality. One of the basic problems of nonverbal communication in hospitality results from the attitude that many hoteliers believe that sincerity can be programmed. Many managers view interpersonal relations as a function of image rather than of sincerity. They pride themselves on knowing their employees' names and walking about the property addressing each individually by name.

What they do not realize is that there is a difference between greeting an employee and asking how he or she is and receiving a response of "Fine, sir", and the response "Fine, sir, and how are you?" In the first scenario, the interaction is somewhat mechanical and insincere, and employees pick up on the unspoken message. In the second scenario, the relationship is pure because the employee feels comfortable enough not only to respond but to show sincere human interest in the manager's welfare as well. Employees view the first form as somewhat patronizing. You're asking them to share with you but you don't really seem to want to hear their answer. You know their names but you don't know them. It's a subtle differentiation, to be sure, but, in effective communications, it is the subtleties that make for sincerity.

THE POSTULATES OF COMMUNICATIONS

You can better use all levels of your communicative abilities by recognizing basic communications postulates defined below:

1. Communication is not random.
2. Communication occurs everywhere, intentionally or unintentionally.
3. Communication occurs on different levels.
4. Communication is continuous.
5. Communication is a transactional process.
6. Communication is the sharing of meaning.

Your communications activities are largely affected by the following:

1. How you perceive your world.
2. How you perceive yourself.
3. How your audience perceives you.

This is best shown by referring to Figure 9.2.

In the ideal model each of the circles will coincide—each of the perceptions will blend into one. Ideally, our audience would perceive us exactly as we would like them to perceive us, and our perception of ourself would be exactly that of our audiences. Few, if

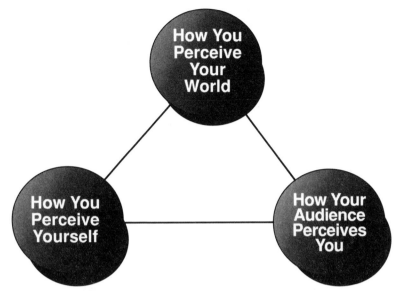

FIGURE 9.2   Communications perception diagram.

any, ever attain that level of perfection but, the closer you can come, the greater your credibility will be. We have all seen the manager who perceives himself (or herself) as the only person in the organization capable of making decisions. In order to reach that euphoric state, in fact, he/she never delegates, often countermands, and always makes certain his/her presence is known . . . and felt! In so doing, the manager is making certain that the audience "has the right perception of both power and talent." In point of fact, the audience perceives that manager as stubborn, unyielding, pushy, loud, and obnoxious! Effective communication begins with knowing yourself and being yourself, consistently, dependably, and honestly!

INTRODUCING THE PROCESS OF DIFFUSION

It comes as no surprise to any of us, of course, that errors cost money (although we may often be startled to learn how much they cost over a period of months or years). The question now arises: how do we proceed to eliminate the errors and cut costs?

Most of us are tempted to tackle the problem the same way we address most performance problems: by hastily issuing new orders to our managers and employees on reservations, check-in procedures, maintenance and housekeeping standards, food service, and so on. But as we'll see in this chapter, that approach is by itself virtually useless; although it may reduce some errors for awhile, it fails over the long haul because it neglects the most powerful factor of all—the creation of positive employee attitudes and a personal pride in one's job performance. That in turn results in a genuine desire to cut costs by making sure that errors simply don't happen in the first place.

How Not To Write a Memo

Suppose for a moment that we're behind the scenes at Big Bucks Inn, a moderately successful resort hotel somewhere in central Florida. Having studied the operations at the front desk, the kitchen, the laundry, the supply room, and the maintenance office, we suddenly come across the following memo posted on the employees' bulletin board:

> Due to the effects of the economy on our occupancy, and because higher productivity is so essential to our success, Big Bucks Inn has engaged the services of Quality Incorporated to implement a new quality assurance program. Beginning September 1, all personnel will become part of this program, which will help department heads and employees develop greater skills in organizational structure, human behavior, and the implementation of innovative ideas. The results of the program will be reported and discussed monthly by the executive committee.
>
> We are confident that all employees will give this program their complete cooperation. If you have any questions, see your department supervisor.
>
> _____
> Walter Headstrong, G.M.

At first glance, this memo seems pretty reasonable and straightforward. In fact, many hoteliers have told me that it reads pretty much like most communications that they themselves have posted on employee bulletin boards or in their company newsletters.

As we'll see in this chapter, however, this particular memo is a recipe for disaster, and probably should never have been written. Although it is clearly designed to announce that some far-reaching changes are under way at Big Bucks Inn, it completely ignores every principle by which such changes are successfully effected. Rather than rallying the staff to a common goal, it creates a fatal division between "us" (the management) and "them" (the men and women who are ultimately responsible for making the new QA program work). As such, the idea is doomed at the outset to utter failure.

At this point, some readers will take exception to such a pessimistic view. After all, they argue, all corporate policy changes are brought about simply because they're ordered from on high; if an executive has to worry about how every directive is interpreted by managers, supervisors, and individual employees, nothing would ever get accomplished.

In most cases, that's absolutely correct. But the introduction of QA is something unique in any organization. Whereas most policy changes demand fundamental changes in behavior and job performance, the launching of a true QA program is a "top-down" process rather than a "bottom-up" process. Also, unlike other changes, QA demands new insights into how individuals perceive themselves and their responsibilities to each other, to the company, and to the customer. As we'll see, such insights do not flow from memos or conventional directives; they arise from a thoughtful, carefully executed process that recognizes not only the similarities that exist in any group, but also the multitude of personal and professional variations.

To illustrate these points, the following are two key principles that are central to the success of what we call QA:

1. The structural and functional characteristics of the so-called "social system."
2. The concept of diffusion—the process by which innovation, regardless of the setting, is ultimately adopted.

SOCIAL SYSTEMS

A social system is formed whenever two or more people join forces to achieve a common goal. Given this simple definition, it's clear that we all belong simultaneously to several such systems; obvious examples include our families, coworkers, communities, political parties, churches or synagogues, and so forth. Within every one of these social systems, moreover, various members not only bear greatly different responsibilities, but they also develop differing methods for reaching the desired goal. (During a football game, for example, the job of the quarterback is much different from that of the half-back, and no football fan would ever confuse the two men on the field. But the players still share a common goal: to win the game.)

Furthermore, every social system can be defined as "modern," "traditional," or some combination of the two. For our purposes, the following six traits are especially characteristic of members of a modern social system but are largely lacking in members of a traditional system:

1. A positive attitude towards change.
2. A well-developed technology with a complex division of labor.
3. A high value on education.
4. Social relationships that are rational and businesslike rather than emotional and affective.
5. "Cosmopolitan" perspectives—that is, members of the system interacting easily and often with outsiders.
6. Empathy on the part of the system's members that enables them to see themselves in roles quite different from their own.

Most important from the standpoint of QA, we can also note that *the adoption or acceptance of innovation is generally most effective in a modern, rather than in a traditional, social system.*

As we might expect, we find a huge variety of social systems and subsystems within the hospitality industry. In most large hotels, for example, the housekeeping function tends to be a "traditional" system, whereas food-and-beverage is actually a relatively complex system made up of several subsystems; the subsystem represented by scullery and stewarding tends to be "traditional" in nature, whereas production and service personnel are more likely to be a mix of "traditional" and "modern" temperaments. Finally, attitudes within the food-and-beverage function usually become progressively more modern as we move through management, marketing, and executive levels.

Nor are these divisions uniform throughout an organization: indeed, production-level personnel in the front office are usually viewed as more "modern" than their counterparts in food-and-beverage. Finally, professionals in sales and marketing are almost invariably "modern" at all levels, not just within upper management.

For the quality specialist, all of this boils down to the following two major points:

1. Although most employees are familiar with the basic principles of QA, they perceive the formal implementation of a QA program as an innovation.
2. The degree to which we accept innovation depends largely on the type of social system to which we belong. If our QA program is to stand a reasonable chance of success, it is imperative that we pay careful attention to the principles and characteristics of these various systems.

DIFFUSION: THE KEY TO IMPLEMENTATION

Once a social system has been defined and characterized, how is innovation introduced to (and eventually accepted by) the members of the system? How do various groups interpret innovation? What are the conditions under which innovation is accepted or rejected?

The answers to those and many similar questions were supplied in 1971 by Dr. Everett M. Rogers and F. Floyd Shoemaker in their book, *Communication of Innovation* (The Free Press, New York 1971). As a former professor of communications at Michigan State University—and more recently at the University of Southern California—Rogers has devoted his life to the study of diffusion. Briefly, diffusion can be defined as the chain of events by which an innovation (which Rogers describes as "an idea perceived as new by a social system") is ultimately adopted and accepted by a social system. And although Rogers' work was not addressed specifically to either QA or the hospitality industry, his findings are extremely relevant for us.

We'll discuss diffusion in some detail in Chapter 10. For now, note simply that Rogers and other investigators have identified five principles that impact on the diffusion process. Don't be misled by the apparent simplicity of these principles. The ultimate degree of success in diffusing an innovation throughout a social system is directly proportional to the extent to which the following are observed:

1. *Relative advantage:* to what degree is the innovation perceived as being better than the idea it supersedes?
2. *Compatibility:* the innovation must be perceived as consistent with the participants' existing values, needs, and experience.
3. *Complexity:* the innovation must be seen to be relatively simple to understand and to put into practice.
4. *Triability:* most of us reject innovations that cannot first be tried on a limited basis.
5. *Observability:* are the results of an innovation visible and readily interpreted?

Let's look at each of these principles more closely, then see how each is violated in the memo written by the well-meaning manager at Big Bucks Inn.

> Due to the effects of the economy on our occupancy and because higher productivity is so essential to our success . . .

The concept of *relative advantage* is usually articulated as "what's in it for me?" But note that our memo offers little or nothing of immediate value to the employee; increasing occupancy and productivity is an important advantage for top management (who will almost certainly be rewarded for their achievements), but what do the employees and department supervisors—the major players in this program—get out of it? Can they lose their jobs? The memo gives no clue.

> . . . Big Bucks Inn has engaged the services of Quality Incorporated to implement a new quality assurance program.

The principle of *compatibility* is also scrapped. Most employees like to think that they not only understand their departments' problems, but can also provide solutions if given a chance. The announcement that outsiders are being brought in to solve the problems (not to mention the call for "higher productivity" and "greater skills") creates a distinct and divisive incompatibility between what the employees believe and what top management seems to believe.

> . . . which will help department heads and employees develop greater skills in organizational structure, human behavior and the implementation of innovative ideas.

Nor does the memo address the need for *simplicity*. Indeed, most line personnel would be confused—and perhaps a bit threatened—by such lofty-sounding terms as "human behavior" and "organizational structure." And what does all that have to do with QA anyway? Why not simply tell employees that the goal of the new program is to reduce the errors that make everyone's job more difficult? There's nothing especially complex about QA; what's the point of making it seem so complicated?

> . . . beginning September 1, all personnel will become part of the program.

There's certainly nothing *triable* about the program; it begins on September 1, period! Wouldn't it be better to introduce the program on a small scale, then assess the results? As it stands now, QA is a "forced adoption" process; that is, employees have nothing to say about it. But if the QA program is to stand any chance of success, that approach simply won't work; as we mentioned earlier, any such program must begin by modifying the attitudes and behavior of every member of the system, beginning at the very top. It must appeal to their personal and professional pride and create a powerful desire to do things right the first time, every time. True, forced adoption may achieve some short-term results; most employees will try to at least create the impression of compliance, if only to save their jobs. But that attitude is light years away from the true acceptance needed for lasting results.

> . . . the results of the program will be reported and discussed monthly by the Executive Committee.

Finally, the memo provides nothing for the participants in the way of *observability*; there is no obvious provision for recognizing or rewarding the contributions of individual managers or supervisors—

never mind those at the bottom of the totem pole. As for the reference to the executive committee, who cares? Chances are that the
managers and their staffs will bear the day-to-day responsibility for
making QA happen, but the credit will go to the executive committee. Isn't that the way it works in every organization? Is there anything in the memo to suggest otherwise?

In Chapter 10, we'll see how the principles of diffusion can be
applied to real-life situations in the hospitality industry. We'll also
see how and why these principles must begin at the very top of the
organization and flow downward in a controlled and orderly way.

10

Work Smarter, Not Harder

Putting Diffusion to Work

Myth #10: THE HOSPITALITY INDUSTRY IS AN ART, NOT A SCIENCE, AND AS SUCH, THE MOST IMPORTANT FACTOR IN SUCCESS IS MANAGERIAL INTUITION.

Whether its a case of "ego" or just lack of understanding, the majority of hospitality management people, in my experience, consider the motivation of employees to be primarily an "art." The favorite claim of hoteliers is "It's in your blood"; in effect, hoteliers are born and success is largely the fulfillment of destiny. Hotel and institutional management schools have to some extent contributed to this attitude in the past, by emphasizing skill needs more than knowledge and attitude needs. Fortunately this seems to be changing in most of the four-year schools, and increasing emphasis is being placed on the management of personnel. When questioning an operation, old-time hoteliers, from force of habit, still tend to inquire about food cost first while younger managers place first concern on labor cost. Lest the reader consider this an indictment of "older hoteliers" I would hasten to add that, in my opinion (shared by many in the industry), today's hospitality graduates have gone too far on the side of technocratic management and are often so "bottom line" oriented that their acquired human relations skills have taken on more of an aura of manipulation than of motivation. A happy medium must be found—one that places in perspective the relationship between the quest for quality, the well-being and motivation of employees at all levels, and the requirement for profitability. That is the essence of the quality assurance principles being set forth. These principles recognize, however, that although there is undoubtedly a large dose of "art" in the practice of hospitality management, there is also a great deal of meaningful "science."

The science of diffusion introduced in Chapter 9 concerns primarily the concept of introducing change to a social system. Quality assurance should not be considered as "change," but unfortunately it is. Whereas the industry has always utilized standards, we will show in subsequent chapters a new approach to the creation, implementation, updating, and monitoring of standards. The cost of error analysis certainly is new, and the modification of employee attitudes to gain real and productive participation in the hospitality operation is also new. Let us, therefore, consider the steps in the diffusion adoption process.

FIVE STEPS IN THE RIGHT DIRECTION

In Rogers' book on diffusion (*Communication of Innovations: A Cross-Cultural Approach*, 2nd ed., NY: Free Press, 1971, pp. 100–101.), he identified the following steps in the "adoption" process:

1. *Awareness stage:* The individual learns of the existence of a new idea but lacks information about it.
2. *Interest stage:* The individual develops interest in the innovation and seeks additional information about it.
3. *Evaluation stage:* The individual makes mental application of the new idea to his present and anticipated future situation and decides whether to try it.
4. *Trial stage:* The individual actually applies the new idea on a small scale in order to determine its utility in his/her own situation.
5. *Adoption stage:* The individual uses the new idea continuously on a full scale.

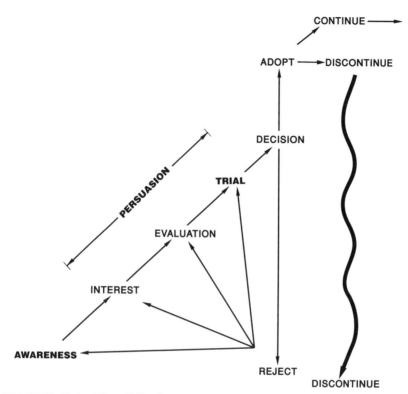

FIGURE 10.1   The diffusion process.

When Rogers was my professor, in 1965–66 at Michigan State, he contended that all adoption processes follow these five steps, with the conclusion that six would be either "adoption," or "rejection." Further, he added that if there is adoption, then two more options are possible: (1) continued adoption ("continuance") or (2) "discontinuance." If "rejection," then two options are (1) "continued rejection" or (2) "subsequent adoption." Let's look at the process in action (see Figure 10.1).

Filling Up the "Big Bucks" Inn

Let us assume that the "Big Bucks" Inn in Central City, Florida reviews its marketing and, by such data as zip code analysis, coupled with information from rental car agencies, airlines, and phone company traffic studies, etc., determines that "Feedertown," southwest USA, is a large source of business to the city but not particularly to the "Big Bucks" Inn. Consequently, a marketing plan is desired.

Obviously, before anyone in Feedertown can even consider staying in our inn, they must know that an inn exists. So ads are run in the Feedertown papers, and radio spots are introduced touting our property. This is the "awareness" stage, and it usually lends itself to mass media communication. If the ads are sufficiently enticing, and if they are aimed at the proper market, listeners and readers will become interested, perhaps enough to call the toll-free reservations number. We have entered the "interest" stage. If interest is cultivated properly, potential customers spend time evaluating what their perception is of the "Big Bucks" versus the inn they usually frequent in Central City. And, assuming that the "evaluation" stage was successful, the client enters the "trial" stage. If we were buying a new car, we would try it by driving it around the block, but is more difficult to "try" a hotel before actually visiting it. Thus we will have a vicarious trial. The customer puts himself or herself into the pictures in the brochures, or into the scene as described by the reservationist, or experiences the hotel through the eyes and words of a friend who may have stayed there. Whatever form the "trial" stage takes, the customer is now ready to decide. Many factors bear on a new guest's decision to adopt the idea of staying at a property for the first time. It could be dissatisfaction with the quality of the last inn or motel used in that city or, if the guest stayed at a chain-operated property during the last visit to the city, and had a bad experience with the same chain in another city, the guest could be switching loyalty. Perhaps the location of the inn is close to where the guest will be doing business. Or it could be a perceived better price-value relationship. Special incentive programs could be the cause of the change. There are many reasons why guests try new inns and motels, however, we can say with great certainty that a guest is unlikely to switch loyalty if the last visit to that city, or to a chain property in another city, was perceived as a quality experience. There are countless examples throughout the U.S. and worldwide of hotels, motor inns, and motels that run high occupancies even though their location, age, accommodations and rates are less advantageous than are those of their competition. Such properties succeed because they have quality. It's that simple!

If, however, the idea of staying at the "Big Bucks" is rejected, all is not lost. It might simply mean that insufficient emphasis was placed on any of the five steps leading to adoption. You still have a chance to attract the customers on the next trip. Assume, however, that the decision is to adopt the idea being diffused. The customer books a room at the "Big Bucks" for the first time. In all probability, if the advertising budget to market Feedertown were divided by the guests from Feedertown who actually adopt the idea to stay with you, you would lose money on their first trip. The nature of the hospitality industry is repeat business. It is absolutely essential that the newly attracted guest be encouraged to return, and to become your word-of-mouth advertiser. This is where quality assurance enters the picture. If the expectations that your promotion has raised in your new guest are met satisfactorily, the guest will return. If not, the guest is lost and, once lost after adopting, it is a difficult task indeed to get that guest back for a second chance.

Figures Do Lie

One major hotel chain with which I am familiar used to spend large sums of money on advertising and promotion each year, and, in point of fact, most years showed improvement. But when the annual chain occupancy climbs from 72 to 74%, it is not necessarily time to celebrate, unless we have more information. It is very possible—in fact, highly probable—that what really happened is a 10-point increase in business combined with an 8-point loss. The net gain, of course, is 2 points of occupancy. Or the figures could be a 15-point gain and a 13-point loss, or 6 and 4, etc. The fact is, if we gained 10 and lost 8, moving from 72 to 74%, we have lost, not gained. For, if we gained 10 points and kept the 8, our occupancy would be at 82%, not 74%! Sometimes hoteliers are so anxious to see good news that they are blinded to what is behind it. One fact is unfortunately prevalent. When occupancy is moving up, it's hard to convince management that quality assurance is important. If the 200-room motor inn with the average rate of $80 and a rooms revenue to total revenue ratio of 65% would only realize that their 2-point occupancy gain added $179,692 of new sales revenue but their 8-point loss cost $718,769, they would appreciate more fully the contribution that quality assurance could make!

The Floating Guest

We discussed the consumer side quality survey by the author in conjunction with AH&MA and Citicorp/Diners Club in Chapter 7. Let us review it briefly as we examine the "floating guest." The study indicated that, when confronted with just 10 leading errors, 1 error occurs among male travelers every 1.06 trips and among female travelers every .9 trips. As a general statement, therefore, we can say that a guest encounters 1 of 10 major errors on every trip. Further, the study indicates that .20 of the guests who encounter an error change hotels on their next trip. This is an awesome percent, but as startling as the information may be, the opportunity it presents should make every hotelier's mouth water with anticipation. The 10 errors used in the consumer perception study were as follows:

1. Unsatisfactory food service
2. Tired facility—poor maintenance
3. Slow check-in, check-out
4. Employees not friendly
5. Room not ready upon arrival
6. Poor overall service
7. Requested room type not available
8. Morning wake-up call not made
9. No record of reservation
10. Over-booked—guest walked

There are many other "serious" errors that could have been added to the list, such as mechanical systems not functioning properly, wrong rate quoted, or lost luggage. If the data indicates that a guest will switch property 20% of the time that 1 of the 10 errors is encountered, we have erred greatly on the side of conservatism in portraying the fragile nature of loyalty among many guests. Let's assume that there are 2,000 available rooms in our city and that the overall annual occupancy of the city is 65%. Further, assume an average stay of 2.2 nights. That means that the city rents an average 1,300 rooms per night or 474,500 rooms per year. It further means that these rooms are filled by 215,681 guests (ignoring double occupancy consideration). (474,500 rooms sold divided by 2.2 nights average stay = 215,681 guests.) Finally, if 20% of all guests are floaters, there are 43,136 guest floaters representing 94,900 rooms nights/year. (215,681 room nights/year/occ. × .20 discontinuance rate × 2.2 room nights per guest = 94,900 room nights per year that are "floating.") If we own a 200-room property, and have a quality assurance program that prevents us from losing 1/5 of our guest loyalty each trip, we would be selling 130 rooms per night if we were at the 65% city average occupancy. That means we have 70 rooms × 365 days, or 25,550 room nights unsold each year. However, there are 94,900 room nights of floating guests available each year. Our prime market, therefore, is in capturing the floating guests by offering quality product and service. And it is immeasurably easier to capture guest loyalty from guests already in your city than to try to advertise nationwide, or in select markets to bring them in.

Recasting the Process

In the third edition of Rogers' book, *(Diffusion of Innovations),* he recasts the diffusion process, noting, among other things, that the five steps mentioned—awareness, interest, evaluation, trial, and adoption—do not always follow in such a logical order but often intertwine and even exchange places. At times interest builds after the evaluation or trial, for example. Thus, Rogers suggests that the new steps be *knowledge—persuasion—decision* followed by *adoption—rejection; continuance or discontinuance;* or *continued rejection or subsequent adoption.* Rogers' new model is certainly more general and probably more accurate, however, I prefer his first paradigm even if the steps do sometimes get out of order, because it helps me to focus on the parts in a more meaningful way.

APPLYING DIFFUSION TO QUALITY ASSURANCE

The same process we used to diffuse the idea of staying at the "Big Bucks" hotel will benefit us in gaining adoption for quality assurance. First we must make all employees "aware" that a quality assurance program is in process. Most employees expect all new programs to be aimed directly at them because, after all, "they" are the "obstacle" to quality. However, quality assurance always starts at the top, for that is invariably where the bottleneck is! One of the strengths of a proper approach to quality is that it does not affect the employees until it has affected the management who, by their example, will encourage production and supervisory-level adoption. Interest will be reached in any process that has a positive effect on employees without requiring effort on their part. As management adopts the idea of quality, the benefits will filter down. Employees will see department heads who start meetings on time and end on time, who travel around their areas of responsibility with regularity, who conduct performance evaluation professionally, on schedule, and with real concern for the welfare of those being evaluated. And it is human nature for employees to want to be part of a successful program. Employees will think about quality if given time and information. By introducing quality to employees in small manageable doses, where they can enjoy early success, you are encouraging their acceptance. Once your employees have adopted the quality assurance program, however, discontinuance becomes a crucial concern. If a quality assurance program is not going to be implemented professionally, with continuity and long-term goals clearly stated, the program will fail. Employer expectations will be let down and it will be most difficult to engage employees in such programs in the future. The cardinal rule for quality assurance is, therefore, "Don't start unless you are prepared and committed to finishing." Quality assurance is not a management game to increase productivity. It is serious business and, treated otherwise, cannot succeed.

THE ENEMY IS US

Walt Kelley, who died in 1973, left a legacy through the sayings of his cartoon character, Pogo, one of which was, "I have met the enemy, and he is us!" One general manager in particular exemplifies this point quite adequately.

As background, the particular property ruled by the manager in question was experiencing constant labor unrest and could never seem to "get it right" in terms of quality. The facility never quite looked clean. Most employees were friendly, but invariably you encountered one with a chip on his/her shoulder. The food was good but not special although the prices were higher than those of competitive properties. The general manager was about 40, in excellent shape, full of energy, coming from a background of considerable experience, and in general the kind of leader you would expect in a resort environment. It was well known among employees that the relationship between manager and his attractive female assistants was based on more than business terms. Frankly, he seemed to take some pride in his prowess as a lady's man and as one who could solve any problem through his ability to verbalize. Normally, a person's private life has no place in a discussion of leadership style, except when it is flaunted in such a way as to say to employees, "I am above the rules that govern your lives"; then it is a problem. I remember quite vividly discussing quality with the executive committee and department heads when the general manager said, "There is no problem in my hotel with quality. The employees do what I tell them or they're fired!" The fact is, they did what he told them whenever they obviously had to. But the minute the opportunity presented itself to do "average" work, that is what was done.

Several things are wrong. The manager made no attempt to create a moral/ethical image of himself, assuming instead that he was immune to the rules of fraternization he inflicted on others. The manager believed in "forced adoption," that is, taking the social system through the steps of the adoption process by force rather than by persuasion. It is a fast way to gain adoption—and a faster way to gain discontinuance! The manager's disdain for his employees was on constant display. He was seen by employees for what he was— a shallow person who placed his own self-interest above both those of the guest and the employees. That property had mediocre quality then, and it still does! And the owners blame it on the economy and "the kind of help you get these days!" Management did not really care about the employees, and the employees picked that up. So, they gave management what management gave them—very little!

But when employees know that management cares about them— sincerely cares—there is no end to the amount of pride they can generate for their work. And pride is the stuff of which quality is made!

Unfortunately it seems almost an occupational hazard of hospitality that some management people consider themselves invincible to the natural laws of human behavior. One large element of leadership is "example." If it is quality we seek, then it must be quality we project. If we want others to live by the standards we set, then we must live by the same standards. Achieving the position of general manager means power, without question. It also means responsibility. Power exerted in a positive and responsible way is a very strong force in the achievement of success. Exerted in a negative way, an irresponsible way, it is equally strong as a force in failure, with this exception. Employees, contrary to the belief of some managers, generally want to do well in their work. They do have some natural pride, perhaps more latent than we would like but, nonetheless, still present. Many an undeserving manager has survived simply because the employees do a good job despite poor leadership. But the difference between "survival" and "excellence" is great, and when excellence is not present, then generally, the enemy has been met—and it is management.

The Role of Opinion Leaders

If it were possible to take a typical hotel or motel and look down upon it as employees go through their daily routines, we would find that there is a considerable amount of interaction going on at all levels. If the interaction could be plotted, we would further discover that some employees have far more interaction than others (see Figure 10.2).

And the amount of interaction does not necessarily correlate with a person's position in the hierarchy; that is, the higher one moves in the organization, the greater the interaction. The kind of interaction that takes place naturally and constantly during the working process occurs not by reason of power or position but rather by virtue of perceived value of one's opinion. Such persons are called "opinion leaders" for just that reason, and they are few in number and located at every level in the organization. There are one or two maids in housekeeping who seem to warrant the respect of most of the other maids. The same is true in engineering, and at the front desk, and among waiters and waitresses in service. Opinion leaders are a crucial part of every organization and, unfortunately, are not always easily identified. They are seldom the loud, talkative, highly opinionated, out-front employees we traditionally view as "opinion leaders." More often, opinion leaders are quiet, reserved persons who do not view themselves as opinion leaders at all, and who would probably be quite embarrassed to find out that they occupied such a

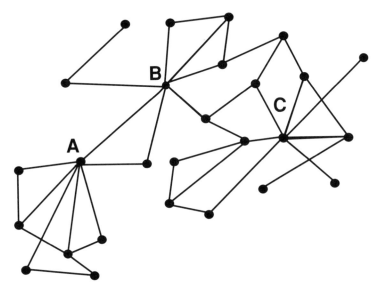

FIGURE 10.2 Opinion leader network showing informal interactions. A, B, and C are strong opinion leader candidates.

role. In short, employees seek and create informal organization charts that invariably differ from the formal ones published by management. Employees informally determine whose opinions they value and seek those persons whenever an opinion is needed. Often the opinion leader is not asked for an opinion directly nor does he/she volunteer one. In the course of the conversation, however, an opinion is perceived by the seeker. For example, assume that management is introducing a quality assurance program and has called the employees together to make them aware of it and to solicit their eventual participation. Employee "A" finds a reason to interact with employee "B," an opinion leader. Employee "A" simply asks, "Are you going to the meeting this afternoon?" The real question is, "What do you think of the new program?" but it isn't asked that way because employee "A" is not willing to admit that he or she needs, or is seeking, help making a decision. But that is the way it really is. In response, employee "B," the opinion leader, might say, "They're paying me to go, so I'll go. But I sure wish I didn't have to!" Translated it says: "The topic being presented, quality assurance, really doesn't hold much interest for me!" Employee "A" now decides that quality assurance is "negative," and the subject has never really been discussed! On the other hand, employee "B" might say, "Everybody's going. They're making a big announcement." Translated it says: "I'm going, and I'm going with an open mind." The opinion leader hasn't sold employee "A" on quality assurance, nor was that even possible, perhaps. But, the opinion leader certainly set the scene for the meeting in positive terms. Let's take another example, this time at a supervisory level. When asked the same question, an opinion leader supervisor might respond, "It's just another productivity program. I wish they would pay us instead of always trying to get more out of us." Translated: "Quality assurance is a manipulative program that we don't need and don't want." Or, the response could be, "It's about time someone started thinking about how we can improve this place." Translated: "Quality assurance is a positive program in my eyes and we ought to give it a chance." It is the "positive—negative" tensions that pervade an organization and make it easy or hard to achieve results. Opinion leaders are critical players in the whole success scene and must not be taken lightly. If they are identified, sought out, and mutually communicated with honestly and sincerely, they are invaluable in communicating positive feelings to the entire organization. Management must be very careful, however. Opinion leaders will know when they are being used insincerely. This should never be done. Bad news travels faster than good news. The value of opinion leadership is in communicating factual, i.e., true, information. Our communications with opinion leaders, therefore, must be honest and true. But, to fail to recognize the value of the opinion leader process is to miss the greatest opportunity to tell your story honestly and factually to all your employees at every level, quickly and effectively.

Will the Opinion Leaders Please Raise Their Hands?

It is interesting to note that opinion leaders do not necessarily view themselves as such. Many, in fact, would shun the label simply because they do not seek visibility and do not view their relationships with other employees as anything more than friendship. Therefore, accepting the fact that opinion leaders are valuable to the diffusion process, how can we identify who they are? Several studies by Rogers and others have resulted in some generalizations about opinion leaders. Taken as a general body of information, and applied carefully and with perception, the generalizations below can help to identify the opinion leaders among our employees:

1. *Opinion leaders have more exposure to mass media than do their followers.*
   We don't know which comes first, opinion leadership or exposure to mass media channels. We do know, however, that once identified, the opinion leaders tend to be more cosmopolitan than are followers and tend to have more contact with change agents, as well as more exposure to mass media.
2. *Opinion leaders are more accessible than are their followers.*
   To be an opinion leader, by our definition, an individual has more frequent interaction with peers than is generally true with followers. Opinion leaders tend to have more social participation than do followers.
3. *Opinion leaders seem to have a higher social status than those of their peers.*
   Studies seem to indicate a natural tendency for followers to seek information from peers of higher social status rather than from those of equal or lower status.
4. *Opinion leaders are more innovative than are their followers.*
   This generalization seems to rest largely on the norms of the social system. In some social systems, opinion leaders actually slow down innovation. The medical field, for example, seems to have a norm of caution among opinion leaders.

In dealing with the preceding generalizations about opinion leaders, the reader should keep in mind that these are relative to the level of the hierarchy under observations. An opinion-leader maid who is perceived to have more contact with mass media might be the maid who has the interest and takes the time to read with perception the employee manuals given to her and also, perhaps, the newsletters and bulletins that are posted. The supervisor opinion leader, perceived as having more mass media contact, might well subscribe to several trade journals. The point is, opinion leaders are present at all levels of the hierarchy and should be sought out and utilized effectively to enhance communication in both directions.

The Adoption Process

We are now ready to examine the process of adoption i.e., the acceptance of an idea perceived as new. The fact that we have the commitment of top management, a quality assurance director, and the Quality Assurance Committee in place, and have identified the opinion leaders and initiated our program means only that we are at the starting line in the diffusion process. Acceptance of new ideas spreads slowly despite our desire or belief to the contrary. Many have been done in trying to identify the various stages in the adoption process. While the conclusions formulated cannot be considered unquestionable, nevertheless, the adopter categories which Rogers and others have identified are helpful in our understanding of the process. The adopter categories are stratified into five parts as follows, with appropriate percentages of participants as a function of total persons in the adopter population.

1. *Innovators—2.5% of total—venturesome.*
   Innovators are eager to try new ideas, and the typical approach among hoteliers is to introduce new ideas to the innovator types in order to gain rapid acceptance. This is not necessarily a good idea. The same venturesomeness that causes the innovator to jump on a new idea also causes him or her to leave an idea for one perceived as more advantageous. Thus, the innovator may well be the first to enthusiastically endorse quality assurance but not the best to sustain the effort.
2. *Early adopters—1.35% of total—respect role.*
   Because early adopters are more stable than innovators in accepting new ideas, they are the most important group to use in diffusing the concept of quality assurance. Basically, they identify themselves in terms of adopting the process by coming on board the concept right after the first small wave of innovators has passed. Numerically (and this is a dangerous way to view the process because it assumes a norm that may not exist), if a hotel has 300 employees, 6–8 will jump on the new quality assurance program immediately and 40–50 will follow as early adopters.
3. *Early majority—34% of total—deliberate.*
   The early majority are generally not leaders but are valuable

because they represent a large group, which gives the adoption process a solid image of acceptance.

4. *Late majority—34% of total—skeptical.*

To be successful, the late majority must be brought on board the adoption process, but it does not happen easily. If a quality assurance program is initiated without a solid dedicated commitment to complete it, it will be missing at this point. The failure of the late majority to come easily on board will discourage the earlier adopters and management as well. Be prepared to spend time, energy, and financial resources to reach the late majority.

5. *Laggards—16% of total—traditional.*

It may be that the laggards never do get with the new quality assurance program or, if they do, it will only be reluctantly after considerable effort. The value of the laggard category is in recognizing that laggards exist and thus in not becoming discouraged when we fail to convert them to our point of view.

ALL OF LIFE IS AN "S" CURVE

Before leaving our discussion of diffusion, we must look at how the process works over time. Change does not normally occur rapidly in any social system. Exceptions are obvious, of course. The change from hotels to motels brought about in the early 50s, primarily by Holiday Inns, was a somewhat rapid change; however, two factors contributed. First, the need was obvious once identified and, second, the traditional thinking of hoteliers had retarded the gradual growth that would have occurred had hoteliers been more modern in terms of innovation. Thus, when the highly standardized Holiday Inn concept burst on the scene, the American travelling public was ready and adopted the concept easily and quickly. On the other hand, a major hotel chain made a quantum leap into computerization in New York City in the 1950s, with disastrous results. That experience helped to retard the computerization of hotels; however, one would never expect that it would take the hospitality industry almost 30 years to enthusiastically adopt the concept of computers.

By and large, ideas follow a normal distribution model during the adoption process. If, for example, an idea takes 10 years to gain

YEAR	1	2	3	4	5	6	7	8	9	10
ADOPTERS	5	7	10	14	19	19	14	10	7	5

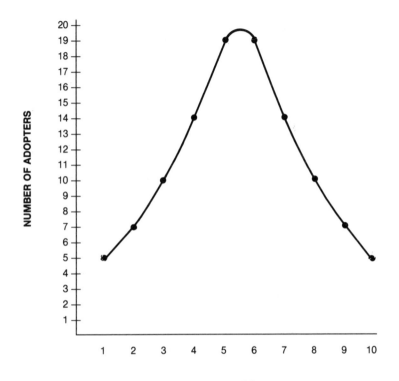

YEARS

FIGURE 10.3   A normal distribution curve.

widespread use, we can construct a curve (see Figure 10.3) by plot-
ting the time it takes the social system member to adopt the innovation.

If the normal distribution curve is correct in depicting our 10-
year diffusion process, then, plotted over time, the "bell" curve becomes the "S" curve as shown in Figure 10.4.

YEAR	1	2	3	4	5	6	7	8	9	10
ADOPTERS	5	7	10	14	19	19	14	10	7	5
CUMULATIVE ADOPTERS	5	12	22	36	55	74	88	98	105	110

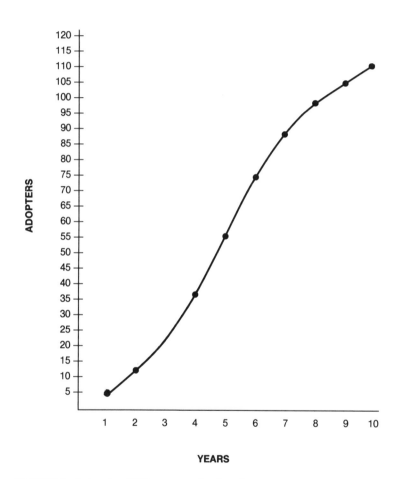

FIGURE 10.4   An "S" curve of adoption.

SUMMING UP

Quality assurance, like any other idea perceived as new, is a diffusion process and, as such, can be enhanced by becoming aware of the stages required for adoption and the value of opinion leaders in the process. The introduction of quality assurance should not be forced or rushed unduly. A slow steady process will give better and more lasting results than will an accelerated process that fails to prevent discontinuance. Hoteliers should realize that it is virtually impossible to gain adoption from every employee and that a proper program could take 2–5 years for successful implementation. Even then, because of turnover within the industry, plus the changing needs and need levels of the consumer, and finally, the constant improvement to standards inherent in a proper quality assurance program, a successful program will never end.

Quality assurance is a continuous process of creation, implementation, review, and recreation. As such it is dynamic in that it is always occurring. Thus, there is no magic button we can push for quality/excellence, for excellence is not an event but a process. Guests continuously enter, pass through, and depart our operation. If our standards and the guests' expectations are in sync, and if we meet our standards each and every time, the guests return and word of mouth fills our rooms. If not, we become one more mediocre hospitality operation just waiting for the competitors to erode our business.

11

The Rules of the Game

Introduction to Standards

Myth #11: *QUALITY ASSURANCE BEGINS WHEN*
MEANINGFUL STANDARDS HAVE BEEN CREATED FOR
ALL AREAS OF THE OPERATION.

DEPENDABLE MEDIOCRITY

The greatest detriment to a successful quality assurance program rests in the misconception we have regarding standards. By way of reinforcement, standards are "required levels of performance," however, today's managers have become too class-conscious in their management perceptions. In simplistic terms, many managers believe that high quality correlates directly with high control of employees. That is to say, they believe that quality assurance is enhanced when discretion is removed from the employees' performances. What results is simply dependable mediocrity. In actuality, the more the control on an employee's job performance, the less motivation he/she has to do a proper job. The net result is employees who do exactly what they are told to do at whatever level it takes to satisfy those who are responsible for supervising them. Further, when employees have too many standards to meet, it becomes

149

impossible for management to effectively measure the results, and without measurement, the system of standards rapidly disintegrates. It is interesting to note that one of the greatest sources of job dissatisfaction among management personnel is not that they don't know the parameters of their decision-making authority, but, rather, that they do not have enough authority to begin with. Frankly, I have never met a manager who complained that his or her boss has not placed enough control over his or her actions! It is a paradox that managers fight for more freedom of action while, concurrently, seeking to control that same freedom for those under them. The obvious question is, therefore, "How many standards are enough?"

HOW MANY STANDARDS?

On many occasions, I have asked managers, "How many standards do you feel would be sufficient for your operation if every standard was met 100% of the time?" The answer usually varies between 100 and 200 standards. This question follows: "Assume you are a manager of a 200-room, average-rate motor inn. If, by some shake of a magic wand, you could be guaranteed that 200 standards would be met virtually 100% of the time, do you feel you could identify those standards and do you agree that you would therefore have a successful operation?" The answer to this question is generally "yes," and most managers feel that they would be in "hospitality heaven." A 200-room commercial motor inn will have between 1/2 and 3/4 employees per room, that is, 100–150 employees. Working with the smaller number, 100 employees will generally include some 25 to 33 job descriptions. If each job description is limited to 10 standards, that property will have between 250 and 330 standards. Yet, most managers will tell you that they could not possibly manage their employees if limited to only 10 standards each. In point of fact, there is no precise limit for the number of standards required. It depends upon job function. The pool lifeguard may have 5, the rooms inspectress 20. However, the fact remains that, to have effective quality assurance, it is better to have fewer standards but have each standard rigidly enforced.

IT'S MORE THAN A NUMBERS GAME

By starting with fewer standards, employees are better able to focus their energies on achieving their standards; in their achievement, they develop pride of accomplishment; in developing pride, they feel like a more meaningful part of the organization; and, finally, their sense of equity fuels their desire to consistently meet their standards. Further, when a small body of standards are met effectively, often the employees themselves will suggest other standards as well as the ways in which existing standards can be improved.

"ON-LINE" STANDARDS MAKE IT POSSIBLE

Prior to the age of the computer, standards were communicated by way of the "operations manual." Most hotels have them, especially the chains. They can usually be found in the managers' offices, covered with dust, seldom used, and almost always out of date. In our seminars, we delight in asking management people to tell us where a maid in their establishment goes to find out the standards that govern his or her work. Ninety percent of the managers respond with answers like "inspector," "housekeeping office," "personnel," "manager's office," etc. The only acceptable answer is "nowhere, my maids have their standards in hand and are trained to use them!" To be sure, operation manuals are impressive (and also expensive). But, on the downside, they generally require the bulk of standards to be created before the manual is published; they are generally out of date at the time of publication, they cannot be updated easily, and they are not geared for general distribution. In my opinion, the hard copy operations manual is to the hospitality industry as the slide rule is to engineering. Its day has long since gone by. There are newer and better ways!

The age of the computer has created outstanding opportunities to effect better quality. The computer also makes it possible to have fewer standards! This seems like a contradiction—we are used to having computers generate "more," not "less." We tend to misuse computers, again because of our misguided notion that more control is better than effective control! We can learn from the Japanese in this respect.

In America, product innovations are generally incorporated into a product at the time the dies are changed and the product enters a second generation. In Japan, on the other hand, product innovations tend to be added to the product as soon as possible. Returning to Jim Bennett's belief that we are only as good as the last 30 minutes, then we should be oriented to making the last 30 minutes the best we can muster. That means that standards, to be effective, must be dynamic—that is, alive and able to be adjusted, added to, and/or deleted easily and effectively. The computer, specifically the word processor, makes this possible. Putting standards "on-line" in the computer makes them effective standards for the following reasons:

1. The system of standards can be built from a base of need.
2. Current and relevant standards can be placed in the hands of the users, where they belong!
3. Decisions are easily executed.

Let's look at each of these three advantages in more detail.

Building Standards as Needed

The first step in the development of standards is to assemble the complete list of job titles in the operation. In a small property, this takes less than an hour. In a larger property, the personnel department already has a list. Either way, it is not a difficult task.

Once the titles are collected, they should be screened and consolidated if possible. You will find in most properties that unique job titles have evolved over the years in response to specific personnel requirements. We call this "job title creep." For example, a new secretary is hired, and Mary, a long-time employee, is given the title of administrative assistant to recognize her value. In time, the new secretary proves to be very good and is rewarded with the title "Senior Secretary." Mary, in the meantime, is approaching retirement after 27 years of service and, frankly, she is slowing down a bit! So, a new administrative assistant is hired and Mary becomes senior administrative assistant. When Mary retires, instead of reviewing the job titles, everyone moves up a notch. Multiply this kind of "creative title mentality" by every department and subdepartment in the hotel and you soon have unique titles for almost everyone. Several years ago, as an experiment, I asked every employee in a 300-room college town hotel, "Whom do you report to?" and "Who reports to you?" The results were astonishing. In many cases, especially at the production level, employees were not certain exactly to whom they reported. And in a few cases, supervisors were ambivalent as to exactly who reported to them! I can readily appreciate how incomprehensible this story seems, yet I wonder what would happen in some of today's properties if the same two questions were asked? Basically, the point is this: "on-line" standards require that job titles be screened not only at the initial setup but every year as well; at that time, standards are reviewed and distributed, and annual reviews will guarantee a proper control on "job title creep!"

Once job titles are consolidated and agreed upon, they are organized in the computer by departments. A simple outline process is used except that each job title should carry a notation "reviewed and approved on (date)." This permits proper reference to the latest and thus most relevant standards when they are distributed to users.

Once job titles are agreed upon and entered in the word processor, each job title is broken down into relevant tasks. Beware! Most people believe they have a myriad of tasks to perform when, in fact, 8 or 10 is the maximum for almost any hospitality position. Creating job tasks is a most educational process for everyone. Not only is the process educational in understanding all that must be accomplished in the property, but it also points up the fact that the essence of quality is a few tasks done to perfection. Consider, for example, a dining room waiter, whose job tasks might look like the following:

1. Report for work
2. Set up tables in assigned area
3. Meet and welcome guests
4. Take guests' orders
5. Service guests
6. Conclude guest interactions
7. Reset tables
8. Break down serving area
9. Conclude work and check out
10. General

The above organizational effort is performed by the Quality Assurance Committee and is best performed with input from department heads, supervisors, and a representative of the particular job title.

The task breakdown is eventually performed for every job title from most senior executive through entrance level positions for production employees. As the tasks are developed by job titles they are fed into the word processor as indentations under the relevant titles. Our program, under Food and Beverage, might look like this:

(5) Food and Beverage Department
    A. Food and Beverage Manager (R&A/Date_____)
    B. Secretary—Food and Beverage Dept (R&A/Date_____)
    C. Dining Room Host—Main Dining Room (R&A/Date_____)
    D. Asst. D. R. Host—Main Dining Room (R&A/Date_____)
    C. Waiter—Main Dining Room (R&A/Date_____)
        1. Report for work
        2. Set up tables in assigned area
        3. Meet and welcome guests
        4. Take guests' orders
        5. Serve guests
        6. Conclude guest interactions
        7. Reset tables
        8. Break down serving area
        9. Conclude work and check out
        10. General
    D. Busperson—Main Dining Room (R&A/Date_____)
    E. Bartender—Cocktail lounge (R&A/Date_____)
    F. Cocktail waiter—Cocktail Lounge (R&A/Date_____)
    [etc. through all jobs titles in F&B Department]

The preceding approach is meant to be general in that there are a wide variety of word processing programs and, of course, job titles and tasks will vary according to each property's operating philosophy. Regardless, the example is meant to illustrate that once the list of job titles has been organized for all positions, the tasks can be input as they are created, and it is not necessary to complete all tasks and standards for your quality assurance program to begin to take shape. Already in the process of creating tasks, you are structuring quality.

Let us assume that we initiated our program by working on the position of dining room waitress because we wanted to make improvements in that area. More specifically, let us assume that the Quality Assurance Committee working with the F & B director, believes that guests are not being fully served (and the property is failing to generate desired profits) because guests are not being offered a chance to include wine with their meal. A standard is now discussed, structured, and set into place under "4. Take guests' orders." It says the following:

> *At the conclusion of the taking of orders for the main course, the waitress will say, "May I bring you a selection of wine to go with your dinner?"*

The property has set a standard to offer every table the opportunity to consider wine with their meal. It is a standard—a required part of the task of serving the guest.

Or perhaps desserts have not been moving well. Under "6. Conclude guest interaction," the following standard can be created that will encourage guests:

> *"May I serve you a selection of outstanding desserts from our pastry chef?"*

Perhaps waiters and waitresses have developed the annoying habit of clearing plates from some guests before all are finished eating. Under "5. Serve guests," the standard below is established:

> *No plates are to be removed from the table until all guests have finished eating their entire course and have placed eating utensils on their plates.*

Admittedly, the above seems simplistic, but it is doing the simple tasks to perfection that builds quality. More to the point, establishing the above three standards for service and insisting on them means that today's service is better than yesterday's (and today's profits are greater as well).

When a standard is created, it is immediately put into effect and monitored. The process permits relevant standards to be fed into the system in meaningful, manageable fashion such that they can be measured, monitored, and met.

PUTTING THE STANDARDS IN THE HANDS OF THE USERS

The greatest problem in achieving standards is lack of communication. Not only do we tend to lay too many standards on employees at one time, we do not utilize systems that put the standards in the hands of the users. By using word processing, the standards for "waiter or waitress—main dining room" can be printed out as they are developed, and a copy of the entire section—title—tasks and standards can be given to the waiters and waitresses as often as changes are made. Obviously discretion is advised. It is best to begin by setting forth the basic, obvious standards for each task in a given job title. Having a representative waiter or waitress present at the quality assurance meeting when the standards are discussed is crucial because a) it will result in meaningful standards based on experience, and b) there will be a sense of participation on the part of the employees, and participation will enhance a positive attitude essential for willing compliance.

REVISIONS ARE EASILY EXECUTED

As the system of generating standards progresses, two things will inevitably happen: a) the employees will suggest ways to improve the standards and/or to add new ones, and b) standards will change as conditions change. The notion that standards do not change is unrealistic. To be sure, some don't. A standard to periodically check fire alarm systems should not change, but standards of service will change as new items are introduced to the market and as guest requirements change. Standards for rooming guests were quite different a few years back before the age of electronic gadgetry, as were standards for room set-ups before the age of amenity baskets and mints on pillows. Further, the age of credit cards and computerized check-in has dramatically altered standards at the front desk. The shift from trains to cars and then to airport limousines has also revised guest reception procedures. The fast food era has changed food service, and instant communications systems have changed the way we handle reservations. In short, standards will change, especially in service industries, and the ability to revise and communicate new standards is crucial. The word processing approach thus becomes the most effective way to achieve consistency, and consistency in regard to standards is essential.

The dynamic on-line approach to standards permits one other essential process to take place. A successful quality assurance program requires a constant awareness of operating standards, which means that no less than an annual review of all standards by every department head and departmental supervisor is essential. Annually, standards by department by job title can be printed and distributed throughout the management positions in every department. They are then reviewed, revisions are suggested, and then they are signed and returned for department head approval. Changes are fed back into the word processor as they apply, and a final printout is made and distributed. The process is impossible with the hard copy operations manual approach.

CONCLUSION

The progressive manager who is truly concerned with achieving quality will have little difficulty agreeing that the quality manual approach is outdated and ineffective. Quality assurance is, bottom line, "behavior modification," and "behavior modification" is not effectively achieved by laying on employees a myriad of standards, ineffectively monitored and measured. Behavior modification is best achieved by slowly and patiently bringing employees into a mainstream where pride of achievement is the empowering force. In effect, "slower is faster." Raising children is a process we all know something about. For children to reach adulthood with ethical values, healthy minds and bodies, a sense of good judgment, and an enthusiastic attitude toward life, we must do more than establish an inflexible, albeit complete body of standards at an early age. Rather, we must constantly nurture their growth and development along value lines we believe in. Quality assurance is no different. We establish our standards slowly and positively. We add them as the situation dictates, revise them as necessary, monitor and measure the compliance, and over time we effect the behavior modification we desire. Perhaps the most important words a general manager can say to his or her Quality Assurance Committee is, "slow down." Take small steps, but make every step meaningful.

12

"On-Line" Standards

Putting Standards to Work

Myth #12: STANDARDS ONLY APPLY TO PRODUCTION-LEVEL EMPLOYEES.

THREE MISCONCEPTIONS

Most discussions of standards become very detailed in areas that are obvious and tend to ignore other areas that are more difficult to codify. This fuels the notion that quality assurance is a process of controlling production-level employees, and this is most unfortunate. In point of fact, standards apply at every level of the hospitality organization. Further, a major misconception of the concept of standards is the belief that they are only valid where there are large numbers of people to whom they apply. Finally, there is a belief among many hoteliers that the need for standards is in indirect ratio to the degree of professionalism. Simply stated, many believe that standards are essential for "those employees," but are not relevant for general managers and department heads. Let us look at each of these three misconceptions in turn.

Standards Are Only Valid in Certain Areas of the Hotel Operation

Hospitality is generally viewed by management as consisting of rooms and food. As such, concentration is placed on the front desk area

158

(which is the source of the largest percent of hospitality "errors"), the guest room, and the food service outlets. In truth, when viewed from the guests' perspective, the quality of an operation is the sum total of all of its parts. A caretaker with a dirty uniform or messy work habits, a garage valet who is impolite, and a newsstand operator who seems totally disinterested in helping you, all contribute to the overall impression of the hospitality experience. Even more subtle, improper receiving and storage could mean wasted food, improper utility monitoring by engineering could add 10–20 percent to utility costs, and inefficient attention to sales call follow-up could lose thousands of dollars of revenue. "Out of sight" may mean "out of mind," but "out of mind" may also mean "out of control," and that means cost! There is no area of the hospitality organization that cannot benefit from the proper application of standards. As the Quality Assurance Committee proceeds through the standards process, the basic question for each task, in every area, is, "If the individual in question is performing this task as I want it performed, what does that mean in terms of a standard?" No job title is immune. If your standard is that no sheet will ever be placed on a guest bed unless it is 100 percent free from tears, holes, or mends, then your folders in the laundry need to know this, or, if you send laundry out, the person who counts it out should be your checker. If your standard is that no guest should wait longer than four rings on the telephone, then this standard must be communicated to all who have telephone responsibility. And, if management believes (as it should) that meetings go faster and more efficiently with agendas, then department heads need to know that agendas are standard items. Standards apply everywhere; they are easier to conceive in some areas than others, but they apply everywhere.

Standards Are Most Effective for Large Groups of Employees

To believe this is to miss the concept of standards, because standards apply specifically to the individual employee. And, frankly, we, as individuals, are judged by our personal standards. What is our personal standard regarding grooming? What is our standard concerning time? Do we begin meetings on schedule and end as promised, or don't we care? What about human relations? Do we practice prejudice, tolerate prejudice, or actively work to prevent it?

What about standards for honesty? Do we tell the guest about a special rate if he or she has not asked? In fact, most of us have personal standards. We don't always meet them, but they are there. Consistency of service and product is the bottom line of quality, and it makes little difference if we receive inconsistent responses from different employees in a multiple-employee department or from the same employee each time we interact with him or her.

Standards Are Less Valid as Education Increases

I cannot count the number of times French hoteliers have told me that they do not need standards for waiters in France because they all come highly trained to begin with. Anyone who has done much dining out in France soon recognizes that standards are often what the waiter or waitress feels like providing at the time—at least it seems this way if you are not French! To be certain, service is good in Europe, but it is not always consistent and, regardless of education and training, consistency is a function of standards. There is a very valid point to be made regarding professionalism, however. Whereas we may need to spell out specifically how the amenities are put into the basket and where the basket is placed in the room, we should not have to be specific in telling our electrician how to wire a three-way switch or troubleshoot a control circuit. Nor should we have to establish a standard for our chef regarding the slicing of celery and carrots for julienne. The on-line approach described in the previous chapter makes such questions academic. In all areas where technique is assumed as part of the trade, we ignore standards until actual performance indicates a need. Standards regarding cleanliness and appearance for both chef and electrician are in order, however, and certainly we want our maintenance personnel to be consistent and professional when they make room calls in response to guests' requests. Let's get right to the heart of the question. Do standards apply to the general manager? They certainly do.

Quality starts at the top. The manager who is to promote standards must live by them. An ITT quality film entitled "Zero Defects—That's Good Enough," (produced by Philip Crosby, 1968) identifies the three main elements of quality as knowledge, attitude, and example. We assume that the most senior executive in a hospitality operation has knowledge, or he or she would not be at the top. And certainly, attitude, as it relates to wanting to do a good job, is generally present. What is often missing is "example." "We have in mind what we want others to do, but that does not apply to us!"

For example, most managers believe that they have what is called an "open-door policy," that is, a willingness to speak with and listen to concerns from within their organization at all levels. Many pride themselves in the fact that few of their employees take advantage of this opportunity, crediting good management as the reason. But it may not be "good management." It may be that managers have no standards for implementing an "open-door policy." Are there certain times when the manager is always available? Or does this vary depending upon what else is happening? Has management communicated standards as to how department heads and supervisors should react when those under them request permission to "talk with the top?" Has management set in place a system of standards governing resolution of issues generated by his/her open-door policy? The point is not whether an open-door policy is "good" or "bad," "desirable" or "undesirable." The point is that to announce such a policy without thinking through what it means and setting in place the relevant standards is simply to render such a policy invalid. And policies that are viewed as meaningless by employees are far more damaging than no policies at all.

The same principles hold true for programs such as "outstanding employee of the month." In many cases, such programs become "PR games" rather than "motivational programs." Behind such awards must be a defined system of standards that truly describe the recipients as worthy under all forms of evaluation. In short, if the prize (usually identifying the selected employee for all to see, including photo) is not truly felt to be earned and deserved, it falls short of its intended purpose.

What about standards regarding management interaction with employees at all levels? Our studies indicate that management interaction, if sincere, is a prime element in employee motivation, and is thus "quality." Most managers claim to have programs that cause interaction to take place on a finite, regular basis, but few, in fact, carry out programs of interaction. Many managers will take issue with this discussion, but the question can be put to rest by simply asking management personnel to identify their written standards in this area and then honestly evaluate their success in meeting these standards.

For quality assurance to take hold, it is crucial that management take the lead by establishing meaningful standards for its own actions and meeting these standards consistently. The hospitality culture is such that little goes unseen and unknown. Employees have seen a multitude of programs aimed at correcting their perceived weaknesses. They have seldom seen, however, programs that are adopted by the top managers long before they are implemented for supervisors, and the production level. Quality is a top-down program, and to attempt to implement it any other way is to court disaster.

Standards apply to every person, at every level, regardless of education, training, or base of power.

THE RELATIONSHIP BETWEEN STANDARDS AND PROCEDURES

Many areas of hospitality operations become hazy when we attempt to write standards to cover them, particularly when the procedure or process is long and involved. For example, let us consider the proper method for making a guest bed. It would be possible to describe every tuck and fold under the job title task "making bed"; however, by the time all elements of guest room cleaning were set forth, we would have a set of standards far too long, far too complex, and far too difficult for the maid to use effectively. If it is important that every bed be made up exactly the same way, then a procedure should be developed covering the exact step-by-step process. The standard for the task "bed making," then, becomes that of making every bed according to the specific procedure, each and every time. Employees are now trained in the procedure, which is totally encompassed by the standard.

Another example would be the fire alarm procedures. Once the process has been worked out in complete detail as a procedure, the standard for every single employee in the property is that they are familiar with the procedure and particularly their specific role within it.

Recall that in our discussion of job tasks in the preceding chapter, we added a category. "General" meant to cover all standards that were not specifically task-oriented. Standards such as those relating to fire safety would come under the "general" heading.

In most large properties, there are rather specific rules, regulations, and procedures covering employee benefits and conduct while on the job. Normally these are set forth in an employee handbook. Theoretically, all items set forth are "standards," however, once again, we could turn our standards program into an overly voluminous listing of procedures and rules by doing so. More to the point is the standard, rigidly enforced 100 percent of the time, that every employee a) be thoroughly trained in the contents of the employees' handbook at orientation, b) have in his/her possession a copy of the handbook, and c) be retrained on its contents each year.

Hopefully, the preceding has put standards into perspective, relative to procedures. By separating the two, the standards manual can be kept short and meaningful while the procedures manual can be revised as needed without causing the standards to be impacted.

STANDARDS VERSUS POLICY

Standards and policies are alike in that both are required 100 percent; however, standards are totally specific whereas policies should be broader. For example, it could be the policy of the hotel to provide clean comfortable rooms to every guest. This is required 100 percent of the time, however, it is the system of standards backed up by a system of procedures that defines what is meant, specifically, by "clean and comfortable." Many managers confuse policy with standards and rules. A good way to view policy is to picture a large umbrella that represents the overall policy of the ownership to "provide excellent service and product at a specific market level and at a profit for the operation." Underneath that umbrella are policies of each department head, who is operating within the overall policy with ones that carry out the main mission specific to their own departmental responsibilities. Under each of the departmental policies are those of the supervisory level. Policies establish the parameters within which the operation is managed. Standards, once again, differ because they are precise and unequivocal.

RESIST THE TEMPTATION

The temptation will always be to take the simple effectiveness of a well-structured standards system and attempt to get more out of it by trying to do more than the system is intended to do. Standards should be kept clear, concise, and relevant and must only be identified when the commitment is towards 100 percent compliance. Start slowly, build steadily and strongly, be patient, and reap the benefits as you progress. This is the proper application of standards—and it works.

13

Up and Running

Implementing QA

Myth #13: IMPLEMENTING QUALITY ASSURANCE IS AS SIMPLE AS LETTING EVERY EMPLOYEE KNOW THAT MANAGEMENT IS COMMITTED, CHOOSING A DIRECTOR AND A COMMITTEE, AND REVISING STANDARDS.

THE WINNING TEAM

Perhaps an analogy to an athletic team will help to solidify the quality assurance process in the mind of the reader.

Before engaging in the first instance of athletic combat, a team must come together, have the positions and responsibilities of each member identified, and practice together until the individual abilities of each member become known to the other members and the overall plan of action is known to all. The team then engages in the contest at hand with two objectives in mind. The first, of course, is to win, and the second is to play the game to the best ability of each member and of the team as a unit. Finally, regardless of the outcome, the good team will evaluate its performance and, returning once again to the practice arena, work to further perfect its skills. This process of coming together around a common goal, engaging in the object of the organization, evaluating the results, and once again coming together to seek additional perfection is an ongoing process and is exactly the same process required of a good quality assurance effort.

THREE LEGS OF THE STOOL

The following are three main parts to the implementation process:

1. Meshing
2. Diffusing
3. Evaluating

These parts, however, must not be viewed as linear to the extent that the process begins with meshing and ends with evaluating. *Quality assurance is forever.* Meshing, or bonding, if you will, between members of the Quality Assurance Committee, between the committee and all employees, and between all employees in general, is a process that never ends. Nor does the process of diffusing the requirements of the program or evaluating the results. Yet each part does have its own specific characteristics and should be viewed in turn.

Chapter 5 suggested nine action steps that will help the newly formed Quality Assurance Committee mesh together into a highly proficient winning team. They are set forth once again in outline form as follows:

1. Discuss concept, definitions, process, philosophy, etc.
2. Perform a needs analysis.
3. Identify 10 areas of potential improvement for the hospitality unit.
4. Cost the 10 areas of improvement in order to gain expertise and confidence in the cost of error process.
5. Collect all existing standards and review.
6. Review existing orientation programs.
7. Collect and review all existing job titles.
8. Select one job title, evaluate its relevant tasks, and create standards for the crucial tasks.
9. Invite the general manager to participate and review performance to date.

The above steps are suggested as ways to immerse the committee into the prime work of quality assurance. There are other events that should also take place during this initial meshing phase.

Who Needs Quality? Studies have shown that hoteliers don't believe, in general, that they have quality problems or that the cost of error is of real concern. In general, hoteliers rely on guest comment cards and tend to balance compliments against complaints, a very bad philosophy to follow. Somehow, before quality assurance can begin in earnest, something has to get the manager's attention—that is, if the influx of foreign ownership in the American hospitality industry isn't of enough import.

The critical question thus becomes, "How do I know I need a quality assurance program?" The answer rests in the performance of a "needs analysis." As a guide, the following areas of the hospitality operation should be evaluated:

1. *Guest comments.* Most hospitality operations solicit guest comments. The creation of a proficient guest comment system will be discussed later; however, suffice it to say at this point, a great comment system, although informative is but one input in the overall needs analysis.

   • Review all guest comments. As a matter of course, all guest comments should pass through the Quality Assurance Committee at some point early in the process. By reviewing all negative comments, areas of concern can be ascertained.

2. *Grievances filed.* By examining the nature of employee grievances filed, it is possible to determine areas where standards can effect solutions. Obviously, a property with numerous grievances is not a "happy" operation, and unhappy employees are prone to cause errors affecting quality.

3. *Turnover.* By first nulling out turnover caused by seasonal considerations, it can be determined whether there appears to be unusual employee dissatisfaction. Dissatisfied employees are, again, error prone. It is not sufficient to blame high turnover on the caliber of employees themselves. For example, a five-star Florida property found that they were terminating a large number of Haitian employees because of poor personal grooming habits, even while acknowledging that they were good workers. By implementing a special training program to teach proper personal grooming to those whose past did not seem to require it, the problem was solved.

4. *Absenteeism.* Most properties do not have good records on absenteeism, and those that do often do not utilize them perceptively. Review absenteeism records to determine if there are underlying causes that proper standards could rectify.

5. *Breakage.* Some breakage is the result of accidents. Other breakage is the result of carelessness. Accidents and carelessness are often caused by a *laissez faire* attitude that can be improved by proper standards.

6. *Insurance claims.* Excessive insurance claims can often be reduced by analyzing the causes and organizing procedures to prevent recurrence.

7. *Repair and maintenance costs.* It is wrong to assume that repair and maintenance costs always result from normal wear and tear on a property. For example, all managers know that a talented, caring maintenance person can keep equipment running properly long after its expected life. A talented maintenance person who does not care, however, will produce different, less desirable results. Caring is a function of attitude, and attitude is a function of a proper quality program.

8. *"No shows."* "No shows" are considered an inevitable part of the hospitality business; however, there is a large difference between a "no show" whose plans have changed and a "no show" who too easily decides to select another hotel or motel in the marketplace. Perhaps a large "no show" number indicates a need for better quality, that is, a more attractive experience for the guest.

9. *Amenities.* Most hospitality operations have processes in which a dissatisfied guest is given some incentive to reassess his or her opinion of the facility and its service. By analyzing the reason for the amenities given under such circumstances, often a quality deficiency can be rectified. "Amenities" should be considered not only a fruit basket, a bottle of wine, and/ or a free cocktail but also discounts and rebates as well.

10. *Cancellations.* As with "no shows," cancellations can be justified or they can result from the selection of an alternate facility where the quality is deemed to be greater. Do not accept cancellations as merely an unavoidable part of the business.

11. *Waste.* An occasional survey of what comes back on the plates of diners and what goes out in the trash barrels from the

kitchens might well give an indication of the quality of the food served and the quality of the produce received.

12. *Inventory.* There is a maxim in the area of consumer preference surveying that says, "If you want to determine which kind of alcoholic beverage a person prefers, don't look in the liquor cabinet, that may only tell what is not preferred" (because it isn't moving!). To know what a person prefers, look in the trash barrel to see what has been consumed. Inventories cost money, money that is not only failing to earn interest but, perhaps, even costing interest!—money that could be much more effective somewhere else. Review what is not moving in the inventory in order to reduce costs and increase guest satisfaction by avoiding unpopular items and utilizing the money tied up in inventory more effectively elsewhere (in the QA program, for example). Stagnant inventory could suggest a need for better purchasing standards and control.

13. *Conversions.* "Conversions" in this instance refers to the sales of functions actually made versus those sought. Lost sales could be the result of improper standards for follow-up on the part of your sales staff.

14. *Walks.* A guest with a confirmed reservation who is "walked" is a guest who, despite efforts to rectify, will in all probability not return. A "walked" guest may result from a situation in which arrivals unaccountably exceeded a well-designed and implemented overbooking policy; or it could result from a problem of communication between reservations and front desk regarding length of stay; or it could even be caused by an overzealous reservations department who abort the overbooking policy. It makes good sense to analyze this problem and to set in place standards to match overbooking more precisely with "no show" experience. Further, when a "walk" does occur, a well-structured system of standards will certainly result in a higher percent of returns.

15. *Capital projects.* Are capital projects completed on time and within budget, or could improvement in the standards for such projects result in better performance?

This list is by no means exhaustive, but it certainly goes beyond the normal exploration of Quality Assurance Committees in their quest to ascertain need. For example, a mature committee could well invite frequent guests to spend a few minutes with the committee, thus instilling in the guest the sincere attitude of the property towards quality. Further, the profit and loss statement itself can guide the committee towards areas of concern and concentration. It is best, however, not to try to analyze everything all at once. It will only result in confusion. We should not lose sight of the primary message in the needs analysis; that is, indications of quality assurance are endless. Ascertaining that absenteeism, for example, does not seem to indicate a problem today does not preclude that it will not be a valid indication tomorrow. A proper committee will establish an on-going process of tracking these and other developed indications on a regular basis. The committee should always remember that although a "watched pot" seems to take longer to boil, it most certainly will never run dry and cause a fire.

Avoiding the Halo.   The work of the committee during the meshing phase is oriented internally and not externally. The natural inclination of management having made a solid commitment to quality is to immediately make the programs public and involve everyone in the process. It takes great restraint to invest 8 to 12 weeks in organization and consolidation, but in successful quality assurance, "slower is faster!" Nothing destroys a program faster than introducing it prematurely. Typically, employees sense that they are perceived as the cause of quality problems and have memories of past programs that have begun in earnest and then withered away into oblivion. It was Machiavelli, the controversial fifteenth-century Italian philosopher—attacked unmercifully but never questioned as an astute recorder of human nature—who said, "Old injuries die slowly." Employees never seem to forget programs that ended in failure and thus will resist any new programs that seem to be similar in nature to what is stored in their memory. The goodwill of all employees is necessary for a successful program, and that goodwill results from trust that, in turn, results from a program perceived as well-defined and adopted wholeheartedly by management before it is imposed upon the employees. It is counterproductive during the meshing phase for expectations of employees to be raised to a level where the committee wears halos in anticipation of wonderful results. It is counterproductive if these same halos are perceived to be around the necks of the committee members! It is best, therefore, that the committee go quietly about its work, not denying the existence of a program of quality, but, at the same time, not attributing to it expectations that are not yet ready to be believed.

Diffusing.   Having gained a sense of the need for quality along with immersion, however shallow, into the process of costing errors, developing standards, and interacting with top management, the committee is now ready to introduce the program to the employees at all levels. Again, the introduction of the program should be without great fanfare. A grand announcement is out of character because there is nothing of instant impact to announce. Quality is an ongoing process, steadily and gradually shaping the attitude of the organization as a growing tree is steadily and gradually shaped by the astute gardener who knows how to gently push and pull in all the right directions, with the right pressure at the right time.

There is another reason why the quality assurance program should not receive visible and widespread publicity, and it has to do with the very essence of quality assurance. Quality is present when there is harmony between the expectations of the guests and the service and product supplied by the organization. When harmony occurs, that is, when the guests' expectations are met with consistency, the result is a solid "word of mouth" phenomenon among guests that, of course, is the ultimate compliment for a successful program. Announcing that either a program is underway or, more frequently, that quality is present creates in the guests an attitude whereby errors take on added importance. In the paraphrased words of a popular wine advertising program, "No quality assurance program should be announced before its time." Because quality is an ongoing process, in which the striving for excellence never ends, there is no time when the property should admit to perfection. Let the guests say it for you. I have never forgotten the following advice given to me by my supervisor at Sheraton when, as a young and eager junior executive, I was being sent on my first project management assignment:

> Always be humble and minimize your knowledge. If you present an image of knowing too much, those who deal with you will be alert and conscious of your errors, whereas if you present yourself as knowing little but eager to learn, others will strive to help you and be favorably impressed when you do offer knowledge that is, in fact, correct.

The same philosophy works for quality. Present the true image of constantly striving for excellence and never being satisfied with any performance less than 100 percent, and guests will be lenient with your occasional errors.

Full Steam Ahead. The production of meaningful, clear, concise standards at every level for every task is the objective of the diffusion phase. Every department head and supervisor now becomes involved. Select a number of specific areas in need of either improvement as to level of performance or improvement as to consistency and, in turn, invite the relevant department head and supervisor along with someone with the job title in question to attend a quality assurance meeting. Do not attempt to write all standards for every task identified, but select the one or two tasks most in need of improvement and, together as an expanded team, develop the standards. It is not necessary that the standards be completed at the committee meeting itself—only that the process be thoroughly communicated and understood and, most importantly, that it be viewed as a total team effort not aimed at criticism but at simply more effective communication. Strive to reach a situation in which the relevant department head, supervisor, and representative can work on the standards outside of the quality assurance meeting, on their own time. Set a time for review and schedule enough time during the Quality Assurance Committee meeting for a thorough review of the subcommittee's work. Remember that the total objective of proper standards for every task for every job title is a massive undertaking best achieved by total participation of all management people in the operation. Concentrate, therefore, on the quality of the subcommittee's performance, not on the quantity. Encouraging the subcommittee to perform the standards writing process to perfection in a small and limited scope results in only a small improvement to be sure, but it is a small improvement done well and in a manner not requiring rework in the immediate future. It also encourages greater output from the subcommittee, which, of course, is the objective of quality assurance. It also places the power where it should be placed, in the hands of the actual performers.

Who Knows Best? Often when the above process is presented to top management the response is: "Employees do not know what I, the manager, want. They will develop standards that are not up to my level of requirement." On numerous occasions, I have then asked management people to write standards for a given production-level task, at the same time asking the relevant production people to do the same. Invariably, the production-level employees set higher standards for themselves than those that management sets for them. This comes about because of the acquired attitude on the part of management that employees are incapable of performing well without direct management involvement at every task. Management standards, however, are, more often than not, poorly defined and poorly communicated. We are talking now about precise standards for those who know the task best, the actual performers. Probably for the first time, they are part of the creation of standards. Given the rules of the game, and supported by a caring management with strong faith in the employees, you will find a hidden energy in employees heretofore untapped. Management has nothing to lose. The ultimate standards must be approved by the general manager so that there is no danger of adopting improper standards. On the other hand, if the process works well, as we know it will, then you have a situation whereby the employees are active participants and they're committed to the process. That, of course, is the bottom line of quality.

Error Identification.   The time is right, in the diffusion phase, to solicit information from the employees. Note that we said "information," not "suggestions." Suggestion systems have never proven to be effective mainly because a suggestion system focuses on the solution to a problem and not on the problem identification itself. For a start, if the employee does not have a solution, there will be no suggestion and, if the solution is not acceptable, you have the problem of telling the employee "no" when much more is to be gained by telling the employee "yes." Every good salesman knows this. They try to get clients and prospects in the mode of saying "yes" by leading them through a series of questions eliciting "yes" answers until finally the point of sale is reached with the client in a "yes" frame of mind. In virtually every case of a problem in a hospitality operation, the solution is easily found once the problem is known. We want from our employees, therefore, the identification of the problem only, after which it can be solved by the Quality Assurance Committee, the department head, or the supervisor, and, in most cases, a standard can be created that will prevent recurrence of the problem. The elements of an error I.D. program are as follows:

1. Creation of a logo for the process. This can either be a name or a symbol that will be identified with the I.D. process. One hotel, the Hotel Captain Cook in Anchorage, used the international symbol of a red circle with the letter "E" in it to signify "error" and an inclined line through the "E" to signify the elimination of errors.
2. Printing of several hundred cards (see Figure 13.1) 3" × 5" or perhaps slightly larger with the simple explanation that they are to be used to identify a problem with which the employee must contend. The following information should be on the card:
   a. Employee's name.
   b. Employee's job title.
   c. Location of the problem.
   d. The problem.
   (Do not try to solicit too much information. It is enough to know who is responding and what the problem is.)
3. Providing a place for depositing the cards. This can be a slot within the department, a box near the employees' entrance/ exit, a mail slot at the front desk, a box in the employees' locker room, or all of the above.
4. Thoroughly communicating the process to all department heads and supervisors and establishing procedure wherein:
   a. All I.D. inputs go to the Quality Assurance Committee without fail, every time. No card is to be short-circuited or returned by any supervisor or department head under any circumstances.
   b. No department head or supervisor will, at any time, place any negative pressure on any employee for any problem written on the card. This is absolutely crucial. It is a meaningful and effective variation of an "open-door" policy and, as such, under no circumstances must the employee be anything but encouraged regardless of the nature of the problem identified.
   c. Managers and supervisors must understand that the purpose of the error I.D. program transcends individual

problems and is part of a larger agenda, that of building an attitude of participation in all employees.

5. Acting upon all cards immediately. As I.D. cards are received by the Quality Assurance Committee, they are assigned a number and logged on a tracking form (see Figure 13.2) containing the following information:

   a. Name of contributor.
   b. Department and position of contributor.
   c. Date of receipt of problem.
   d. Nature of problem.
   e. Person to whom assigned for follow up, date of follow up, and by what means.
   f. Corrective action taken, plus date and method of communicating corrective action.

6. Communication with the originator of the error—crucial to the error I.D. system. Once received, a member of the Quality Assurance Committee is assigned the responsibility to acknowledge receipt to the originator. A personal acknowledgment is best by far, but if the choice is between a personal interaction and a slow or worse yet, no acknowledgment, a standard form should be developed that can be easily and quickly initiated.

7. Analysis of the type of error received, which will fall into one of three basic categories:

   A. *Maintenance errors* that can be corrected easily, such as valves that don't work, broken rolling stock, shelving required, loose carpet, etc. Errors of this nature should be corrected immediately and once completed, the originator should be contacted in person, thanked for participating and encouraged to submit other errors as they arise.

   B. *Process errors* that require evaluation, analysis, and decision such as changes in desk room procedures, luggage handling, room service process, check-out procedures, etc.

      1. Such errors normally require a working subcommittee consisting of the assigned quality assurance member either as a participant of the subcommittee or as its liaison, the department head or his or her designee, a person holding the relevant job title under discussion, and others, depending upon need. One of these "oth-

ers" could be the originator of the error communicated; however, care must be taken not to use the subcommittee as a means to punish or sidetrack the originator. Whether the subcommittee uses the originator as a member is of far less importance than treating the error seriously, working to effect a solution, and communicating properly.

2. When either a new process is developed, or no new process is deemed necessary, the originator must be contacted by the committee liaison and told the results of the quality assurance analysis.

C. *Nuisance errors*, which fall into many categories such as personality conflicts, general complaining, unreasonable requests, etc. Two points must be kept in mind concerning nuisance errors.

1. An employee expressing animosity toward the error I.D. process is an opportunity to modify the employee's behavior by indicating a sincere interest in him or her as a person, not as an employee of the hospitality operation.

2. Unreasonable requests (such as increased employee parking in the company garage or air-conditioning the dishwashing room) often lead to other solutions that truly solve errors. For example, a request to park in the company garage may be based on animosity or may indicate a transportation problem innovatively solved by a remote lot near a bus or subway line or with pickup by the hotel van. The air-conditioned dishwashing room may only be a communication that the exhaust fan is not working or that the make-up air system filter is dirty and thus obstructed. In other words, consider all errors submitted carefully with an open mind, and act on each, regardless.

8. The file or tracking sheet must not be closed on any error until the error has been resolved or considered thoroughly. If it should develop that the error cannot or should not be resolved, then it should not be considered an error.

9. Finally—the ultimate object of the error I.D. process—putting in place standards that prevent a recurrence. Broken items

 **HOTEL CAPTAIN COOK
ERROR IDENTIFICATION**

PLEASE DESCRIBE ANY PROBLEMS THAT MAKE
YOUR AREA OF WORK MORE DIFFICULT

NAME _____ JOB TITLE _____

DEPARTMENT _____

PUT CARD IN QA BOX AT EMPLOYEE ENTRANCE.

FIGURE 13.1   Sample error identification form.

suggest standards for improved inspection and/or preventive maintenance. Process errors often result in specialized training. For instance, in our example cited while discussing standards, whereby we required more emphasis on promoting wine, knowledge training on types of wine offered and skill training on the proper techniques of service are required.

The Power of Suggestion.   The error I.D. process must not be taken lightly. Start with the assumption that errors exist; large or small, they exist. And solving them will improve our quality. Four actions, listed below, can take place around the error:

1. Management discovers it and solves it.
2. Guests find it and are dissatisfied.
3. No one discovers it and it continues to be a problem.
4. Employees identify the errors, and they are resolved that the guest sees and enjoys only our best product and service.

Management's role is to solve problems. Finding them, although within the scope of management responsibility, is normally not within the scope of management's time limitations. Thus, management is not the best source of error identification. Doing nothing or making

| FORM 3 | Error Tracking | I.D. NUMBER: |
| | | DATE: |

O P P O R T U N I T Y	
C O S T	
S O L U T I O N	

	IDENTIFIED BY:	
	DEPARTMENT:	
T R A C K I N G	ASSIGNED TO:	DATE:
	ACKNOWLEDGED BY:	DATE:
	HOW:	
	SOLUTION APPROVAL BY:	DATE:
	FINAL ACKNOWLEDGEMENT BY:	DATE:
	HOW:	
	IMPLEMENTATION DATE:	FOLLOW-UP DATE:
	FINAL REPORT BY:	FILE CLOSED DATE:

STEPHEN HALL ASSOCIATES 1984

FIGURE 13.2   Sample error tracking sheet.

our guests our inspectors is totally unsatisfactory. Seeking the input of every employee is the only intelligent solution, and employees will participate if they believe management is serious in seeking the errors and diligent in resolving them.

There are other activities that are carried out by the Quality Assurance Committee during the diffusion process, and they are discussed in following chapters. However, the key activities are to create standards at every level for every job title and to identify errors at every level as a catalyst to the creation of standards. We now move on to the third phase—evaluation.

Evaluating

We have discussed the fact that quality assurance is forever, that it never ends but is a constant process of evaluation, correction, reevaluation and recorrection. The quality assurance program is best viewed as a wheel with the hub or center being total management commitment. Obviously, with anything less than total management commitment, the wheel, i.e., the quality assurance program, does not exist. Around the hub, we find the quality assurance structure, that is, the quality assurance director, the committee, the process by which standards are written and disseminated, the error I.D. process—in short, all of the mechanics of the program. The meshing process, i.e., the process by which all of the parts and pieces of the quality assurance structure come together to form a smooth, effective program, takes place constantly around the structure and holds the structure together (see Figure 13.3). The next level is that of diffusion and, finally, the outside of the wheel—the evaluation phase.

As previously discussed, a standard is not a standard unless it can be measured. It is in the measurement process, however, that we see one of the major differences between quality control (quality related to manufacturing) and quality assurance (quality related to service). The service industries do not lend themselves to the same intensity of measurement as does manufacturing. For example, every hotel or motor inn with bellhops should have a well-defined standard for rooming a guest; however, whether that standard is followed can be measured by a) sending along an observer or b) asking each guest. Observation is unwieldy, very expensive, and totally impractical. Asking the guests in specific terms is an imposition and in

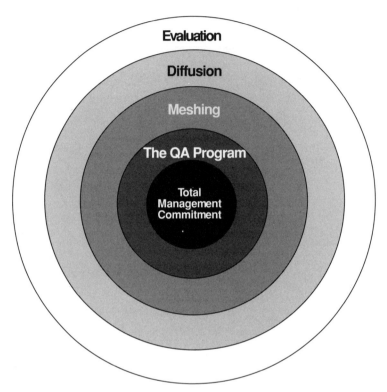

FIGURE 13.3   Elements of quality diffusion.

general terms, insufficiently accurate. Another approach to measurement must be adopted, and we call it "selective measurement." Perhaps the following will illustrate the concept.

When I was teaching quality assurance at the International Center at Glion, Switzerland, access to the school, located above the city of Montreux, was by cog railway, automobile, or an inclined railway, called a "funiculaire." The funiculaire ran every 15 minutes between the hours of 7:00 A.M. and midnight, sometimes with no riders and sometimes with 15 to 20. The funiculaire consisted of two cars, one at the top and one at the bottom, connected by cable, riding on a single track with a passing station of two tracks precisely in the middle of the run. The ride took five minutes. It was impractical and expensive to have a conductor on both cars on each trip to check tickets, so the control was effected by random checks at the top and/or bottom of the ride. A one-way ticket obtained automatically by machine at top and bottom cost approximately $1.50. Being caught without a ticket resulted in a fine of almost $20.00! To be sure, there were those who took their chances of being discovered, but, by and large, all riders had tickets, and the cost of measurement was held to an absolute minimum. In the same fashion, it is not necessary to measure every standard every time. But it is necessary to check frequently enough and completely enough to know that each standard is being met.

Three Ways to Measure.   Some standards (Class A) lend themselves to finite, constant measurement. The following are examples:

1. Guest complaints. Keep in mind, however, that only a small percent of dissatisfied guests bother to complain. They just don't return—and tell all their friends why!
2. No shows and walked guests.
3. Maintenance calls.
4. Amenities given.
5. Accident claims.
6. Grievances filed.
7. Rebates given.
8. Skippers (those who leave without paying).

Where finite measurement is available, the Quality Assurance Committee should establish a regular schedule of data input.

Other standards (Class B) may be easily measured but require a conscious act to do so. Some of these follow:

1. Long check-in, check-out lines.
2. Long waits to be seated in the food outlets.
3. Periodic guest room inspections (over and above the normal housekeeping controls).
4. Dining room service.
5. Cleanliness—back and front of the house.
6. Maintenance of equipment in the back of the house.

Class B standards require the delegation of a finite responsibility for measurement. For example, in long check-in/check-out lines, whether the standard is based upon number of people in line, or, more appropriately, a maximum "wait time" objective, someone who is in the vicinity of the desk frequently enough to measure conformance should be delegated to do so. This could be a concierge, an assistant manager, or even the bell captain. Regardless, the assignment must be definite and the data must be fed back to the Quality Assurance Committee.

Still other standards (Class C) are almost impossible to inspect and/or measure in constant fashion and generally fall into the category of guest contact with employees taking place in non-public areas. The rooming of a guest is, as mentioned previously, a prime example. Hoteliers have identified employees lacking knowledge of the facilities as the single, most frequent error. With bellhops, there exists a tremendous opportunity to train in all available information on the facility and to impart this information, in a general way, as the guest is taken to the room. In other words, the bellhop is one of the most important communicators in the operation *if* the bellhop has the correct attitude and does his or her job well. But how can this effort be measured? Practically, it cannot. What is required of processes such as this, in which measurement is difficult, is creativity. Management should institute the following procedures:

1. Create precise standards as to what the bellhop is expected to say to each guest roomed.
2. Train all bellhops thoroughly in the application of the standard.
3. Role play when the opportunity presents itself, i.e., have a bellhop act out the rooming of a guest (an assistant manager) all the way from lobby to completing the process in the guest room.
4. Periodically check specifically with the guest either by calling the guest to inquire as to the effectiveness of the rooming process, or by placing in the guest's mail slot a specific questionnaire on the process. This should be done automatically on a rather infrequent schedule, unless data such as guest comment cards, or direct complaints indicating problems in the process, make it necessary for more frequent checking.

Other areas where management is difficult are those listed below:

1. Valet delivering laundry or dry cleaning.
2. Bellhop delivering messages.
3. Maintenance calls.
4. Room service.
5. Inspector performing room checks.

This quickly becomes unwieldy when you consider that a 100-room hotel could easily have 400-500 standards, minimum (and this would only be an average of 12 to 15 standards per job title!) Thus the philosophy should be to display compliance regarding all major class A standards, which, of course, are easily available in finite form. Again, by exception, other standards should be displayed as well. For example, if the concentration is on improved courtesy among employees at all levels, then specific measurement techniques should be implemented and the results displayed. You might consider polling 10 percent of all registered guests one week each month with a short survey form aimed directly and specifically at the issue of employee courtesy. The results should be published for all employees to see.

Using the Measurement Rate.   Errors indicate one or more of the following:

1. The standard is not properly communicated, thus not properly understood.
2. Employees have not been properly trained in the application of the standard.
3. Employees do not have the proper "tools" to comply.
4. The standard is wrong.
5. Employees don't care.

Errors, therefore, require analysis and reevaluation on the part of the committee. Persistent errors should result in a task-force approach that includes one or more of those persons for whom the standards have been written. The task is to get to the root cause of the error, the bottom-line reason for nonconformance. Once that has been determined, the direction becomes obvious and yet another source of guest dissatisfaction is eliminated.

CONCERN BY EXCEPTION

The multiplicity of interactions taking place within the typical hotel or motel would, if permitted, result in measurement overload for the Quality Assurance Committee. The committee's own standards for measurement, therefore, should state that all negative measurements be brought to the attention of the committee. Thus, it will hear of all errors but will be spared concern when things are going correctly. In many properties, much emphasis is placed on positive comments, even to the extent of finding certain satisfaction when "positive" comments outnumber "negative" ones. Such a philosophy misses the intent of quality assurance. The goal is to eliminate all errors, and that should be the sole objective. Positive comments, though nice to hear, are like money in the bank. It is the money we spend because of the lost opportunities and hard costs related to errors that we must work to capture.

This does not say that relevant department heads and supervisors should not be cognizant of all measurement relating to them. It simply says that the Quality Assurance Committee should focus on errors and let the reward for standards met be "word of mouth."

SEEING IS BELIEVING

Whenever possible, measurements should be displayed in graphic form for all relevant parties to see.

The most common problem associated with graphs is a tendency to make them more complicated than they should be, that is, trying to display too much data. To be effective, particularly in a social system such as a hotel or motel where there is a heavy traditional orientation among employees, particularly at the production level, the graph must be kept very basic. There are three basic kinds of graphs in common use—the bar graph, the line graph, and the circular graph, or "pie" chart. All three have one basic requirement in common; they must be simply but thoroughly labeled. The basic labeling is the heading which must show the following:

1. Title of graph indicating simply but precisely what the graph shows. For example, a graph showing "Coffee Shop Complaints Received."
2. Period covered by the graph, as in "For the Year 198__," "For the Month of _____," etc.
3. Notation when the graph shows a comparison with a prior period that should read: "Compared With Same Period Last Year," etc.
4. Notation if a scale is involved, such as "in thousands of dollars" or "per 100 guests," etc.
5. Vertical and horizontal axes, in bar graphs and line graphs. In circular graphs, the segments must be labeled.

The use of color in graphs is most helpful in attracting and holding attention. Graphs for public display should be placed in high traffic areas and must be kept absolutely current. Graphs should be large in size and lettering and should stand out prominently. Special display boards dedicated to quality assurance graphics are very helpful. The process of graphics today, with the advent of computers, is much easier. Simplified programs are capable of displaying data in a variety of graphic forms and can even, in the case of line graphs, project trend lines in response to a simple command. A computer dedicated to statistical recording and graphic display does not need a powerful memory and is well within reason as a tool of the Quality Assurance Committee.

In our discussion of selective measurement, we hypothesize that it is better to do a good job of measuring suspected problem areas as the need arises than to try to thoroughly measure every standard constantly. Selective measurement recognizes the need to control labor cost and also the difficulty people have in absorbing extensive data on a constant basis. The same principle applies to graphic display. A few graphs, well done, showing data relevant to the majority of employees, is the way to display quality progress.

One other way to display progress is by simply posting a numerical indicator. For example, guests' comments should be structured as yes-no responses, i.e., we either met our standard 100 percent or we did not! The percentage of "no" responses to total responses is a meaningful measure, displayed in positive terms, i.e., 100 percent minus the "no" percent. In such a display, non-responses may be handled either as assumed "yeses" or ignored as a response. The value of such a display is that one single number, which can be changed daily, reflects the overall index of the guest comment system and ignores the confusion that results from trying to display averages as in "How did we do?, Rate us 1–5," etc.

In general we have been discussing graphic display of data affecting all departments. Each department will have its own data to communicate as well. Data such as "guest roomed—room not ready," "maintenance calls from guest rooms," "reservation not found," "room inspected—discrepancy found," etc., are representative of departmental quality checks. The committee must establish the need for measuring with all department heads and work with them to develop meaningful displays. In the mature program the department heads will initiate the measuring and implement the display, keeping in communication with the committee but not waiting for the committee to initiate the process.

14

The "Enlightened" QA Committee

Innovations That Make QA Successful

Myth #14: ONCE A PROGRAM IS IMPLEMENTED, IT, LIKE EVERY OTHER QUALITY ASSURANCE PROGRAM, BASICALLY RUNS ITSELF.

By definition quality assurance is conformance to standards, and excellence is conformance to standards that are both ethical and moral. However, concentration solely on standards will not produce true excellence any more than can a symphony orchestra, focusing strictly on the notes, play beautiful music. The task of the symphony conductor is to instill emotion into the process—to create the desire not just to play the right notes, but to do so as a matter of pride. So it is with excellence. Meeting standards rigidly without desire, emotion, enthusiasm, and pride will certainly result in failure. Quality cannot be forced on employees any more than can a piece of string be pushed across a table. Leadership is required, leadership that results in a behavior modification. Unfortunately, production-level and supervisory-level employees are generally regarded by management with less respect than they are due. This poor attitude on the part of management has been verified through many studies, and it must

187

change if excellence is ever to take root. Managers won't change by thinking or saying "right" things but rather by doing "right" things. As the first step in excellence, managers must modify their behavior. Here are areas in which my studies have indicated that management behavior must be modified.

FACTORS THAT INFLUENCE QUALITY

The basis for the following data came from a study done for AH&MA by the author and published by AH&MA in December of 1982. As a result of a nationwide personal interview of more than 40 recognized "quality oriented" hotel executives, a 43-question survey form was mailed to 357 hotels, motels, and motor inns of 80 rooms or more. A 24.6 percent response resulted from 40 of the 50 states in the U.S. The distribution of the response was the following:

Casinos	2%
Destination resorts	29%
Hotels over 300 rooms	25%
Hotels under 300 rooms	16%
Motor inns	13%
Motels	14%
National parks	1%

Fifty percent of the responses were from chains, 21 percent of all respondents were seasonal properties, and, in terms of rooms, 2.92 percent of all AH&MA member hotels were included in the results. Room rates varied from $21.88 per night to $165. The average number of employees per room was .94, with the lowest reported being .14 and the highest 2.52. Annual employee turnover for the respondent group was 37.31%. In order to ascertain the affect of different elements on overall quality, a basis for measurement of employee turnover was used, the assumption being that higher quality operations will have less turnover than those of lower quality. The results were the following:

1. Turnover rates among properties that used turnover and absenteeism reports in their daily operations rated 32% lower than did those of properties where reports were not used.

2. Turnover rates among properties with a structure of inter-action with production-level employees were 27% lower than were those of properties with no interaction.

3. Properties in which managers spent a large amount of time interacting with employees had turnover rates 7% higher than had those who spent the average amount of time in employee interaction.

4. Properties with a system of standards had average turnover rates 19% lower than did those with no system of standards.

5. Properties with production-level interaction, standards, and turnover/absenteeism reports averaged turnover rates 57% lower than had those in which all three programs were non-existent.

6. Properties with performance evaluation systems for employees at all levels had turnover rates 35% lower than those of properties with no evaluation system at all.

7. Thirty-six percent of all respondents claimed to have a quality assurance program in place. No attempt was made to qualify the elements or effectiveness of the alleged programs; however, properties that claimed to have a program had turnover rates 46% lower than did those properties where no program existed.

8. Respondents were asked to advise the acceptable level of conformance to standards they would tolerate in food and beverage, housekeeping, maintenance, and morning wake-up. Respondents who would not accept a level less than 98% in all five categories had turnover rates 48% less than had those respondents who would accept less than 98% in all five categories.

9. Properties conducting ongoing training had turnover rates 45% lower than those of properties doing no training.

10. Properties with orientation programs had turnover rates 41% lower than those of properties without orientation.

11. Properties with continuing education programs for employees had turnover rates 22% lower than had properties without continuing education programs.

12. Properties of managers who had a high index of civic involvement had turnover rates 33% lower than those of properties where the manager did not have a high civic involvement.

13. Properties with guest comment card systems had turnover rates 23% lower than had properties without a guest comment card system.
14. Respondents were asked to rate the value of their guest comment system to their quality assurance program. Properties in which the guest comment system was rated above the average had turnover rates 26% higher than those of respondents who rated their comment system below the average of the group for value.

The 14 elements, in more simplified form are listed below:

ELEMENT	TURNOVER RATE
1. Turnover and absenteeism reports	↓ 32%
2. Employee interaction	↓ 27%
3. Excessive employee interaction	↑ 7%
4. System of standards	↓ 19%
5. Interaction, T&A reports, standards	↓ 57%
6. Performance evaluation systems	↓ 35%
7. Quality assurance program	↓ 46%
8. Demand for higher conformance	↓ 48%
9. Training	↓ 45%
10. Orientation program	↓ 41%
11. Continuing education program	↓ 22%
12. Civic involvement by manager	↓ 33%
13. Guest comment card system	↓ 23%
14. Excessive emphasis on guest comment	↑ 26%

The reader must keep in mind that the data indicates effects of various elements on quality. It does not represent finite effect; that is, the effects are not additive in any way. For example, items 1, 3, and 4, taken separately, add to a 78% reduction of turnover, but when analyzed together as in item 5, the effect is 57%. For the properties "doing things right," many of the elements were present, and it is not possible to isolate the exact value of each element in quantitative terms. What can be said, however, is that any single positive impact element will probably be a plus to the quality assurance program, and all of them will most certainly be a plus!

THE MANY HATS OF THE QUALITY ASSURANCE COMMITTEE

The Quality Assurance Committee is, in effect, the board of directors of the quality assurance program and, as such, must be involved in every aspect, well beyond simply developing standards. Taking each relevant element of excellence in turn, let us look at ways for the Quality Assurance Committee to get involved.

Turnover and Absenteeism Reports

Taking the quality assurance pulse, so to speak, of your employees is crucial to excellence. The committee should track both turnover and absenteeism on a weekly basis. The data should be made visible in graph form to all employees not only to indicate that management cares but also to show the numbers coming down as the quality assurance program progresses.

Turnover is defined by the U.S. Department of Labor as:

$$\frac{\text{Number of Employee Separations During the Month}}{\text{Number of Employees at Midmonth}} \times 100$$

The definition is not very helpful to us. Employees leave for a variety of reasons, not all bad. Their reasons could be seasonal flexing, promotion, transfer, health, termination, retirement, or resignation. Seasonal flexing, as in a summer resort, is planned turnover. Promotions and transfers within the organization are positive turnover relating to cause. Health reasons, if not occupationally related, are beyond the control of management. Retirement generally is a plus in terms of employee satisfaction. Termination and resignation, however, are indications that the system has failed. Somewhere in the chain of events beginning with hiring, orientation, training, supervision, evaluation, compensation, and motivation, we failed. This is the issue to be faced by the Quality Assurance Committee. One way to get to the heart of the turnover question is to have meaningful exit interviews. With little prodding, terminated or resigned employees will tell you what they don't like about your organization. The committee should review every exit interview.

Absenteeism is defined by the U.S. Department of Labor in the equation below:

$$\frac{\text{Number of Person Days Lost Through}}{\text{Average Number of Employees} \times \text{Monthly Days Worked}} \times 100$$

The condition "unauthorized" has been added by the author to produce a figure that is more purely negative in its makeup. Absences for legitimate health reasons, if not job related, and/or officially sanctioned absences, albeit important pieces of information, do not generally indicate job dissatisfaction. The Quality Assurance Committee should seek to identify the root cause of unauthorized absenteeism so that corrections can be put in place.

Some companies with high absenteeism, normally in the form of sick days taken, have developed plans to "reward" employees who don't use up their sick leave. This is a classic example of solving the symptom rather than the "root cause." It is a blatant attempt to buy the employees' "loyalty" and it simply will not work. In fact, it is totally counterproductive to quality assurance. In organizations in which a strong sense of pride and responsibility is present, management has a difficult problem—a problem of preventing stress! What is the basic difference between a company with excess absenteeism and one in which employees are too conscientious? You will generally find that it is a management that truly and sincerely cares about each and every employee.

The Process of Structuring Interaction

The attitude of true caring between management and employees, in both directions, is crucial to employee attitudes, behavior modification, and excellence! Yet it is poorly done in many organizations. Either management consciously decides that "power would be lost" if there is too much familiarity between management and labor, or the interaction is done insincerely and in a patronizing fashion. To reemphasize our discussion of power in Chapter 6, *true* power is only possible when freely granted by followers to leaders. Some managers believe that interaction with employees means walking around greeting employees with a "Hi, how are you?" This is a standard stimulus and elicits a standard response, usually "ok," or "not bad," or "fine." But, it is not the kind of interaction we mean, for with this model, if an employee ever did say, "Not good, my house burned down this morning," the manager would probably respond "That's good" and be halfway out of the room! The kind of interaction we need is the kind that goes, "Good morning, Sam, how are you today?" "Fine Mr. Jones, and how are you?" Or, if things aren't "fine," Jones takes the time to really listen and help. In other words, sincere, caring interaction. Does it erode your power? No, it strengthens it!

The task of the Quality Assurance Committee is to encourage meaningful management interaction with the ultimate goal of fusing the objectives of both management and labor in one direction, that of 100 percent conformance to standards, thus meeting the needs of the guests. There are several ways to achieve this goal. The following are a few:

1. Robert Beck, the revered former dean of the School of Hotel Administration at Cornell, is a master at interaction. Rumor has it that he had standing orders to be reminded every morning of the first main class break, even if he was occupied. He would then make himself prominent in the main hallway, to greet and interact with students. Standing order or not, he always seemed to be there! And he enjoyed being there! Students knew who the dean was and considered him a sincere friend. Hotel managers could achieve the same results by spending a few minutes near the employees' entrance when shifts change.
2. Many hotels and larger motels and motor inns have a policy that all management takes their lunch meal in the employees' dining room. This is great interaction, providing executives don't simply congregate at one table in the corner. It also assures the quality of the food!
3. Peter Van Kleek, President and Chief Operating Officer of Saunder's Hotels, has a monthly lunch, in his office, with 8 or 10 employees. Peter is the only manager present. Participants are selected from the different departments, specifically invited by the manager, and the rules are that any and every topic is considered fair and open discussion. Employees like the idea and even the unions support it. Each participant re-

ceives a special coffee mug as a thank-you gift and an informal photo is taken and displayed throughout the hotel. I would add that this is only one approach to interaction by Mr. Van Kleek. I have walked the property with him from function room to boiler room. He knows everyone and they know him!

4. Scott Morrison, when general manager of the Boca Raton Resort in Florida, held a monthly coffee hour at shift change time, with all department heads and employees invited.

5. Wally Hickel, Jr., general manager of the Hotel Captain Cook in Anchorage, Alaska, considered the finest hotel in the state, took his entire Quality Assurance Committee on a "fly in" fishing trip and cook-out on a remote lake just to solidify the committee and express his support. He also publishes a house organ called the "Wally Street Journal," and he tours his property daily, speaking to every employee on a first-name, informal basis. It's one big, happy family at the Hotel Captain Cook, and the bottom line reflects it! Even when the economy of Alaska has been depressed, the hotel marches on, the best in the state and every employee proud of it. Incidentally, the hotel was built by Walter Hickel Senior, former governor of Alaska, and former secretary of the interior. Walter Sr. also tours the hotel on occasion, starting in the engine room. "If that's clean," he says, "I know the rest of the hotel is clean." He's right.

There are many ways to achieve meaningful interaction with all employees. Don't just rely on the annual company outing or the monthly photograph with the "employee of the month." Get out, on a regular basis, and meet the folks, at every level, in every department, who carry your image with them in all they do.

Excessive Employee Interaction

A paradox can be found in element #3—"excessive employee interaction." Note that the turnover rate is higher where excessive interaction takes place. I interpret this as meaning that when sincere and caring interaction does not take place, then confrontive and nonproductive interaction must take place, and this takes more time.

Standards

The importance of standards has been discussed and need not be repeated except to say that the survey proves that standards and turnover are related. This becomes even more prominent when we discuss "demanding high performance."

Interaction, Turnover/Absenteeism Reports, and Standards

The message here is, in fact, the message of excellence—it is not doing one big thing well, but rather, it is doing the combination of many small things well. There's nothing "small" about the three elements that are combined, but the concept is proven. Studies have shown what is important to the achievement of quality/excellence. With each and every element brought on line and perfected, quality/excellence increases. Resist the temptation to try to do everything well at the same time. Quality assurance is a process. Take each element and perfect it, setting in place systems to perpetuate its effectiveness. It may take a year, or two, or more to have the parts and pieces of quality/excellence in place, but with each step, the operation improves. Be patient.

Performance Evaluation System

Every study seems to certify the value of a meaningful performance evaluation system for every employee, however it is rarely done and when done, rarely done well. Everyone needs to know how they are doing. They need to be appreciated or shown objectively how to gain appreciation. Generally, employees only see the boss when things go wrong. The Quality Assurance Committee must take the lead in seeing that an evaluation system is in place and functioning properly. Not only will it prove beneficial in setting reasonable goals for all employees, it is a fine element in the process of interaction as well. You don't need fancy forms and exotic systems to have an effective performance evaluation system (PES). But you do need time, objectivity, open-mindedness, and optimism.

Effective employee evaluations should take place no less than every six months on a precise and regular schedule. Every quarter is better but too time-consuming for most properties. Better the process is done right than frequently—better quality than quantity. The performance reviews should be between immediate supervisor and the employee supervised—at every level from general manager down. A basic form can be developed with standard items such as grooming, tardiness, cooperation, attitude, communication, etc., but the most important benefit of the program is the objective discussion that takes place as supervisor and supervised talk over what the strengths and weaknesses of the relationship are, and what can be improved upon. The PES interaction should take between 15 and 30 minutes and should be conducted in an environment of total trust and honesty. Keep in mind that if the standards for the particular job title in question are completed, that, and that alone, becomes the basis for evaluation. The standards are either being met or they are not. If they are, praise and commendation are the order of the day. If not, praise the good achievements and be specific in discussing and making note of deficiencies and the agreed-upon path to resolution. And be optimistic that good results will occur. Remember, if you want people to be something, treat them as if they are, and they will rise to the occasion!

One standard for every employee from supervisor upward is to conduct the PES in a totally professional manner, on time, and exactly as prescribed. Most evaluators tend to view the process as not meaningful, rush through it just to get it over with, and, consequently, do more damage than good. It is the Quality Assurance Committee's responsibility to see that a system is in place and operating effectively.

Quality Assurance Program

It should come as no surprise that quality assurance and turnover are directly and strongly related. Let's look at some economics to seal the relationship. Let's say that a 300-room property has 300 employees and no quality assurance program. The average turnover in our survey, which included properties with quality assurance programs, was 37.31%; since we have no program, let us assume a turnover of 40%. If quality assurance can reduce turnover by 46%, and if it costs an average $5,000 per turnover (which many argue is too low), then a quality assurance program in our 300-room property would save:

300 employees × 40% turnover × 46% reduction with quality assurance × $5,000 per turnover = $276,000 per year saved.

Many managers will argue with this figure, but they cannot do so objectively unless they have analyzed the cost of turnover in great detail. When such an analysis is done, it may well be that the cost is low! However, if we are only half correct, the savings are still several times more than the total cost of an effective quality assurance program.

Demand for High Conformance

During the nationwide survey, hoteliers were asked to name the most significant event in their lives that allowed them to succeed as managers. You would expect to hear about college education, or a mentor somewhere, or a break getting that "right job" along the way, or just being in the right place at the right time. Instead, the majority of respondents mentioned a particular manager they had worked for during their early years in the hospitality industry. The manager was pictured as tough, demanding, unyielding, and consistent. The responses generally were like this: "I really disliked working for _____, but I learned a great deal and later on I realized he was right!" However, these same managers have a tendency today to view employees as incapable of performing consistently good work, so they, the managers, attune themselves to accept less than perfection. You would think employees would be happy under this situation. Quite the contrary. Turnover is less, by 48 percent, where the demands for perfection are highest. In fact, of all the elements affecting quality/excellence that were studied, the demand for high conformance to standards resulted in the greatest decrease in the turnover rate. The conclusion is inescapable: employees are happier and perform better when the rules of performance are fair and precisely spelled out, and when the employees are recognized for their compliance. You don't win employee loyalty by being lax. You simply teach employees that standards aren't important.

The Quality Assurance Committee will have to work constantly to get this message across to all supervisors and department heads.

An integral part of high conformance is reward and recognition. For many managers, reward and recognition is a picture of the "employee of the month" displayed in the back of the house. Often it is a picture of the general manager presenting the award to the employee. I would encourage eliminating the singling out of individual employees and instead basing rewards on a work-unit basis such that all members win if the team wins. Further, we should not pit one work unit against another, but rather, pit every work unit against itself. Suppose in the dishwashing room there is too much breakage, too much overtime, and too many plates which aren't clean and rejected by the dining room. After discussing the situation with the dish crew or representatives therefrom, and creating standards for performance, the manager should create three graphs and post them in or near the room. Plot the breakage week by week. Also plot the overtime. Instead of allowing waiters and waitresses to place unfit plates in their dirty dishes tub, have the dishes put in a special tub marked "rejects." Count the rejects daily and plot the results. When the results are looking good, a visit by the general manager, or at least the director of food and beverage to the area to give a personal thank-you will pay handsome dividends.

Avoid money as a motivation. It seldom works equitably across the board and, once initiated, it is difficult to remove.

I recall, during the survey portion of the Quality Index© at the Wilmington DuPont Hotel, listening to five members of the stewards' department complain and make sarcastic comments as they completed the questionnaire. When they were finished, I asked them to play a game with me. "If," I told them, "I had a magic wand and could grant one wish for the stewards who worked the dishwashing room, what would they wish for?" I expected to hear "more money," or "shorter hours," or "air-conditioning," or "better equipment." What I heard instead was, "We wish management knew we were there!" I passed this on to management who, interestingly, acknowledged that the people in the dishroom were forgotten, and a conscious effort was made to visit the area periodically and talk with the employees—an easy solution without cost!

Training

Proper training not only enhances skill, knowledge, and attitude, but it also makes employees feel that management cares. Training is crucial to quality/excellence, and the Quality Assurance Committee must insure that it is being performed when needed, properly, and effectively. The Quality Index© survey process is geared to providing relevant data, in a convenient and cost-effective manner, as to where training is required and what type.

Orientation Programs

According to our national survey, the average length of orientation program for the 65 properties responding that they had orientation programs, was 59.34 minutes. That probably equates to 9.34 minutes of lecture followed by a 50-minute tour of the property. This is totally unacceptable.

When a new employee arrives at the hotel for his/her first day of work, they are anxious, excited, and highly motivated to please. That is the exact time to gather them together, give them a motivational talk about the property, explain the quality assurance program, go over company regulations and benefits, establish the do's and don'ts, and solicit feedback. You may recall that the #1 error stated by managers is employees not knowing what the property offers by way of services. With a good orientation program, this will be a minor problem.

Following a general orientation program, employees are taken on a tour and then taken to their departments for a departmental orientation. A minimum of three to four hours of orientation is time well spent.

Here is a point to remember. When we did the Quality Index© at the Hotel Captain Cook, the results indicated, among other things, that employees did not like the orientation program. This struck us as strange, because it had been installed four months prior and was an excellent program. What was concluded, correctly so, was that the employees responding were older employees who were relating to the old, less effective program. To solve the problem, older employees were recycled through the new program. Don't overlook this point. Long-time, loyal employees don't appreciate being left in the dark on new programs. The Quality Assurance Committee must take the lead in implementing orientation programs both on an overall basis and in each department. And the progress must be monitored to ensure success.

Continuing Education Programs

Without continuing education, we all grow stale. Programs that encourage employees to study on their own time to improve themselves will, our data shows, positively affect quality in their job performances. Many hotels offer tuition assistance plans for qualified courses. One other idea that is beneficial is to call in experts from time to time to interact with the committee. It could be a quality assurance director from a local manufacturing plant, or a college professor, or even a member of the committee leading the discussion in a related field. The idea is to a) show the committee that management cares, b) increase the knowledge level of the committee, and c) stimulate new ideas. The cost to bring in so-called "experts" is not great. In most cases, the true cost is little more than a lunch or a dinner for two, small enough price to pay for a turned-on committee.

Civil Involvement of Managers

A manager that is involved in the community is certainly a visible promotion for the property, but it goes beyond that. An involved manager is one who has his/her antenna up in all the right places to gain feedback on customer needs and likes or dislikes. And it does not only have to be the manager. Department heads and supervisors can become active as well. There must be someplace, however, to collect and work with the data gathered, and that someplace is the Quality Assurance Committee. New ideas can result in new standards that result in new levels of excellence and thus new business. The Quality Assurance Committee should be aware of the various civic involvements of the staff and orchestrate a program in which feedback can be extracted regarding the property and its image.

Guest Comment Cards

For many properties the guest comment card is the sole means of gaining input from the customer. Properly designed, it can be an effective tool; however, few guest comment cards are properly designed. First, they often require too much writing and therefore are not filled out in great numbers. Second, they generally ask guests to rate various activities of the operation on a scale of 1 to 5, with 1 being poor and 5 being outstanding. This falls into the trap of dependable mediocrity, because we are generally happy if we are on the plus side of the mean and unhappy if we are on the negative side. But quality/excellence is not a case of being better than average, it is a case of being *right*. In other words, a score of 4 on a scale of 5 could be considered 80 percent and pretty good when, in fact, it means we have a 20 percent error rate, and that's pretty bad. There is only one way to structure a quality report card, whether it be performance evaluation, guest comment card, or a selective measure of a particular function, and that is to state the standard and solicit a yes/no response. Either we met the standard 100 percent or we failed to meet it. Would you drive your car if the brakes were guaranteed 90 percent reliable? Would you fly an airplane with an absolute guarantee to reach your destination 95 percent of the time? Of course not. So why talk of quality in any other terms than 100 percent?

Further, it's nice to get guest comments that tell us how wonderful we are, but if our quality assurance program is working correctly, every card will be positive. So, don't dwell on the cards that say "yes," dwell on the ones that say "no." Remember the statistic that only four percent of the people who are moderately dissatisfied will bother to tell you. You will, of course, hear from a much higher percentage of the highly dissatisfied. Thus, negative responses must be taken very seriously. The committee should develop a program, manual or computer, to record all comment cards, and by categories, calculate the negative responses as a percent of total. Perfection is zero, of course. Guest comment cards should go directly to the quality assurance director, who analyzes and distributes the results. A few minutes of every quality assurance meeting should be devoted to reviewing the guests' comments.

The guest comment system should be viewed as a friend. The property must try to maximize the number of cards received. This can be enhanced in a number of ways. First, design an attractive comment card. Avoid the cliché, "All comments go directly to the general manager." Whether true or not, it's sadly overworked. Better that the manager says, "These comments will go directly to the Quality Assurance Committee where they will be reviewed and corrective action taken immediately." This is more believable and indicates a team in action. Having promised action, however, see that it is done. The fact that a guest complains does not indicate a negative guest, especially if handled correctly. A fast letter to the guest acknowledging the error and the guest's willingness to share comments, along with the action taken, and you have probably converted a guest with a problem into a guest who tells others how much you care.

Managers speak with pride about their system of form letter responses to problems. Few people are fooled by form letters. If the number of negative complaints is large enough to warrant form-letter responses, you have serious problems. On some of the more negative comments, a personal phone call is a very persuasive response.

More to the point of generating more responses, have the bellhop make particular note of the card before rooming the guest and, upon picking up the guest's bags, again remind the guest of the card.

Have your front desk clerk give each guest a 15-second spiel on the guest comment system.

> We're very proud of our quality assurance program, Mr. _____ and we would like to ask you to take a minute towards the end of your stay to fill out this comment form for our Quality Assurance Committee.

As a final step, the cashier could ask the guest to fill out the form as he/she is processing the bill. If the form is easy and simple, the guest won't mind. It even makes sense to have a speedy quality assurance comment form for the check-out and a more extensive form in the room; the idea is to solicit the guest's comments and then listen!

One major southern resort spends several thousand dollars each year mailing a rather elaborate form to selected guests. The results are tabulated and an exhaustive report is generated for management. It's great guest relations but it doesn't do much for quality assurance. The data is out-of-date by the time it is received, and memory for detail on the part of the guest has faded.

One final point on guest comment systems. We have minimized the positive comments as not being as helpful to quality assurance as are the negative comments. Occasionally, however, a positive comment will mention a particular employee who has performed well. By all means, tell the employee and show them the comment. And, take the time to write the guest, thanking them for their comments, and telling them that you have passed their thoughts on to the relevant employee. There is no better way to make friends than to acknowledge the input of others as important and meaningful.

Excessive Emphasis on Guest Comments

It was surprising at first to see the results of the question, "What happens to turnover when excessive emphasis is placed on the guest comment system to achieve quality/excellence?" Upon reflection, however, it should not be surprising. A meaningful quality assurance program does not wait for guests to respond. A meaningful quality assurance program consciously goes out to seek feedback. A meaningful quality assurance program is not afraid to ask the basic question, "How are we doing?" Therefore, properties that rely extensively on the guest comment system are missing a valuable input, and quality assurance suffers as a result. Some other ways to gather information follow:

1. Invite guests to attend a quality assurance meeting. This is rather difficult to do in the normal situation because guests are busy during the day. If, however, you have regular guests, you might inquire as to whether or not they would like to join the quality assurance team in a discussion of quality. And, if you are a resort property, or have functions where spouses attend, there are opportunities to include some of the curious in the quality assurance discussions. Discussing directly with guests is the very best way to learn about your quality assurance success.

2. Invite outsiders who are frequent travelers to attend. The general manager or department heads will generally have a

pretty good idea of people who travel extensively, even though not with you. Such people can certainly give you the customers' side of needs.

3. Have a program as do some hotels, of subsidizing an overnight or weekend stay by an employee and spouse in competitive properties. There is no question of ethics involved any more than if a manufacturer buys a competitor's product to compare it with their own. It does provide insight into customer needs and possible new and/or better ways to meet those needs consistently. The Quality Assurance Committee should be a part of any such program as well as encouraging input from employees who, in their travels, have discovered new and/or better ways of service. The key issue is the involving of all employees in the quality effort by soliciting their input.

There is a caution to all of this. Some managers argue, with good reason, that they do not want to find out how they are doing from the guest because the guest has a right to quality treatment without having to serve as the property's quality inspector. Thus, having no guest comment system is one extreme. On the other extreme we have extensive polling, which eventually disturbs the guest. Common sense must dictate a common ground. We all agree that the guest is the final judge of our success, but waiting until memory of our facility has eroded away is foolish. Therefore, we need to know constantly how we are doing both from internal measurement of our standards from our own resources and external measurement as provided by the guest.

SUMMARY

I have tried to illustrate in this chapter that the Quality Assurance Committee needs to be aware of, and involved in, far more quality assurance areas than just the creation, monitoring, and re-creation of standards. The elements affecting quality/excellence are field proven. Ignoring them, or minimizing their importance, will result in a mediocre performance, the only consolation being that you can, for a while at least, be the best among the mediocre: that is, until the competition initiates a meaningful quality assurance program, and then you will fast become the average among the very good, and that is definitely the wrong road to success!

15

"Let Me Show You"

Training the Trainers

Myth #15: FULL-TIME TRAINING ONLY WORKS FOR BIG HOTELS, WITH TRAINING DEPARTMENTS AND BIG BUDGETS.

Training employees has become a paradox in the hospitality industries. On the one hand, training is the most essential ingredient in a quality assurance program. On the other hand, the traditional approach taken towards the training process by the hospitality industry has proven to be very detrimental to the process of quality assurance.

There are many definitions for the word "training." However, in the final analysis, we would propose the following:

Training is the process by which a desired, predictable response or action is created in an individual over time.

Whether training an athlete, a medical technician, a front office clerk, or a busperson, the objective is to create, in the individual, both the motivation and the skills such that we have total confidence that the individual will respond and act in precisely the manner we require. Training is, therefore, a behavior modification.

What has been missing in the discussion thus far, and is the element causing the problem relative to the industry's approach to

206

training, is time. Through the efforts of our training, we want behavior to be modified for a certain length of time. For example, the training of a quarterback for a specific game must take place in the period of approximately one week, and we expect the quarterback to give us a predictable response in terms of action for a period of between two and three hours, after which a new training process takes place, oriented toward the next week's game. In terms of an Olympic athlete, the training would take place over a period of several years, during which we expect the athlete to perform in predictable fashion in all of the competition leading up to and including the Olympic event. In terms of a front desk operation, we want the training to last for as long as the individual is employed at the front desk. In terms of training for attitude and motivation, we expect the training to last for as long as the individual is employed by the organization. On the other hand, the process of education, which is a training process, would seek as its result a predictable response that would last virtually a lifetime.

The problem with the hospitality industry and other industries as well is simply that training is viewed as a single event and not as a process. One of the greatest complaints in the industry is that substantial sums of money have been invested in "training" without lasting results. This occurs because of an event known as the "extended ego."

THE EXTENDED EGO

People live and work in an environment of power, and they respond to it. In short, people tend to become what they are expected to become in the particular environment in which they find themselves. When employees are called together for a training session, particularly when their superiors have initiated the process, they tend to become very receptive and cooperative. They adapt to the training environment. When the training is completed, however, they once again return to their normal environments and the adaptation process takes place all over. We hope, of course, that the training process has modified their behavior such that they can operate in their normal environments in a more efficient and more consistent manner. However, this is often not the case.

There are individuals and companies who are extremely well

qualified to conduct training sessions. Such individuals and companies are in great demand and command large fees. And, the performances of these individuals and organizations are most impressive. The enthusiasm of the participants runs high, and the feedback, relative to the value of the training, is normally outstanding. To be sure, some behavior modification will take place. However, unless there is a conscious and dedicated effort to seek as an objective a behavior modification keyed to the time requirements we desire, there is, in fact, absolutely no guarantee that the finest of training sessions will result in a successfully trained employee. To repeat, the problem is a function of the extended ego. The employee has become a very enthusiastic trainee, and both the trainer and employer have become misled by the trainee's attitude and participation during the actual training. Therefore, the behavior modification is only temporary unless we consciously work to make it otherwise.

QUALITY ASSURANCE AND TRAINING

In previous discussions, we have outlined the duties of quality assurance directors and quality assurance committees in an environment of total commitment by management and the publication of meaningful and measurable standards. In effect, what we have done is to set in place the mechanisms for a) continually monitoring the effects of the training process against b) a constant known and measurable standard, which takes place over time. Management's commitment, together with the constant leadership and energy of a capable quality assurance director as strengthened by the participation of a well-organized and dedicated Quality Assurance Committee, all of whom are working with a properly defined system of standards, is the overall ingredient that will guarantee the effectiveness of the training process. In short, a quality assurance program is management's guarantee that training dollars are invested properly and have the greatest return on that investment.

The trend, in fact, among hospitality organizations that have implemented quality assurance is to steer away from the use of the term "training" in deference to "quality assurance." Just as the sales function is a part of overall marketing, the training function is part of overall quality assurance.

WHO DOES THE TRAINING?

A major misconception within the hospitality industry as well as in other industries is that training is performed by either a training director or an outside consulting entity. Some organizations view the department head as a trainer, and the training seldom goes beyond that level. This is a misconception that must be remedied immediately. The fact of the matter is that every single employee in the organization—with the exception of new entrance-level employees, and even then only for a short period of time—is, in fact, a trainer. The most outstanding orientation program, coupled with the best departmental training program, will still be mitigated by the new employee's view of fellow employees performing their tasks during the actual work process. For example, let us assume that every busperson has been thoroughly trained in the process of clearing a guest table without excessive noise as the dishes are placed on the tray to be taken to the kitchen. If a newly hired and trained employee begins work in the dining room only to see buspersons clearing the tables in a noisy and undesired fashion—and if the busperson learns that the waiters and waitresses place a premium on speed and, therefore, that noise is overlooked—how long do you think it will be before the new employee learns to perform to the norm rather than as he or she was trained to perform? And, what about the bellhop who has been properly instructed to explain the various components of the guest room to each check-in so that the guest will know how to operate the heat and air conditioning, how to send out laundry or order room service, etc? Once on the job, the bellhop learns that there are peaks and valleys relating to check-ins and that it will cost tip money to take too much time rooming a guest during a busy period. If the bellhop discovers that no one else is following the proper procedure, then it will not be long before he stops following it as well.

Obviously, supervision is involved in both instances. However, supervisors themselves are trainers by example. A supervisor who constantly arrives late for work and takes longer than allowed for coffee breaks is, in fact, training his or her employees to do likewise. A manager who does not dress neatly or present himself or herself professionally is training the assistant managers and department heads to perform in the same fashion. Everyone is a trainer by example, and that concept must be driven home to every employee in the organization.

THE FORMAL TRAINING PROCESS

Books have been written about the methodology for proper training. It is not the purpose of this chapter to present a comprehensive course in training, but rather to refresh the reader's memory of some of the crucial elements in the process. The foundation for all effective training is in the development of a proper and thorough training plan. There are many approaches to the creation of training plans. This chapter will deal with a formal training plan that has proved to be effective in our experience.

Train According to a Plan

Before the first trainee arrives at the training site, the trainer must have a fully developed plan, showing exactly what the objectives of the training session are and the processes to be used to achieve them. If the trainer and trainee had equal knowledge about the subject, there would be no trainer and trainee! This simply means that the trainer is more knowledgeable than the trainee at the point in time of the training process. This creates a tendency on the part of most trainers to be somewhat casual in their approach. Nothing could be more detrimental to successful training.

Prior to beginning the training, the trainer should think through the following elements:

1. What goal or goals do I want to achieve with this training?
2. Who is my audience?
3. What will motivate this audience most effectively?
4. Against what standard will I measure the results?
5. What are my space and equipment needs?

Each of these points can obviously be broken down into many more minor points. However, they will serve as an overview.

Most trainers like to make a few notes on a note pad and then stand up and talk for an excessive length of time. However, the results will not be satisfactory. As basic as it sounds, or seems to the trainer, each and every step of the training process should be thoroughly planned out and committed to a training plan. For each segment of the training process, the trainer should ask the question, "When I am done with this section, the trainees will . . ." Each segment should also have the means by which the success or failure of that segment can be measured. The overall schedule should be flexible enough to allow time to go back over some items when it is obvious that they have not been completely communicated initially. In short, training is far too important to be left to chance. The creation of a formal training plan achieves the following objectives:

1. It clarifies the training process in the mind of the trainer.
2. It organizes the effort, thus increasing effectiveness.
3. It guarantees that all subsequent training in that area will be to the same standards.
4. It assures that important elements of the training will not be overlooked.
5. It places emphasis on the training and less on the trainer.

Many managers do not want to take the time to create a formal plan; however, time is actually saved by the plan. With a formal plan, effectiveness can be evaluated and changes and/or fine tuning can be directed specifically to the area in need. The use of word processing also makes the storage and updating of plans relatively easy.

A formal training plan consists of two parts:

1. Master plan
2. Segment detail

Master Plan.   The *master plan* answers the following questions:

1. What is the designation (title) of this training?
   For example, if we wanted our maids to be more familiar with the facilities and services we offer, we might title the training "Maids—Knowledge of the Facility." Or if we wanted to train our fire brigade to be more responsive we might designate the training "Fire Brigade—Response Skill." A third

example might be to improve the attitude of our buspersons, in which case we would designate the training, "Buspersons—Attitude Training."

Note that we have established three words—knowledge, skill, and attitude. Training falls into these three areas, and each area requires a different approach. Our designation should be specific as to the area of training we are affecting.

2. What is the purpose of the training?
   A. There should be a clear, thorough statement of purpose as to the objective of the training. The statement should end with an answer to the question, "When the training is completed, those trained will . . ."
   B. For example, in the case of our maids the statement might be the following:
   > It has been brought to the attention of management that our chambermaids are generally unable to answer basic questions regarding the facilities and services we offer. It has been determined that the problem is one of knowledge and not of attitude. The orientation program for new employees is being refined to include more knowledge regarding property. The housekeeper and inspector have been asked to establish interdepartmental training of facility and service; however, the general maid staff should be brought up to an acceptable level of knowledge as soon as possible in order to provide better service and increase profits. When the training is completed, all maids will be knowledgeable regarding the physical facilities we offer and will have specific knowledge regarding times of operation, cost, availability and special instructions, or will know how to direct the guest to someone qualified to answer his/her inquiry.
   C. Note that the statement answers the basic "why" question that enlightened management should always ask.
3. Who will be trained?
   Be specific. Are we training all maids? Day maids? Call maids? New-hire maids? Are we training the specific fire brigade members or others who relate and interact with the process as well? Is our busperson attitude training for every busperson or just those in the main dining room or the specialty restaurant? etc.

4. Who will do the training?

The first decision is, "Who is best qualified to train?" This must be considered carefully. It's nice to be able to do training "in-house" but, if it is not as effective as if done by an outside consultant, you have wasted your training. Consultants often do not have good images, often for valid reasons; however, many are superb in what they do and represent the maximum training cost effectiveness. *Keep an open mind.* Remember the definition we proposed. You want "a desired, predictable response or action over time." The issue of "who trains" is simply a question of who can provide the best results. Saving a few dollars by doing the training in-house is often counterproductive. Having said this, I would argue, on the other hand, that in-house training can be very productive and cost effective *if organized properly.* Generally speaking, what in-house trainers lack in terms of training skills are more than adequately made up for by the fact that they are known, they know the facility intimately, and they have real incentive to succeed, because it will affect their own future.

5. "When" and "where" is the training held?

"When" is primarily a function of availability of trainer and trainees. In a hotel, where there is constant 24-hour activity, it is often difficult to get all trainees together at one time. Further, there is always the question as to whose time is used for training, i.e., whether the employees are paid during the training, or not. Managers are sometimes shortsighted on this question. The number one error as communicated by managers across the U.S. is employees who do not know the services offered by the hotel or motel. Managers believe that that error alone can result in an increase of more than 2 percent of sales. We believe that the figure is much higher. Regardless, a 100-room property, doing 2 to 2½ million dollars per year in total sales, should be willing to spend some amount in order to increase sales $40,000 to $50,000 per year, conservatively. By thinking through the "when" question in detail, ahead of time, there will be few, if any, surprises.

"Where" is a critical question as well. It is always best to train in the environment of the process for which you are training, but this is not always possible or not always acceptable. Assume you are training for knowledge, and you are familiarizing your maids with other services of the property. If you want the maids to be familiar with and understand the room service function, they should really see it in action, but that may not make sense for two reasons. First, such areas don't lend themselves to many extra persons during the busy times and, secondly, a training environment should be comfortable, quiet, and conducive to good communication. Thus, you would organize your training to perhaps tour the room service area during an off-peak period and then do the training in a designated area more conducive to the exchange of information. The point is simply that the difference between effective training and ineffective training is planning.

Good training in today's environment requires the use of audiovisual equipment. The number of good tapes and videos concerning training is growing exponentially. It is the enlightened manager who takes a space somewhere on the property and dedicates it to training. Equipment can be purchased, training material gathered, and, over time, the result is not only an effective training process but an appreciation on the part of the employees for a management that cares not only in words but in actions.

6. At what time will the training begin and end, and what is the elapsed time?

It is now time to establish the duration of the training in some precise terms. In order to be accurate in planning total time required, the segments of the master plan covered in #9 of this section should also be considered (see Figure 15.1). Taken together, the topics to be covered and the time available to cover them will result in the blocking out of time for the training process. In some cases, perhaps exact start-stop times are not known, but overall time required is. That presents no problem. Given only the required elapsed time, we can develop the segments. Remember the axiom, "The brain can absorb about only as much as the seat can endure." Good training is a mix of lecture, demonstration, participation, and discussion. Resist the temptation to train by lecture alone.

The assumption is that the trainees are listening and better yet, retaining, but it is a wrong assumption. The best training takes place when trainees see, hear, do, and discuss. So, allow time for trainees to become involved.

7. What are the special requirements of this training process?

Training is governed by all the rules of quality assurance, i.e., every training standard must be met every time. This applies to all special requirements such as equipment needed (flip charts, tripods, projector, chalkboards, etc.). List all needs and then list what can go wrong. Is there a spare bulb available for the slide projector? (They never fail until one minute before you need them!) Can room lights be dimmed? Is there a refreshment break? What about achievement certificates? Any special people attending for any particular part of the process? Make a list of *all* special requirements and also note where they will come from and who is responsible for providing them.

8. What is the cost of training?

Formal training generally costs. We should have a notion of how much, especially if there are unusual components such as special equipment to be rented or special aids to be produced. By understanding the cost of training, greater emphasis is placed on making it effective. Calculating the cost also aids in the decision to do it "in-house" or with consultants. There are, of course, two kinds of costs—direct out-of-pocket and intangible costs. Renting a VCR system would be an example of the former. Charging for the space used on some pro-rata basis would be an example of the intangible costs. It is not intended that cost analysis be overly formal or official. Rather, it is intended that a good, defensible analysis of costs be done.

9. How much time will the training take, listed by item?

In #6 we developed the elapsed time and did so with some consideration to the various topics we must cover. It is now time to list the topics in finite form and to estimate the time required for each in a *segment outline*. Be absolutely thorough in your list. Every minute of the overall master plan should be covered by a segment. Schedule administrative time, refreshment break, lunch, group team sessions, etc. Detail is not required on each segment at this point; that comes next. For now, simply list the segments and allot time to each.

10. How can a top manager gain approval of the training program?

It is very important that the formal master plan be done prior to scheduling the training and that it be discussed with the relevant decision maker. Among many managers there is an inherent resistance to training, primarily the result of it not having been done well and effectively in the manager's experience. By presenting a well-thought-out, organized outline of the particular training proposed, management approval and enthusiasm can be gained. A further benefit of proper planning and approval is that, given a good plan as a base, management can input its thinking and experience to make the plan even better. Proper training is everybody's concern, and the more involvement and concurrence you have, the better the process and more successful the results. Management should approve the master plan before the segment detail is created.

Creating the Segment Detail.   The *segment detail* is the precise plan that rules the training process. Most trainers do not do a good job on the segment detail. This is particularly true because most trainers believe that they know their subject so thoroughly that an outline is not necessary. They should take their cue from an airplane pilot. Whenever I go flying in my single-engine Cessna, even though I have close to 1,000 hours as pilot in command, I still do my preflight check according to a printed outline. Commercial pilots do likewise. Familiarity breeds sloppiness—and sloppiness, in the case of airplanes, results in accidents. So, no matter how many times a pilot has flown a particular aircraft, he or she will always flight check the plane against a finite outline so that nothing is forgotten. A trainer who forgets to cover a particular training point in proper detail will be in far less danger than will a pilot who forgets to check the oil level, but quality assurance seeks perfection, and perfection results from discipline, and discipline comes from structure. The segment detail will guarantee that what you want to cover in your training will, in fact, be covered.

The segment detail takes each and every part of the master plan–segment outline and plans it in precise detail. The actual training is

Stephen Hall Associates
SPECIALISTS IN QUALITY ASSURANCE

**TRAINING ORGANIZER
MASTER PLAN**

COMPLETED BY: _____

DATE: _____

1. TITLE:

2. PURPOSE:

3. TRAINEES:

4. TRAINER:

5. LOGISTICS:

6. SPECIAL REQUIREMENTS:

© 1989 Stephen S.J. Hall

FIGURE 15.1   Sample Master Plan form, front.

217

7. COST:

8. SEGMENT OUTLINE.

		TIME REQUIRED	ELAPSED TIME
1.			
2.			
3.			
4.			
5.			
6.			
7.			
8.			
9.			
10.			
11.			
12.			
13.			
14.			
15.			
16.			
17.			
18.			
19.			
20.			

9. APPROVAL:

FIGURE 15.1   Sample Master Plan form, back.

taken from the segment detail worksheet. The heading of each segment detail worksheet contains the following information.

1. Master Designation _____
2. Segment Number _____
3. Segment Designation _____
4. Segment Start Time _____ End Time _____
   Elapsed Time _____
5. Segment Leader _____
6. Segment Objective _____
7. Objective Measurement _____
8. Special Requirements _____

1. *Master Designation:* This is simply the overall title for the master training program in question.
2. *Segment Number:* Each segment is given a progressive number beginning with 1. Every minute of the master plan must be covered with a segment number—even those where nothing occurs such as "Breaks for messages and/or calls." Certainly there is not much by way of organization required for such a segment, but it must be planned into the program if necessary, and, if part of the program, it must receive a number designation.
3. *Segment Designation:* Give each segment a title. For example, a two-hour training program on engineers answering a guest room maintenance call might have the following segments:
   - Welcome and outline of training to come.
   - Ice breaker.
   - How requests for maintenance are received.
   - Planning the service call.
   - Arriving at the guest room.
   - Coffee break.
   - Unusual situations and how to handle them.
   - Leaving the guest room.
   - Reporting on the project.
   - Question-and-answer period.
   - Summary.

Note that even the coffee break is titled and scheduled.

4. *Segment Start, End, and Elapsed Time:* Each segment is given a specified amount of time. The total time for all segments, of course, equals the elapsed time set forth in the master plan.

5. *Segment Leader:* The person doing the training for this particular segment should be written here.

6. *Segment Objective:* The segment objective answers this question: "When this segment is completed, participants will . . ." Simply put, what is to be achieved by this segment? Possible answers might be: "Understand how to prepare for a guest room maintenance call," "Be able to handle difficult situations that commonly arise while answering guest room maintenance calls," "Have individual guest questions answered to the guest's satisfaction." The segment objective portion of the outline seems at times a bit silly. But, if there is no objective to the training, how can results be evaluated? No matter how silly the process looks or feels, force yourself to play the process through regardless. It will be a habit worth its weight in gold as you grow and progress as a trainer.

7. *Objective Measurement:* How will you know when you have achieved your objective? There are three main ways to test:
   - A short, written quiz.
   - An informal, verbal quiz.
   - Calling on trainees to demonstrate.

   Never eliminate or minimize the measurement portion of training. It is the feedback you require. To train without testing to see if you are effective is as silly as driving your car without looking at the dashboard. While you may luck out and do a good job of driving, the chances are that you will go too fast, run out of gas, overheat, forget to turn on or off your turn signals, and more. The essence of quality assurance is to know what is happening around you. Test each segment of your training. How do you know when the coffee break has been meaningful? When everyone is back in their seats, ready to go, on schedule! How often have we attended seminars that fell behind schedule because no one worked to maintain it? Every segment has an objective, and every objective is tested!

8. *Special Requirements:* Anything special about this segment? Write it down. If you require a break-out area with pencils and pads

at each place, list it, or you may well forget. If you need special equipment to demonstrate, list it.

Now that the segment outline heading is complete, the segment detail is developed (see Figure 15.2). There are three columns in the segment outline process. *Time, outline,* and *notes.*

TIME

For each part of the segment that lends itself to a specific time, note the time in column 1. For example, let us suppose that under "Welcome and outline of the training program" there are four basic parts. First, you, as trainer, welcome the trainees (assume 2 minutes). Second, the general manager issues a greeting (assume 5 minutes). Third, you outline the training agenda (assume 6 minutes), and fourth, you have each trainee fill out a brief background form ending with the trainee's one-sentence statement of what he or she expects to accomplish during the entire training program (assume 5 minutes). The total time for segment 1, "Welcoming trainees and outlining the program," is 18 minutes. If this segment takes 30 minutes, we are in trouble. Chances are it won't take much less than 18 minutes, but if it does, and we achieve all of our objectives, we are in great shape. Incidentally, the statement as to what the trainee hopes to accomplish during the training is a form of measurement of the objective of segment 1.

We are now ready to schedule segment 1. If the training begins at 2:00 P.M., then that is the first time in column 1. In column 2—Outline we write "Introduction—John Doe." Under the heading in column 2, we put all of the outline notes we need to do our 2-minute welcome—For example, notes on the background of the general manager.

After the notes for the first part of segment are complete in column 2, we move back to column 1 ("Time") and we enter the starting time for part 2. In column 2, we write "Comments by general manager." Obviously we can't outline the manager's comments in column 2, *but* if there are special points the manager should make, after consultation with the general manager note them in column 2.

Now move on to part 3. We enter 2:07 P.M. in column 1, and in column 2 we write "Outline of training program." We follow that heading with notes on all we intend to say regarding the program.

Stephen Hall Associates
SPECIALISTS IN QUALITY ASSURANCE

TRAINING ORGANIZER
SEGMENT DETAIL

COMPLETED BY: _____

DATE: _____

1. MASTER TITLE: _____ 2. SEGMENT #: _____

3. SEGMENT DESIGNATION: _____

4. SEGMENT START TIME _____ END TIME _____ ELAPSED TIME _____

5. SEGMENT LEADER _____

6. SEGMENT OBJECTIVE: When this segment is over, participants will

_____

7. MEASUREMENT:

_____

8. SPECIAL REQUIREMENTS:

TIME	OUTLINE	NOTES

© 1989 Stephen S.J. Hall

FIGURE 15.2   Sample Segment Detail form, front.

222

TIME	OUTLINE	NOTES

FIGURE 15.2   Sample Segment Detail form, back.

223

Lastly, we enter part 4 by writing 2:13 P.M. in column 1 and "Data and feedback" in column 2. Then enter the outline for "Data and feedback" in column 2. Finally, we write 2:10 P.M. in Column 1, and in Column 2 write "End." We have finished our plan for segment 1.

TOPIC

We have discussed column 2. It contains in outline form all you want to cover. Such detail does three things:

1. Nothing is left to chance. Points to be made are written down.
2. Training follows a logical course.
3. All training is consistent over time, i.e., the next time this training is performed, it is done the same way regardless of who does it.

NOTES

This column is where any and all special notes are written. For example, you may make this note as a reminder: "Recognize other special guests present." This reminds you to mention the department head, or resident manager. You will *probably* remember to do so without a note, *but* with a note you *undoubtedly* won't forget. During the data and feedback stage, you may wish to remind yourself to ask if there are questions. Remind yourself with a note, "Questions?" in column 3.

When segment 1 is outlined, go to segments 2, 3, 4, etc. until they are all done. Your training outline is now complete for the planned training program. If you are really up to speed, it can all be entered in the word processor. Now it can be refined and fine-tuned and can proceed towards perfection. And, incidentally, the better the segment details are done the first time, the easier will be the training the second time around. So, take your time, do it right, and become an expert trainer!

TYPES OF TRAINING

We have mentioned the three types of training: *skill, knowledge,* and *attitude.* When done formally, all three require the same diligence required for master planning and segment detail; however, the three vary in their basic approach.

Skill Training

The steps to effective Skill Training generally follow the model below:

1. *Introduce the program and break the ice.* Tell the group what is to happen and help them to relax and interact.
2. *Prepare the trainees.* Facilitate the training by helping the trainees to internalize a valid reason or reasons why this training is necessary. Refer to the discussion of diffusion at the end of Chapter 9. Give trainees answers to one or more of the five following elements:
   - Relative advantage
   - Compatibility
   - Complexity
   - Trialability
   - Observability
3. *Tell, show, observe, correct.* Tell the trainees how to perform the skill you are teaching. Show them how to do it. Let each try the skill themselves. Correct their errors. Remember, we learn by our mistakes. "To err is human, to ridicule error is to fail as a trainer!" Try the two for one rule. Before you say something negative, say two things positive. It works!
4. *Reward.* Be quick to hand out rewards or compliments to all who participate.
5. *Summarize.*

Knowledge

With knowledge training we follow the same outline except that often there is nothing physical to demonstrate. Knowledge training lends itself more to the written or spoken word. So, we show *visually* and tell *verbally* whenever possible. Then we elicit feedback through questions and discussion. The essential difference between skill and knowledge training occurs in the feedback and measurement process. With skill training, the feedback comes from observing the trainee perform; with knowledge, a quiz is a more effective means of measurement.

Attitude

By far, the hardest training process is that of changing attitude. It is so because few people believe their attitudes need changing! So, the task becomes that of helping employees to see themselves, and this can happen best by open discussion with peers or role playing. We can't begin by telling our trainees that we are going to change their attitudes because they will immediately "tune out," lose interest, resist the change. So, we talk in general terms about general problems and help the trainees to see themselves. Measurement is difficult. Perhaps it is best achieved at the end of the training by simply exploring "What we have learned today!" Obviously, the best feedback occurs on the job when the employee is observed with a "new attitude." More to the point, however, is that attitude training is ongoing. Training not only makes bad attitudes good; more importantly, it keeps good attitudes good!

THE IMPULSIVE, COMPULSIVE TRAINER

Thus far we have been discussing formal training. It is important, but the very best training is not formal. It is informal, impulsive, compulsive training. It is the kind of training that takes place over a 2–3-minute time frame as supervisor, department head, or anyone in a position of responsibility sees something that can and should be done better. The principles, listed below, are the same:

1. Prepare the trainee.
2. Tell, show, observe, correct, test (observe *skill*). Tell and show, test (*knowledge* verbally). Mirror, discuss, suggest, test (observe *attitude*).
3. Reward and recognize.
4. Summarize.

Remember, we are talking about 2–3-minute training, or less. Obviously, there is no master plan or segment detail. Suppose we see a kitchen helper wiping up a spill with a dining room napkin. We can do the following:

1. Tell his/her boss.
2. Threaten the employee.
3. Ignore the situation.
4. Do some instant training!

The employee is using the napkin either because a) he doesn't know better (knowledge), or b) he knows better but doesn't care (attitude). So we ask: "Why are you using a napkin to clean up the spill?" The answer will tell you what you are dealing with.

"You know, I did the same thing once when I worked in the kitchen, that is, until someone told me how much napkins cost and how hard it is to clean them. Is there a problem keeping utility cloths handy?" (There might be, you know; then the problem is one of laundry distribution!)

"I need your help keeping the napkins clean and in the right linen bag after they have been used."

"I'll help you with the utility cloth supply if you help me to keep the napkins clean."

"A deal?" A deal! Done. Elapsed time, one minute.

This is a simple example, perhaps, but it's the way really effective training works! We have standards. They aren't being met. We have to train. And so we do, quickly, confidently, impulsively, compulsively. And, we get everyone in a position of authority to do likewise. The fact is, everyone is a trainer. We either train properly and correctly by our actions, or improperly and incorrectly. Doing nothing trains improperly. Demanding something from a base of fear does nothing but train improperly. But stepping in with two minutes of instant, well-intended training is the stuff that leaders are made of and the stuff of winners! Can you think of other areas where instant training is required? If not, just keep the concept in mind next time you walk around. You'll be surprised at the opportunities!

A FINAL CAUTION

Many managers will respond to this approach negatively. They believe that the most effective way to "train" is simply to demand. There is no question that the kitchen helper will stop using the napkin as a cleaning cloth if you simply say, "If I see you do that one more time, you're fired!" There's no question that forced adoption is the quickest way to alter an action behavior, *but* what does it do for attitude? And, attitude is the biggest complaint of the consumer *and* the hardest training to do effectively. There are times, of course, when you must be direct and firm, but those times will be less and less if you practice good training technique as a way of life.

CONCLUSION

This has been a very quick run-through of very basic training. The main message is that good training, effective training, is no accident. It occurs by hard work and attention to detail. It occurs by building an attitude for training. It occurs when all employees realize that "doing the job better is better for everyone!" This is the essence of excellence. I do my own job well, and the whole team does better.

It would be a great error for the reader to assume that he or she can now train effectively and thus stop learning. There are many good books, many good videos, many good trainers to learn from. Pursuing the knowledge that is available is what will make you a better trainer. This is but a beginning!

16

Passing Through the Minefield

Handling the Roadblocks

Myth #16: A QUALITY ASSURANCE PROGRAM IS JUST LIKE A NEW SHIP; IF THE DESIGN IS RIGHT, THE WORKMANSHIP PROPER, AND EVERYTHING READY AT LAUNCH TIME, THE ENTIRE PROGRAM WILL BE A SUCCESS.

IF IT WERE ONLY TRUE!

The keys to success of quality/excellence are commitment, planning, and energy. In short, the organization must want excellence and commit time, money, people, and power of office to the development of a program. The program must be carefully planned out and, once initiated, sufficient human energy in the form of enthusiasm, motivation, and effort must be brought to bear. These requirements, however, do not guarantee a successful quality/excellence program. At times, even when everything seems to be going well, the program shifts into idle and progress ends. The causes of failure are not complex. Let us look at some of the following gremlins that can creep into quality assurance, and discuss their cures:

1. **THE COMMITTEE DOES NOT GEL INTO A SOURCE OF ENERGY FOR THE PROGRAM.**

The first sign of an ineffective committee is poor attendance at quality assurance meetings. The excuses always seem to be valid and rational. Even when attendance is relatively good, the meeting hour is filled with considerable conversation, generally of the complaint nature, and very little productive work is accomplished. Look for the following reasons:

A. The commitment of the most senior executive is not, in fact, real, or is not perceived as real. In such an environment, committee members will not participate with sincerity! The most senior executive must now attend the quality assurance meeting to reinforce his/her dedication to the program and plan, in the short run, to sit in on sessions. The most senior executive must read each meeting's minutes and immediately restate his/her commitment to all who miss meetings. Committee members who lack the ability to make one prescheduled hour available each week for quality assurance should be replaced. Management must move decisively if their commitment to quality is not perceived as real. If, on the other hand, the commitment is in fact, not real, the program cannot proceed, for failure is the only result!

B. Meetings are disorganized and uninteresting. Agendas and minutes are important organizational tools. So too is perceived contribution on the part of members. The quality assurance director must not permit a group's natural inclination to talk about everything but the task at hand to disrupt the quality assurance progress. Set objectives for each session. It's not important that they be major objectives. What is important is slow, steady progress. It is possible that the wrong person has been selected as quality assurance director. This is a damaging error, but not nearly as damaging as permitting the situation to linger. Time spent at the onset by the most senior executive to assure that the quality assurance director is performing effectively will save hours and hours of frustration, even failure, later on.

C. The committee not operating on a consensus basis. Decisions of the committee cannot be unilateral; they must be by consensus. All members must participate. If this is not happening, correct it! Inactivity will cause members to lose interest fast. And that will destroy the committee.

D. Meetings don't start and end on time. Meetings must start on time and end one hour later. Hoteliers are notorious for meetings that start "when everyone is there" and end "when everyone is tired of talking." Interest will surely erode. Establish the standard as to when meetings start and end and practice what you preach! It works!

2. **THE COST OF ERROR PROCESS IS NOT ACCEPTED AS VALID.**

Generally the symptoms are substantial criticism concerning the validity of the process. "It isn't accurate," "It's not in tune with the 'real world'," "Error is inevitable," "We don't have that many errors," "Calculations don't prevent errors, managers do!"

A. The process is misunderstood. It is not meant to be a solution, but rather a process of awareness of the following facts:

1. Errors affect everyone.
2. Errors cost.
3. Errors can be eliminated.

Don't raise the cost of error process to halo status. Use it as a tool but don't make it the prime tool around which the program is structured. In one colossal failure, the quality assurance director worked diligently to calculate more than one million dollars of error cost, then proceeded to publicize the program as if those costs represented savings, even going so far as to demand higher status and salary because of his "success." Establishing the cost of an error does not solve the problem; it only identifies it as worthy of solution.

B. Department heads often view the identification of errors as an admission of their own failures. Having errors is not failure, failing to correct and prevent them is! Get the point across to department heads that their stock will improve as it is perceived that they are willing to identify and eliminate errors.

C. Top management minimizes the effect of cost of error on the basis that the costs are not "real" or "accurate." The key is to be conservative. To minimize the fact that some guests won't return is to be blind to reality. To question whether "lost time" is a cost is to misunderstand time management. Can cost of error costs be objectively defended? No. They are subjective, based on probability and some speculation. But, the concept of "offsetting errors" is very real. The fact that 50 costed errors are individually questionable does not take away from the fact that some will be too high and others too low; thus, the overall effect will be far more accurate than imagined. Nothing talks to management like the bottom line. Cost of error emphasizes the relationship between bottom line and error. This link is crucial!

3. **EMPLOYEES ARE NOT PARTICIPATING IN THE ERROR I.D. PROCESS.**

The process has been communicated, the cards distributed, and the deposit process established. However, few cards are received and those that do come in seem to contain more complaints than error identifications.

A. The process was established too soon. Employees did not have sufficient time to see the quality assurance process in action and become believers in the program. Remember, quality assurance is an ongoing process. Proceed slowly and steadily.

B. Department heads and/or supervisors are stonewalling the process because they perceive that errors reflect on them. Make certain that department heads and supervisors view the process as a benefit. Use management to solve the errors and compliment them on their successes. *Never* permit errors to filter up through the ranks where they can be quietly and effectively stifled. Errors are identified directly to the Quality Assurance Committee, which then works cooperatively and appreciatively with supervisors and department heads to effect solutions, giving credit to employees and supervisors for their help and success.

C. Employees see no reward for identifying errors. The process of acknowledging error inputs and communicating successful solutions is absolutely crucial. Imagine the situation in which every employee willingly identifies errors affecting quality that, in turn, are solved by a motivated management. Would you stay there instead of at a property where errors are swept under the rug as inevitable? Of course you would, and you would pay more for the privilege. Gaining employee participation is gaining employee equity in the organization's success. Work for it!

4. MANAGERS ARE HAVING TROUBLE WRITING STANDARDS.

The concept of quality standards requires a new way of thinking about employees. Standards are not job descriptions; rather, they are required levels of performance for tasks that we, as management, decide have specific requirements. Fewer standards are better than more standards. More standards means less concentration on monitoring and measuring. Cooks should know how to slice onions and dice parsley. Electricians should know how to wire switches, and plumbers understand how to sweat copper tubing. No need to write standards for such tasks. Further, we might hold training sessions to show waiters and waitresses how to stack and carry a serving tray, but this need not, necessarily, be a standard. If it is not important to us that plates be served from the left and removed from the right, don't make it a standard. If, on the other hand, it is important, make it a standard and insist upon 100 percent compliance.

Many standards do not fit job tasks conveniently. For example, every employee should understand the property's fire procedures 100 percent. If the procedures are somewhat standard for all employees regardless of job title, then, in all probability, a separate general fire procedure should be created. Under the "General" section of the individual employee's tasks, there would be a universal standard, "Read and be thoroughly familiar with the hotel's fire procedure found in Bulletin _____." In this fashion, we have made knowledge of a rather extensive set of instructions a standard. The same would hold true for such areas as the employees' handbook. As another example, assume that the kitchen has rather specific standards for each menu item regarding portion size, placement on plate, garnish, etc. Assume that there is even a book of photographs showing exactly how the plate should look. We would not incorporate all of this material in each relevant kitchen job title; we would simply note under "General," "Be totally familiar with Food Service Handbook #_____ and adhere to it 100 percent of the time."

5. **GOOD STANDARDS ARE DEVELOPED, BUT PERFOR-MANCE IS STILL ERRATIC.**

   In short, the standards are in place but the employees aren't consistent in their application.

   A. The concept that "standards are *required* levels of performance" has not been instilled in supervisors, department heads, and top management. This usually results from far too many standards that are not enforced. Cut down on the number of standards and insist that they are met every time. Require that supervisors consistently promote the standards and are as willing to compliment success as they are to criticize failure.

   B. Management perceives that standards only apply to supervisors and production employees. Consequently, they, management, do not follow their own standards. An open-door policy isn't really open door. Meetings scheduled for a specific topic and time, end up unfocused and run overtime. Promises made are not kept. Performance evaluation sessions are done unprofessionally. Scheduled training is poorly organized. The list goes on. Employees will not respond willingly to standards enforced solely by power. Management must set the example.

   C. Training is not properly understood and performed. Listing standards is hardly enough. Employees must understand them and know how they are to be applied.

   D. Measurement is ineffective. *Every* standard must be measurable, and all standards that are, in any way, erratically administered, must be measured, results communicated, and reinforced.

   E. Nonconformance is viewed selectively. Nonconformance is nonconformance and is to be viewed equally in every case, with the same response regardless of who the employee is. It is said that employees know how well they are doing by how their mistakes are evaluated. If the evaluation is forgiving, that employee's stock is high. If the evaluation is harsh, the employee knows his or her time in the organization is short. This cannot exist in quality assurance. A breech of standards is just that, and the evaluation is the same for all errors regardless of who is involved.

F. Standards are not published annually and distributed. Employees need their standards in hand, and those standards should be refined and republished each year. This maintains emphasis and exhibits commitment on the part of management.

6. TURNOVER AMONG DEPARTMENT HEADS AND SUPERVISORS INCREASES ONCE THE QUALITY ASSURANCE PROGRAM IS UNDERWAY.

This is not at all uncommon! For some management folks, their job is very nice indeed. They have learned how to avoid the mines and crossfires that exist in virtually every organization. They become almost like chameleons, able to change color and shape depending upon the situation. This was described to me once by a corporate executive in discussing the behavior of another long-time employee of questionable competence as an example of "the water fountain syndrome." When things got sticky, the questionable employee simply "turned into a water fountain" for the duration of the crisis, reemerging when things settled down. Such employees are very talented at becoming invisible. Quality assurance, with its emphasis on real performance, strikes fear in their hearts and, often, they simply move on rather than face the hassle of having to open themselves and their performances to objective evaluation. Better that they go—they have not been big contributors anyway. And, as a postscript, most production employees see this situation very clearly and will applaud the fact that the nonperformer has finally been discovered.

7. ENTHUSIASM IS NOT BUILDING FOR THE PROGRAM.

Considerable effort has been expended but the acceptance level is just not filled with energy.

A. Chances are the opinion leader process has not been utilized properly. Opinion leaders are the eyes and ears of the organization and must be taken seriously. They are not ever to be manipulated, but rather, recognized and used effectively not only to diffuse correct information but also to analyze feedback. Opinion leaders are not spies or tools of management. They are persons who others respect and from whom others seek advice. Not to recognize them and their role in the organization is pure ignorance on the part of management. Check with them individually or call a group meeting. Discuss the objectives of quality assurance and solicit their input. Then listen! A management that believes it alone has all the answers often fails to understand the questions! Quality assurance is, in the final analysis, an employee program—all employees at all levels. Let the employees speak for themselves!

B. Remember that laggards exist in every organization. Some people just never get with any program. Over time, they will identify themselves and eventually they will need to be replaced because they will tend to retard total quality/ excellence.

C. Reward and recognition is not present. We all need to feel wanted as a viable part of the organization to which we belong. Be as quick to recognize and reward as you are to criticize.

8. THE PROGRAM IS TAKING TOO LONG TO PRODUCE RESULTS.

A manager once asked me to install a quality assurance program and said he wanted it in three weeks! He obviously did not understand what he wanted. Unfortunately I could not convince him.

A. Quality assurance is an ongoing process. It will move at different speeds in different environments. The issue is not total, big success but rather continuous, small success. We are modifying behavior, and it doesn't happen quickly when others demand rapid change from us, nor will it happen when we demand rapid change from our employees. Standards are never fully written. They will be candidates for revision, usually higher, before they will be entirely written. Two years for a mid- to large-size hotel is not too long for standards to be written, communicated, trained for, and implemented for every task. Victory belongs not necessarily to the most swift but to those who persevere. On the flip side of the coin, progress begins with the first written and implemented standards. The number of standards in effect can be easily measured and plotted. Using eight tasks per job title and four good standards per task is not a bad quality assurance goal. In a 200-room commercial hotel this would be:

200 rooms × .33 job titles/room × 8 tasks/job title × 4 standards/task = 2112 standards

Over a 2-year period, allowing 8 weeks for the "meshing" process, we are looking at implementing 22 meaningful standards per week.

Now the conclusions are the following:

1. 2112 effective standards in place and conformed to consistently would certainly result in excellence.
2. 22 standards per week is a very ambitious goal.
3. It's worth it, so . . . be patient, do it right!

B. The effectiveness of quality assurance comes from word of mouth, and that takes time. Results are not always immediate, but when they come they are solid. I once had a dedicated salesman who quit after one year because he "couldn't see results." His successor earned more than $100,000 in sales commissions less than two years later, based largely on the work of salesman #1. Be patient!

9. **KEY PLAYERS ARE PROMOTED, REASSIGNED, OR LEAVE FOR BETTER JOBS.**

This is not only a serious problem, it is compounded by the fact that employees experienced in quality assurance are in greater demand. Thus, the more effective the program, the more pressure on key employees to move up or leave. One consolation: with an effective quality assurance program in place a replacement moves into a well-defined environment, thus minimizing the impact of the change. The fact that a key employee moves does not detract from the fact that proper standards transcend individuals. If management turnover is a problem, quality assurance is an absolute requirement. Not only will the environment tend to keep key people happier, but, should they leave, the replacement process will cause a minimum of change.

A. Standards must reflect the goals of the organization, not of individuals. Managers who become "indispensable" are costly employees indeed. Not only must you pay dearly to keep them, but, when they leave, their standards tend to go with them. Considerable time and effort is expended in finding and settling the replacement. Where organizational standards prevail, managers do what they are employed to do, *manage*. If and when they leave, the standards remain. Replacing them is greatly facilitated.

B. Standards make leaving possible! I have always operated on the theory that the most important person in the organization is the #2 person because that frees up #1 to manage more effectively and to be promoted as opportunities are presented. A great standard for every manager, therefore, is "to train and develop a competent assistant fully capable of carrying on effectively in the absence of the one to whom the assistant reports."

10. **THE UNION RESISTS THE QUALITY ASSURANCE PROGRAM AT EVERY OPPORTUNITY.**

Every standard is challenged, and employees are instructed to resist and withhold cooperation. In effect, the quality assurance program becomes a battle of wills, with no winners, only losers, and they are: first, the customers and second, the bottom line of the property.

A. There is a failure in communication between management and union leaders. If union resistance is encountered the problem rests squarely on improper communication. The prime announced objective of every union is fair and equitable treatment for every employee coupled with fair compensation for acceptable performance.

To be sure, there will be questions of what is "fair"; however, programs that work to establish precisely the tasks and performance levels of every employee are not programs that unions reject if they understand them and if they feel they are involved with the process. In fact, the modern trend in union-management relationships is for unions to insist that management have an effective quality assurance program. American labor has been taking a rather sound beating lately in questions of quality assurance. American labor is being blamed for what is essentially an American management problem. A program that improves quality assurance levels, creates better communication or expectations in both directions, improves profitability, reduces grievances, and results in fair evaluations of performance is certainly not a program that unions can reasonably oppose. At the start of the program, even before the committee has been chosen, call in the union leaders and explain the objective and process of quality assurance. Quality assurance is a management program; unions do not have a vote as to whether the program is implemented, but they do have a right to understand it, and most certainly we want their cooperation. *Do not be talked into including supervisors, production-level employees, shop stewards, or union leaders on the committee.* Explain carefully, but decisively, that quality assurance starts at the top. Once the program is fully conceived, then, and only then, will it be taken to the supervisory and production levels. And don't be quick to establish quality circles. They will come in due time.

B. Union resistance is unrelated to the quality assurance program. It is possible that union resentment in other areas is causing resistance in the area of quality assurance. After years of tooth and nail fighting between union and management, it is quite conceivable that the unions would resist virtually any new program introduced by management. This fact should be ascertained early on. It will not be easy to undo years of animosity, but, if any program can do it, it will be quality assurance. The confrontation word is "productivity." The tendency will be for labor to view the program as another attempt by management to increase productivity without increasing wages. A second confrontation word is "efficiency." For labor, this means layoff. If quality decreases errors, it also decreases manhours and that means layoff. This is not true. Concurrent with reducing manhours, quality increases sales, which, in turn, increases manhours. Proper quality assurance won't reduce staff. It will only ease tensions, increase sales and average rates, and result in greater financial health that benefits everyone. When we were kids, it was fun to play with magnets. Align positive poles in opposite directions and the magnets repel each other. Aligned in the same direction they attract, and the overall force is increased. Quality assurance aligns the positive forces of both management and union. Work to make it so!

11. **THE QUALITY ASSURANCE PROGRAM BEGINS STRONG BUT SOFTENS AFTER ONE OR TWO YEARS.**

We sometimes become complacent with our success, expecting it to continue ad infinitum. The causes for reduced effectiveness can be as follows:

A. A change in commitment. A new manager takes over without the same commitment as that of his/her predecessor. Sometimes changes in emphasis result from the desire of the new person to change what has been done for change's sake. Hopefully this is not the case. More probably it is a case of different style or priorities. Generally management changes occur in properties belonging to chains or where there is off-premises ownership. If the program has been strong, ownership will want it to continue, and, in fact, quality assurance will be a policy requirement of the ownership. If changes begin with the new manager, it is important to establish a policy quickly regarding quality. Management should be forewarned; employees used to working within a sound quality assurance program won't be happy without it!

B. Standards are not upgraded and republished annually. This must be done, for the following two reasons:

1. Employees should have the latest set of standards in their possession.

2. Quality emphasis will be recommunicated to every employee and, because of the annual attention, the program will maintain its energy.

C. Conditions have changed, but standards have not kept pace.

1. Perhaps competition or the economy has caused more emphasis to be placed on bottom-line cost reduction, thus detracting the focus from quality.

2. The property has changed its orientation from, for example, a budget, non-food operation to a mid-priced, full-service operation, and the quality program has been put on hold for the time being.

In both cases, the quality assurance program becomes even more required. As standards are affected by external sources, it is crucial to soften the impact of change by surrounding employees at all levels with a solid structure of standards. To do otherwise is to compound the anxiety that comes from change.

D. Assumption by management that once quality habits are established, they will remain and thus the cost to maintain quality can be reallocated. There is no more successful fast-food operation than McDonalds, and few companies invest as much in continuous advertising. Why? Because McDonalds knows that staying at the top is often more difficult than getting there. The same applies to quality assurance. Having achieved quality/excellence, emphasis must be continued if quality assurance is to be maintained.

17

Short and Sweet

General Principles for Quality/Excellence

MYTH #1

QUALITY ASSURANCE CAN ONLY BE DONE EFFECTIVELY BY PROPERTIES WITH A LARGE STAFF AND A TRAINING DEPARTMENT.

Quality is an individual attitude and thus applies equally to organizations of all sizes.

MYTH #2

QUALITY IS IN THE EYES OF THE BEHOLDER AND MUCH TOO NEBULOUS TO LEND ITSELF TO A PRECISE DEFINITION.

To be valid, quality must be measured; to be measured, quality must have a valid working definition.

MYTH #3

WHEN YOU HAVE ACHIEVED QUALITY, YOU HAVE ASCENDED TO THE TOP OF YOUR CHOSEN PROFESSION.

Quality is a function of conformance to standards. Standards may be good or bad—the difference is a function of ethics.

242

MYTH #4

PROGRAMS ARE ALL RIGHT, BUT QUALITY WILL REALLY ONLY START WHEN THE GENERAL MANAGER DEMANDS IT.

Management by dictate will produce results in the short run, but effective quality is a long-range process.

MYTH #5

THE ONLY ROLE OF THE QUALITY ASSURANCE COMMITTEE IS TO SOLVE PROBLEMS THAT ARE PRESENTED TO IT.

The true essence of quality is not "solving" problems but preventing them.

MYTH #6

GROUPS ARE INEFFECTIVE VEHICLES FOR ACHIEVING ORGA-NIZATIONAL OBJECTIVES.

Group decisions are always better than individual decisions *if* the group has true consensus.

MYTH #7

IT IS IMPOSSIBLE TO CALCULATE THE COST OF AN ERROR IN HOSPITALITY; THE INDUSTRY IS TOO LABOR-INTENSIVE AND ERRORS ARE TOO COMPLICATED TO BE ANALYZED.

Hospitality is a very subjective process. So too is the process of costing hospitality errors. Thus, a new process is required!

MYTH #8

QUALITY OCCURS WHEN THE GUESTS, OUR CUSTOMERS, COMPLETE THEIR INTERACTIONS WITH US WITHOUT ERROR HAVING OCCURRED.

Concentrating completely on customer-based quality without due attention to the process can be unduly expensive.

MYTH #9

IN THE SERVICE INDUSTRIES, QUALITY ASSURANCE IS SIMPLY A MATTER OF HAVING EMPLOYEES FOLLOW THE RULES SET DOWN BY MANAGEMENT.

Forced adoption is the fastest way to gain compliance with an idea. It is also the fastest route to discontinuance.

MYTH #10

THE HOSPITALITY INDUSTRY IS AN ART, NOT A SCIENCE, AND AS SUCH, THE MOST IMPORTANT FACTOR IN SUCCESS IS MANAGERIAL INTUITION.

The more management knows how things really are, the better the decisions will be. Gathering and disseminating information is largely a science.

MYTH #11

QUALITY ASSURANCE BEGINS WHEN MEANINGFUL STANDARDS HAVE BEEN CREATED FOR ALL AREAS OF THE OPERATION.

Excellence is not achieved by writing standards. It is achieved by implementing them effectively at every level.

MYTH #12

STANDARDS ONLY APPLY TO PRODUCTION-LEVEL EMPLOYEES.

Excellence is a top down continuing process, and thus standards apply to every level.

MYTH #13

IMPLEMENTING QUALITY ASSURANCE IS AS SIMPLE AS LET-
TING EVERY EMPLOYEE KNOW THAT MANAGEMENT IS COM-
MITTED, CHOOSING A DIRECTOR AND A COMMITTEE, AND
REVISING STANDARDS.

Likewise, baking a cake is simply flour, sugar, eggs, milk, flavoring,
temperature, and time. Success, however, is a function of technique.

MYTH #14

ONCE A PROGRAM IS IMPLEMENTED, IT, LIKE EVERY OTHER
QUALITY ASSURANCE PROGRAM, BASICALLY RUNS ITSELF.

A quality assurance program with a personality of its own will be
better received and far more effective.

MYTH #15

FULL-TIME TRAINING ONLY WORKS FOR BIG HOTELS, WITH
TRAINING DEPARTMENTS AND BIG BUDGETS.

Training is everybody's responsibility. Even the newest employee
who is not trained will, by example, train others—to perform improperly!

MYTH #16

A QUALITY ASSURANCE PROGRAM IS JUST LIKE A NEW SHIP;
IF THE DESIGN IS RIGHT, THE WORKMANSHIP PROPER, AND
EVERYTHING READY AT LAUNCH TIME, THE ENTIRE PRO-
GRAM WILL BE A SUCCESS.

Yes, providing the tide is right, the wind is right, and there are no
obstacles, submerged or otherwise!

THREE REASONS FOR ERRORS

1. Employees have not been trained to know what standards are expected of them.
2. Employees have been trained, but they have not been given the proper tools to meet the standards.
3. Employees have been properly trained and equipped, but they just don't give a darn because no one seems to give a darn about them.

ETHICS/MORALITY IS "KNOWING WHAT WE OUGHT TO DO, AND HAVING THE WILL TO DO IT."

Three possible conditions spring from this definition, as follows:

1. We do not know what we ought to do, and thus we do not (cannot) do it (education is required).
2. We know what we ought to do but we do not do it (a greater will is required).
3. We know what we ought to do and we do it! (excellence results).

FIVE TESTS FOR ETHICS AND MORALITY

1. Is the standard fair?
2. Is the standard legal?
3. Does the standard hurt anyone?
4. Have we been honest with those affected by the standard?
5. Can I personally live with a clear conscience with the standard or action taken?

SEVEN WAYS TO RATIONALIZE UNETHICAL BEHAVIOR

1. It's not really "very wrong."
2. We're in business to make a profit, and that's the bottom line.

3. It really doesn't hurt anyone.
4. If I don't do it, I will suffer or lose my job.
5. Everybody else is doing it, so I will too.
6. If I don't do it, I'll have far greater problems than if I do!
7. Who will ever know?

CONCLUSIONS OF A NATIONAL SURVEY OF ETHICS AND MORALITY IN HOSPITALITY*

1. *Hoteliers believe themselves to be highly ethical.*

   Hoteliers were asked to rate 18 industries, including news media, retail clothiers, funeral directors, government officials, investment counselors, etc. in terms of "being ethical," and hoteliers rated the top four as (1) hotel industry, (2) medical profession, (3) motel industry, and (4) restaurant industry.
2. Respondents believed the following principles:
   - A greater knowledge of ethics is highly desirable.
   - Ethics can be taught.
   - The application of ethics improves profitability.
   - Teaching schools are doing only a fair-to-inadequate job of teaching ethics.
3. There is ambivalence between what is a "business decision" and what is an "ethical/moral decision."
4. Ethical decisions are made most often *after* a situation arises and *if* the situation poses a potential problem or threat to the establishment.
5. The foundation for ethical/moral judgment is believed by hoteliers to come mainly from parents and not from school, church, work, self, or other sources to any great extent.

INTERPERSONAL ETHICS

Interpersonal ethics fall into the following four categories:

1. Hierarchical—up and down the organizational chart.
2. Promotional—how we project our image.
3. Transactional—between employee and guest.

---

*Hall, Stephen, S. J. "Ethics and Morality in Hospitality—An Original Survey." Master's thesis, Harvard Divinity School, 1988.

4. Contractual—between the organization and non-guest out-siders, in written or informal form.

CHARACTERISTICS OF A SUCCESSFUL QUALITY ASSURANCE DIRECTOR

1. Someone who wants the position and the responsibility.
2. Someone who is able to devote at least one day per week to quality assurance alone.
3. Someone who has the respect of his or her peers.
4. Someone who is upwardly mobile.
5. Someone who is politically astute.
6. Someone with administrative skills.

CHARACTERISTICS OF A SUCCESSFUL QUALITY ASSURANCE COMMITTEE MEMBER

1. Should be either a department head or an assistant depart-ment head.
2. Should be willing and have time.
3. Can accept constructive criticism and productive change.
4. Has diverse skills.

POINTS TO BE COVERED IN A PROPER QUALITY ASSURANCE POLICY STATEMENT

1. Complete standards in writing at every level.
2. Total training for all in the implementation of standards.
3. Total commitment to measuring performance.
4. Commitment of time and money to the QA program.
5. Total support for the QAD and the committee.

THREE GROUPS WHOSE SUPPORT IS ESSENTIAL BEFORE STARTING A QUALITY ASSURANCE PROGRAM

1. Executive committee
2. Department heads
3. Union(s)

THREE AREAS TO BE COVERED IN QUALITY ASSURANCE COMMITTEE MEETING MINUTES

1. Items of information
2. Items of action
3. Items of decision

NINE ACTIVITIES TO BE PERFORMED DURING THE MESHING STAGE OF IMPLEMENTATION

1. Discuss in general the concept of quality, the basic definitions, the committee process re: times, schedules, agendas, minutes, overall philosophy, etc.
2. Perform a needs analysis on quality.
3. Discuss and try to identify the top 10 areas in the property in which specific improvement could be made.
4. Using the cost of error process, cost out together three or four of the top 10 errors and then ask each member to cost out one of the remaining errors individually. Discuss each cost of error calculation.
5. As much as possible, collect and review whatever is available as existing standards.
6. Review existing orientation programs.
7. Collect all job titles and organize in outline form.
8. Select one job title that the committee believes will make the greatest progress in standards.
   - Call in the relevant department head and someone with that job title.
   - Discuss that particular job title.
   - With the department head and job title representative, identify the job tasks for that job title.
   - With the department head and job title representative, write standards for the most crucial tasks within the job title.
9. Invite the general manager to a meeting and review progress on the above in order to do the following:
   - Demonstrate the director of the committee.
   - Illustrate the value of the process.
   - Solicit the approval of the general manager for the process.

POINTS TO BE COVERED
IN THE MANAGER'S INITIAL MEETING
WITH THE QUALITY ASSURANCE COMMITTEE

1. I (the GM) believe in quality and give total support to the committee—time, people, money, and power of office. (Presenting the quality assurance policy of the property at this point is a real plus!)
2. I (the GM) have total faith in ——————, the QA director, and in the committee, and the QAD has access to me whenever needed.
3. I (the GM) am sincerely appreciative of the willingness of the committee members to take on the quality responsibility.

COROLLARIES UNDERLYING THE WORK OF
THE QUALITY ASSURANCE COMMITTEE

1. Quality Assurance Committees need time to develop into a team.
2. Quality Assurance Committees need to operate on the basis of total consensus decision making.
3. The quality assurance director's role is that of team building and not of group directing.
4. Forced adoption is to be avoided at all cost.
5. Feedback is a crucial element in all communication.
6. Relevant employee input is essential throughout the quality assurance decision-making process.
7. The fastest way to achieve meaningful excellence is to establish a slow, steady, thorough pace and be diligent in its execution.

COROLLARIES THAT BUILD TEAMS

The effectiveness of a group cannot be one-dimensional. Functionality depends upon productivity, satisfaction, and development.

A crucial emergent factor in any group is the degree to which members turn out to like each other and the group.

TEN COROLLARIES THAT AFFECT GROUP PERFORMANCE

1. The greater the interaction among people, the greater the likelihood of developing positive feelings for one another.
2. The greater the positive feelings among people, the more frequently they will interact.
3. The greater the interaction required by the job (task), the more likely that social relationships and behavior will develop along with the task relationship and behavior.
4. The more cohesive the group, the more eager individuals will be for membership and, thus, the more likely they will be to conform to the group norms.
5. The more cohesive the group, the more influence it has on its members.
6. The less certain and clear a group's norms and standards are, the less control it will have over its members.
7. Group cohesion will be increased by acceptance of a superordinate goal subscribed to by most members.
8. Group cohesion will be increased by the perceived existence of a common enemy.
9. Group cohesion will be increased when there are low numbers of external required interactions.
10. The greater the cohesion of the group, the higher the productivity will be if the group supports the organization's goals, and the lower the productivity will be if the group resents the organization's goals.

COROLLARIES THAT AFFECT MEMBERS WITHIN THE GROUP

1. Members who contribute most to task accomplishment are accorded the most respect of the group, whereas members who contribute most to social accomplishment (developing of relationships) are accorded the most liking in the group.

2. The higher the background of external status, the higher the emergent internal status of a group member. Lower status members defer to higher status members, allowing higher status members to initiate interactions, make statements without being challenged, and administer informal rewards and punishments. Higher status members will usually "talk for the group" in public situations, make more contact with outsiders, and usually have the widest number of connections with the group. The lower one ranks in a group, the more one defers to others.

3. The more one individual group member fails to conform to the group norms, the more frequently negative sentiments will be expressed towards him or her. The less a member conforms to a group's norms, the greater will be the interaction directed at him/her for some time. Should the interaction fail to bring the member into conformity with the norms, interaction will sharply decrease. The greater a member conforms to the group's norms, the greater the group's liking for the member.

4. The member(s) who conform most closely to a group's norms have the highest probability of emerging as informal leaders of the group. Informal group leaders may occasionally violate norms without punishment, provided that they have earned their leadership by general conformity to the group's norms.

FIVE NEGATIVE ROLES THAT CAN IMPACT ON THE QUALITY ASSURANCE COMMITTEE

1. The *dominator* tries to run the show, asserting real or alleged authority, demanding attention, interrupting others, making arbitrary decisions, and insisting upon having the last word. "Now I've had some experience at this sort of thing, and let me tell you what to do . . ."

2. The *blocker* is often a frustrated dominator. When he finds his authority is not conceded, or when the majority is moving in another direction, he becomes stubborn and resists the group on every count. "That idea will never work; you might just as well throw it out . . ."

3. The *cynic* sometimes succeeds the blocker. Thwarted in his isolated position, he scoffs at the group process, deliberately provokes conflict, or becomes painfully nonchalant. "It's obvious that you people will never agree; let's call it quits."
4. The *security seeker* may want sympathy, or just personal recognition. In one case he becomes self-deprecatory about his own plight, in the other, he continually calls attention to his own apparently unique experiences and accomplishments. "I had worse than that happen to me once . . . and I wish you'd tell me what I should have done."
5. The *lobbyist* is continually plugging his own pet theories, or pleading the special interests of other groups to which he may belong, although he is seldom willing to register as a lobbyist. "Now you understand this makes no difference to me, but don't you think we're being unfair to . . . ?"

FIVE CAUSES OF BURNOUT

1. The boss who is never satisfied.
2. The boss who never gives recognition.
3. The boss who does not give clear directions.
4. The boss who demands more than can be accomplished.
5. Stress and fatigue.

THREE TYPES OF COSTS
THAT RESULT FROM ERROR

1. *Hard costs*—money that must be expensed at the time of the error and as a direct result of it. Examples would be amenities, rebates, transportation (as in the case of transporting a "walked" guest to another hotel), letters written, phone charges, and such costs as replacing a guest's shirt or jacket lost in the cleaning process.

2. *Soft costs*—costs relating to events required as a result of an error in lieu of the normal manner in which the money is spent. For example, we pay a maid to make up rooms, but when the maid is spending 15 percent of her time correcting errors, then her productivity is decreased by 15 percent, and that is a soft cost of error. The

same applies to the front desk personnel, bellmen, waitresses, assistant managers, and others. There's a saying in quality, "Why is there always enough time to do things over but never enough time to do things right the first time?"

3. *Opportunity costs*—future sales lost as a direct result of an error. For example, statistics developed from a nationwide study by the author in 1985, in conjunction with AH&MA and Citicorp/Diners Club, indicate that some 20 percent of frequent male and female travelers "float," that is, change lodging accommodations because of errors encountered. Whenever a guest does not return because of an error, it is an opportunity cost.

ELEVEN STEPS OF THE COST OF ERROR CALCULATION

1. Define the error.
2. Determine the consequences.
3. Establish a cost for each consequence.
4. Establish the frequency (probability) of consequence per error.
5. Calculate the expected cost for each consequence. Post the expected cost in the appropriate column.
6. Total the expected consequence costs by category.
7. Calculate total possible chances for error to occur/year.
8. Estimate frequency (probability) of error occurring/year.
9. Calculate number of times error occurs per year.
10. Calculate error cost per year by categories.
11. Calculate total cost of error per year.

FOUR POINTS TO REMEMBER IN A "CUSTOMER DRIVEN" PHILOSOPHY

1. Quality assurance is *not* an event, it is a process requiring the active, willing, proficient participation of internal human resources, as well as of external suppliers. Focusing totally on the "end" and ignoring the "means" ignores the process and without proper process, successful conclusions are impossible.

2. Providing a perfect end product can often mean accepting considerable waste if focus is placed too strongly on final inspection and interim inspection is ignored.
3. Many elements of the service equation have no direct relationship to the customer. For example, proper engineering management in the production of heat and hot water can reduce costs 10–20%. If we focus totally on delivering hot water and not at all on the efficient transfer of heat in our boiler, guests will be happy, but we will be wasting financial resources.
4. Many elements of hospitality service are areas in which gratuities play a major role in employee compensation. Ethically, every guest deserves the same treatment whether he/she is a large tipper or a non-tipper. If the philosophy of end-user satisfaction is overstated, it could become the *raison d'être* for preferential treatment.

SIX ELEMENTS IN A PROPER COMMUNICATION PROCESS

Sender—the originator of the communications.

Channel—the means by which the communications are transmitted.

Receiver—the person or persons who receive the communications.

Message—what is communicated. It may or may not be the same for the sender and the receiver.

Feedback—the sender's perception of the effectiveness of the transmission.

Environment—the combination of elements that establish the attitude of the sender. The receiver is also affected by the combination of elements that surround him or her. The environments of sender and receiver are often different and are, at times, even in conflict.

THREE ELEMENTS THAT ARE PRESENT
IN THE SENDER AND RECEIVER

Decoding—the process of perceiving the message in the case of the receiver or the feedback in the case of the sender.

Sorting and selecting—the act of analyzing the output of the decoding process.

Encoding—the process of structuring the message in the case of the sender and the feedback in the case of the receiver.

TWO MAIN TYPES
OF COMMUNICATIONS

One-way communications are those in which there is no instant feedback capability.

Two-way communications are those that generally take more time but are significantly more effective. In this form, the receivers have a chance to provide instant feedback, allowing the sender to make changes in subsequent messages to achieve total understanding.

TWO MAIN TYPES
OF COMMUNICATIONAL INTERACTION

Interpersonal communications—those occurring between two people (dyadic), or between a person and a small group, or between a small group and another small group. The interpersonal form permits the most effective feedback of all forms.

A-personal communications—those occurring between one person and a large group of receivers, such as in a speech or between one person and a mass audience as in a media approach such as newspaper or television. The speech will allow feedback, albeit difficult at times, but the use of media, as already discussed, makes feedback very difficult.

SIX POSTULATES OF COMMUNICATIONS

1. Communication is not random.
2. Communication occurs everywhere, intentionally or unintentionally.
3. Communication occurs on different levels.
4. Communication is continuous.
5. Communication is a transactional process.
6. Communication is the sharing of meaning.

THREE PERCEPTIONS THAT AFFECT COMMUNICATIONS

1. How you perceive your world.
2. How you perceive yourself.
3. How your audience perceives you.

SIX TRAITS OF A MODERN SOCIAL SYSTEM

1. A positive attitude towards change.
2. A well-developed technology with a complex division of labor.
3. A high value on education.
4. Social relationships that are rational and businesslike rather than emotional and affective.
5. "Cosmopolitan" perspectives—that is, members of the system interacting easily and often with outsiders.
6. Empathy on the part of the systems' members that enables them to see themselves in roles quite different from their own.

TWO POINTS RELATING TO QUALITY ASSURANCE AND INNOVATION

1. Although most employees are familiar with the basic principles of QA, they perceive the formal implementation of a QA program as an innovation.

2. The degree to which we accept innovation depends largely on the type of social system to which we belong. If our QA program is to stand a reasonable chance of success, it is imperative that we pay careful attention to the principles and characteristics of these various systems.

FIVE ELEMENTS AFFECTING THE ADOPTION OF A NEW IDEA

1. *Relative advantage:* To what degree is the innovation perceived as being better than the idea it supersedes?
2. *Compatibility:* The innovation must be perceived as consistent with the participants' existing values, needs, and experience.
3. *Complexity:* The innovation must be seen to be relatively simple to understand and to put into practice.
4. *Triability:* Most of us reject innovations that cannot first be tried on a limited basis.
5. *Observability:* Are the results of an innovation visible and readily interpreted?

FIVE STAGES IN THE ADOPTION PROCESS

1. *Awareness:* The individual learns of the existence of a new idea but lacks information about it.
2. *Interest:* The individual develops interest in the innovation and seeks additional information about it.
3. *Evaluation:* The individual makes mental application of the new idea to his present and anticipated future situation and decides whether or not to try it.
4. *Trial:* The individual actually applies the new idea on a small scale in order to determine its utility in his/her own situation.
5. *Adoption:* The individual uses the new idea continuously on a full scale.
   - *Continuance*—the individual continues to adopt the new idea over time.

• *Discontinuance*—the individual sees his or her expectation not met and discontinues the new idea.

TEN TOP ERRORS USED
IN THE CONSUMER PERCEPTION STUDY

1. Unsatisfactory food service
2. Tired facility—poor maintenance
3. Slow check-in, check-out
4. Employees not friendly
5. Room not ready upon arrival
6. Poor overall service
7. Requested room type not available
8. Morning wake-up call not made
9. No record of reservation
10. Over-booked—guest walked

FOUR GENERAL QUALITIES
OF OPINION LEADERS

1. Opinion leaders have more exposure to mass media than do their followers.
2. Opinion leaders are more accessible than are their followers.
3. Opinion leaders seem to have a higher social status than those of their peers.
4. Opinion leaders are more innovative than are their followers.

FIVE GROUPS IDENTIFIED
IN THE ADOPTION PROCESS

1. *Innovators*—2.5% of total—*venturesome.*
2. *Early adopters*—13.5% of total—*respect role.*
3. *Early majority*—34% of total—*deliberate.*
4. *Late majority*—34% of total—*skeptical.*
5. *Laggards*—16% of total—*traditional.*

THREE REASONS FOR "ON-LINE" STANDARDS

1. The system of standards can be built from a base of need.
2. Current and relevant standards can be placed in the hands of the users, where they belong!
3. Decisions are easily executed.

THREE MISCONCEPTIONS OF STANDARDS

1. Standards are only valid in certain areas of the hotel operation.
2. Standards are most effective for large groups of employees.
3. Standards are less valid as education increases.

THREE MAIN PHASES OF IMPLEMENTING A QUALITY ASSURANCE PROGRAM

1. Meshing
2. Diffusing
3. Evaluating

FIFTEEN SOURCES OF INFORMATION ON THE NEED FOR QUALITY ASSURANCE

1. Guest comments
2. Grievances filed
3. Turnover
4. Absenteeism
5. Breakage
6. Insurance claims
7. Repair and maintenance costs
8. "No shows"
9. Amenities
10. Cancellations
11. Waste
12. Inventory

13. Conversions
14. "Walks"
15. Capital projects

NINE ELEMENTS IN THE ERROR I.D. PROCESS

1. Creating a logo for the process.
2. Printing several hundred cards, $3'' \times 5''$ or perhaps slightly larger, with the simple explanation that they are to be used to identify a problem with which the employee must contend. The following information should be on the card:
   - Employee's name.
   - Employee's job title.
   - Location of the problem.
   - The problem.
3. Providing a place for depositing the cards.
4. Thoroughly communicating the process to all department heads and supervisors and establishing procedures wherein the following occurs:
   - All I.D. inputs go to the Quality Assurance Committee without fail, every time.
   - No department head or supervisor will, at any time, place any negative pressure on any employee for any problem written on the card.
   - Managers and supervisors must understand that the purpose of the error I.D. program transcends the nature of individual problems and is part of a larger agenda, that of building an attitude of participation in all employees.
5. Acting on all cards immediately. As I.D. cards are received by the Quality Assurance Committee, they are assigned a number and logged on a tracking form containing the following information:
   - Name of contributor.
   - Department and position of contributor.
   - Date of receipt of problem.
   - Nature of problem.
   - Person to whom assigned for follow-up, including date of follow-up and by what means.

- Corrective action taken, including date and method of communicating corrective action.
6. Communicating with the originator of the error—crucial to the error I.D. system.
7. Analyzing errors received, which fall into three basic categories.
   - Maintenance errors
   - Process errors
   - Nuisance errors
8. Not closing the file or tracking sheet on any error until the error has been resolved or considered thoroughly. If it should develop that the error cannot or should not be resolved, in that case, it is not considered an error.
9. Finally, maintaining the ultimate object of the error I.D. process, which is to put in place standards that prevent a recurrence.

FOUR ACTIONS THAT CAN TAKE PLACE AROUND EVERY ERROR

1. Management corrects an error that it happens to find.
2. Guests find it and are dissatisfied.
3. No one discovers it, and it continues to be a problem.
4. Employees identify virtually all errors, and they are resolved such that the guest sees and enjoys only our best product and service.

THREE WAYS TO MEASURE CONFORMANCE TO STANDARDS

1. Class A standards lend themselves to finite, constant measurement. For example:
   - Guest complaints. Keep in mind, however, that only a small percent of dissatisfied guests bother to complain. They just don't return—and tell all their friends why!
   - No shows and walked guests.
   - Maintenance calls.

- Amenities given.
- Accident claims.
- Grievances filed.
- Rebates given.
- Skippers (those who leave without paying).

2. Class B standards may be easily measured, but they require a conscious act to do so. For example:
   - Long check-in, check-out lines.
   - Long waits to be seated in the food outlets.
   - Periodic guest room inspections (over and above the normal housekeeping controls).
   - Dining room service.
   - Cleanliness—back and front of the house.
   - Maintenance of equipment in the back of the house.

3. Class C standards are normally related to a guest-employee interaction out of public view and are extremely difficult to measure. For example:
   - The interaction between bellhop and guest en route to guest room.
   - The interaction between maid and guest.
   - The interaction between laundry and valet delivery person and guest.
   - The interaction between guest and engineer making room maintenance call.

FOURTEEN ELEMENTS
THAT AFFECT TURNOVER

1. Turnover rates among properties that used turnover and absenteeism reports in their daily operations rated 32% lower than those of properties where reports were not used.
2. Turnover rates among properties with a structure of interaction with production-level employees was 27% lower than those of properties with no interaction.
3. Properties in which managers spent a large amount of time interacting with employees had turnover rates 7% higher than had those who spent the average amount of time in employee interaction.

4. Properties with a system of standards had average turnover rates 19% lower than had those with no system of standards.

5. Properties with production-level interaction, standards, and turnover/absenteeism reports averaged turnover rates 57% lower than those of properties in which all three programs were nonexistent.

6. Properties with performance evaluation systems for employees at all levels had turnover rates 35% lower than had properties with no evaluation systems at all.

7. Thirty-six percent of all respondents claimed to have a quality assurance program in place. No attempt was made to qualify the elements or effectiveness of the alleged programs; however, properties that claimed to have a program had turnover rates 46% lower than those found in properties where no programs existed.

8. Respondents were asked to advise the acceptable level of conformance to standards they would tolerate in food and beverage, housekeeping, maintenance, and morning wake-up. Those respondents who would not accept a level less than 98% in all five categories had turnover rates 48% less than had those respondents who would accept less than 98% in all five categories.

9. Properties conducting ongoing training had turnover rates 45% lower than had properties doing no training.

10. Properties with orientation programs had turnover rates 41% lower than those of properties without orientation.

11. Properties with continuing education programs for employees had turnover rates 22% lower than had properties without continuing education programs.

12. Properties of managers who had a high index of civic involvement had turnover rates 33% lower than had properties where the manager did not have a high civic involvement.

13. Properties with guest comment card systems had turnover rates 23% lower than those of properties without guest comment card systems.

14. Respondents were asked to rate the value of their guest comment systems to their quality assurance programs. Properties in which the guest comment system was rated above

the average had turnover rates 26% higher than those of respondents who rated their comment system below the average of the group for value.

FIVE MAJOR CONSIDERATIONS
BEFORE BEGINNING TRAINING

1. What goal or goals do I want to achieve with this training?
2. Who is my audience?
3. What will motivate this audience most effectively?
4. Against what standard will I measure the results?
5. What are my space and equipment needs?

FIVE ACHIEVEMENTS
OF A PROPER TRAINING PLAN

1. The plan clarifies the training process in the mind of the trainer.
2. The plan organizes the effort, thus increasing effectiveness.
3. The plan guarantees that all subsequent training in that area will be to the same standards.
4. The plan assures that important elements of the training will not be overlooked.
5. The plan places emphasis on the training and less on the trainer.

A FORMAL TRAINING PLAN
CONSISTS OF TWO PARTS

1. Master plan
2. Segment detail

TEN PARTS OF A TRAINING MASTER PLAN

1. Designation (title) of the training
2. Statement of purpose
3. Person being trained

4. Person doing the training
5. Logistics
6. Training schedule
7. Special requirements
8. Cost of training
9. General segment outline
10. Gaining approval

EIGHT SEGMENTS OF A PROPER SEGMENT DETAIL TRAINING PLAN

1. Master designation
2. Segment number
3. Segment designation
4. Segment start time, end time, and elapsed time
5. Segment leader
6. Segment objective
7. Objective measurement
8. Special requirements

SAMPLE SEGMENT PLAN FOR A TWO-HOUR TRAINING SESSION FOR ENGINEERS ON HOW TO ANSWER A GUEST COMPLAINT

1. Welcome and outline of training to come.
2. Ice breaker.
3. How requests for maintenance are received.
4. Planning the service call.
5. Arriving at the guest room.
6. Coffee break.
7. Unusual situations and how to handle them.
8. Leaving the guest room.
9. Reporting on the project.
10. Question-and-answer period.
11. Summary.

THREE WAYS TO TEST THE EFFECTIVENESS OF A TRAINING SEGMENT

1. A short written quiz.
2. An informal, verbal quiz.
3. Calling on trainees to demonstrate.

FIVE STEPS IN SKILL TRAINING:

1. *Introduce the program and break the ice.* Tell the group what is to happen and help them to relax and interact.
2. *Prepare the trainees.* Facilitate the training by helping the trainees to internalize a valid reason or reasons why this training is necessary. Refer to the discussion of diffusion. Give trainees answers to one or more of the following five elements:
   • Relative advantage
   • Compatibility
   • Complexity
   • Trialability
   • Observability
3. *Tell, show, observe, correct.* Tell the trainees how to perform the skill you are teaching. Show them how to do it. Let each try the skill themselves. Correct their errors. Remember, we learn by our mistakes. "To err is human, to ridicule error is to fail as a trainer!" Try the two for one rule. Before you say something negative, say two things positive. It works!
4. *Reward.* Be quick to hand out rewards or compliments to all who participate.
5. *Summarize.*

FOUR STEPS IN IMPULSIVE-COMPULSIVE TRAINING

1. Prepare the trainee.
2. Skill—Tell, show, observe, correct, test (observe *skill*).

Knowledge—Tell and show, test (verbal or written).
Attitude—Mirror, discuss, suggest, test (role play or direct observation).
3. Reward and recognize.
4. Summarize.

Glossary

A-Personal communications Communications between one person and a large group of receivers (as in a speech) or between one person and a mass audience.

Adoption (of an innovation) A decision to make full use of a new idea as the best of courses of action available.

Amenities Items or acts in which the prime purpose is to bring pleasure to others. For example, a basket of soap, shampoo, bath salts, cologne, etc., in the guest bathroom is meant to bring added pleasure.

Awareness The point in the diffusion process at which the individual recognizes the idea being diffused.

Blocker A negative group role in which an individual becomes frustrated and resists group progress on every count.

Burnout A condition that develops when an individual becomes immobilized and unable to function properly, brought about primarily by a feeling of helplessness to improve his/her situation and secondarily by stress and fatigue.

Capital project A project, usually large in scope, that is depreciated rather than expensed. For example, a rooms renovation project.

Change agent A professional who influences innovation-decisions in a direction deemed desirable by a change agency.

Channel The process by which a sender communicates a message to a receiver. Channels can be mass media or interpersonal, written, oral, symbolic, nonverbal, and/or a combination of the above methods of communication.

Code The form in which the message in a communicational process is structured.

COE (cost of error) A process used to calculate the annual numerical cost of an error by identifying consequences and using probability to compute the expected frequency of each consequence and the error itself.

Compatibility The degree to which an innovation is perceived as consistent with the existing values, past experience, and needs of the receivers.

Complexity The degree to which an innovation is perceived as relatively difficult to understand and use.

Concierge A knowledgeable person, well versed in human relations, whose prime function is providing guest services such as information regarding all guest services, helping with schedules, reservations and tickets, special guest needs and/or problems, and, in general, representing the goodwill of the operation.

Consensus decisions A form of group approval in which all members favor and/or can accept without reservations the decision made. Consensus decisions require more analysis time than do majority decisions, but consensus decisions are generally better decisions.

Contractual ethics Used in the case of the needs analysis; "conversion" refers to the fact that a signed contract has resulted from a sales lead.

Conversions Factors, used in the case of the needs analysis, that cause a sales lead to become a signed contract.

Customer driven In extreme terms, giving the customer what he/she wants when he/she wants it. In more moderate terms, designing your product and service to fill the needs of your customer and making customer satisfaction the sole judge of the success of the process.

Cynic A negative group role in which the individual scoffs at the group process, deliberately provokes conflict, or becomes painfully nonchalant.

Decision The point in the diffusion process at which the individual decides to either accept or reject the idea being diffused.

Decode The receiver's perception of the message received in the communicational process.

Department heads Persons considered senior management within the organization, who are charged with the management of personnel, finances, and product within a specific area requiring both the interpretation and enforcement of policy.

Diffusion process The process by which an idea perceived as new is spread through a social system.

Diffusion stage The stage in the implementation of quality assurance in which the program is taken to the supervisory- and production-level employees. The diffusion stage usually begins at the sixth to eighth week and lasts as long as it takes to produce all relevant standards and disseminate the same.

Dominator A negative group role in which an individual asserts real or alleged authority and tries to "run the show" at the exclusion of others.

Early adopters Individuals who adopt an innovation early on in the process of diffusion. (Represented by minus one standard deviation to two standard deviations from the mean. *Early adopters* are approximately 13.5% of the total group and are characterized by the word "respectable.")

Early majority Individuals who adopt an innovation only after they see that the innovation is being adopted by those whom they consider to be opinion leaders. (Represented by the mean minus one standard deviation. Early majority are 34% of the total group and are characterized by the word "deliberate.")

Empowered Causing the latent energy in other people to be released by granting them relevant authority.

Error A standard not met.

Error identification The process by which employees at all levels are encouraged to submit errors and/or problems that are having a negative impact on the performances of their tasks.

Ethics Knowledge of what is right and the will to do it.

Evaluation   The point in the diffusion process at which the individual analyzes all of the relevant information collected on the idea being diffused.

Evaluation stage   The stage in the implementation of quality assurance when standards have been written once and disseminated to all employees and the processes of monitoring, measuring, reevaluating, rewriting, and redistributing take place. The *evaluation stage* begins long before the *diffusion stage* ends, and the *evaluation stage* remains in effect as long as the quality assurance program is in place.

Excellence   Quality plus ethics.

Expected value   The value of an event at full cost multiplied by the probability that the event will occur. If one in every ten passers-by gives an average of fifty cents to a street beggar, the probability of a donation is 10 percent, and the expected value is five cents.

Extended ego   The state in which individuals temporarily become what is desired of them by the social system or environment in which they find themselves. Upon returning to a normal environment, they generally do not retain what was.

Feedback   The sender's perception of the effectiveness of the communication transmission.

Floating guests   Guests who change loyalties (estimated at 20 percent) to hospitality entities because their expectations have not been met; i.e., errors are present in sufficient numbers to cause a discontinuance.

"Golden Rule"   "Do unto others as you would have others do unto you." In Christianity, the *Golden Rule* is found in Matthew 7:12 and Luke 6:31; however, close variations are found in virtually every major religion.

Group dynamics   The behavior exhibited by individuals when placed in a group environment.

Hard costs   Error costs that represent actual money expended as a result of an error. For example: a rebate issued.

Hierarchical ethics   Ethics involved with interpersonal relationships up and down the organizational chart.

Innovation   An idea perceived as new by a social system.

Innovators   Individuals who are first to adopt an innovation. (Represented by minus two standard deviations from the mean, innovators are 2.5% of the total group characterized by the word "venturesome.")

Interest   The point in the diffusion process at which the individual desires to seek more information on the idea being diffused.

Interpersonal communications   Communication between two people (dyadic), a person and a small group, or a small group and a small group.

Job title creep   The process wherein job titles proliferate within an organization without a meaningful or significant difference in job descriptions.

Laggards   Individuals who adopt an innovation last, if at all. (Represented by plus 1 to plus 3 standard deviations. Laggards are 16 percent of the total group and are characterized by the word "traditional.")

Late majority   Individuals who adopt an innovation when it has become obvious that the majority of the group is adopting it. (Represented by plus 1 standard deviation from the mean. Late majority are 34% of the total group and are characterized by the word "skeptical.")

Lobbyist   A negative group role in which an individual is continually plugging his/her own pet theories or pleading the special interests of other groups to which he/she belongs.

Majority decisions   Decisions made by a group in which approval results from a favorable vote of 51% or more of the group voting. Majority decisions are reached faster than are consensus decisions, but they are generally not as good either in substance or to implement.

Market level   The particular segment of consumer needs selected as the focus for dedicating the property's physical, financial, and human resources.

Mean   The mathematical average of a group of samples. (The *mean* of the numbers 1, 3, 6, 10, and 15 is 7.)

Median   The midpoint number in a sample of ordered numbers. (The *median* of the numbers 1, 3, 6, 10, and 15 is 6.)

Meshing stage   The initial phase of the implementation of quality assurance in which the prime objective is for the quality committee to come to know each other and develop the working relationship necessary for team building. It usually takes 6–8 weeks.

Message   Information initiated by the sender in a communicational process either intentionally or inadvertently.

Modern norm   The point at which a strong acceptance of a willingness to change prevails, characterized by an appreciation for technical and scientific methods, rationality, cosmopolitan ideas, and empathy.

Most Senior Executive (MSE)   A term used because titles have become so proliferated within the hospitality industry that "general manager" often does not define the top executive within the property.

Needs analysis   An evaluation process that creates or denies credibility to an intended action.

Norm   A rule or authoritative standard; model; type or pattern.

Observability   The degree to which the results of an innovation are visible to others.

One-way communication   A communicational process in which the receivers have no immediate opportunity to respond to the message. Television, radio, and the newspaper are examples.

Open-door policy   The process of making oneself accessible to those falling below on the reporting line. The policy is normally characterized by a professed willingness to objectively listen to negative comments, however strong, without retribution, and is viewed by most managers as a meaningful feedback process.

Opinion leader   An individual who is able to informally influence other individuals' attitudes or overt behavior in a desired way with relative frequency. In general, opinion leaders, relative to other members of the social system, are 1) more exposed to all forms of external communication, 2) more cosmopolitan, 3) have higher social status, and 4) are more innovative.

Opportunity costs Error costs that represent highly probable future losses of revenue. For example: money lost because a guest will not return due to an error such as "lost reservation."

Orientation program A program designed especially to familiarize either new employees with an existing process and environment, or existing employees with a new process or environment. In hospitality, there are generally two orientation programs, one for overall familiarization with the facility and a second to familiarize the employee with the department.

Parameters The finite values or limits set on a specific situation. A bank supervisor able to make loans up to $500, thus has a $500 parameter.

PLE Production-level employee.

Policies Set parameters established by senior management within which subordinates are expected to perform. *Policies* permit individuality to prevail at all levels as long as it remains within the limits established. Whereas *policies* are general by nature, the standards, rules, and regulations that fall within them are more rigid.

Probability The likelihood of the occurrence of any particular form of an event, estimated as the ratio of the number of ways in which that form might occur to the whole number of ways in which the event might occur in any form.

Production-level employees Employees whose function is to perform physical and/or mental tasks but who are not responsible for the supervision of others.

Promotional ethics Ethics relating to how the hospitality entity projects its image to the market and/or the public at large.

QAC Quality Assurance Committee.

QAD Quality assurance director.

Quality 100 percent conformance to standards.

Quality assurance The process by which all errors are eliminated.

Quality circles Groups of people, usually from the same work area, who meet regularly on a voluntary basis to identify, analyze, and solve quality and other problems in their area.

Receiver   The individual or agency that is the recipient of a communication.

Rejection   A decision by an individual not to adopt an idea being diffused. A rejection may result from a conscious denial of the idea, or from the fact that the idea has simply not been diffused well enough to cause its acceptance over the situation that it attempts to supersede, in which case the diffusion process may still be valid.

Relative advantage   The degree to which an innovation is perceived as being better than the idea it supersedes.

Security seeker   A negative group role in which an individual seeks sympathy and personal recognition by calling attention to himself/herself to the detriment of group progress.

Selective perception   Seeing, hearing, and/or feeling only what we want to see, hear, and feel.

Selective retention   Remembering only the parts of a communication that we want to remember.

Sender   The individual or agency that initiates a communication.

Social system   A collectivity of units that are functionally differentiated and engaged in joint problem solving with respect to a common goal.

Soft costs   Error costs that represent the reallocation of existing costs as a result of error. For example: lost time.

Sorting   The process of selecting and analyzing the perceived relevant elements of a received message that has been communicated.

Standard deviation   A standard calculation that indicates the dispersion of samples around the mean of all samples. The smaller the standard deviation, the greater the consensus of the group sampled. The larger the standard deviation, the less the consensus of the group sampled.

Standards   Required levels of performance.

Stress   A situation in which an individual is subjected to internal forces that, when excessive or present for prolonged periods, can cause burnout.

Supervisors   Individuals whose prime duty is to supervise others but who have little or no responsibility to change or interpret policy.

Traditional norm   The point at which a strong resistance to change prevails, characterized by a nontechnical or scientific mode of thinking, emotionalism, generally local ideas, and a lack of empathy.

Traditional/modern continuum   The finite path connecting the polar traditional norm with the polar modern norm. All individuals' thinking falls at some point along the path; the ability to adopt new ideas is indirectly related to the distance from the modern norm, i.e., the less an individual's distance from the modern norm, the greater the individual's willingness to adopt a new idea.

Training   The process by which a desired, predictable response or action is created in an individual over time.

Training master plan   The overall training plan for a specific area of training, indicating rationale, logistics, and segments to be covered. For example, training a waiter to serve a guest properly may involve six segments over a three-hour period.

Training segment detail   The finite point-by-point plan for each segment of a master training plan, showing, among other things, start time, elapsed time, measurement techniques, as well as the complete detail of material covered. For example, one segment of training a waiter how to properly serve a guest might be "writing the order properly," and it might require 20 minutes of a three-hour "Serving the Guests" training master plan, involving that and other segments.

Transactional ethics   Ethics involved in relationships between employee and customer within the hospitality environment.

Trial   The point in the diffusion process at which the individual gains personal experience with the idea being diffused, either actually as in test driving a car or vicariously as in imagining oneself staying at a resort known only through the brochure.

Trialability   The degree to which an innovation may be experimented with on a limited basis.

Two-way communication   Communication in which there is the opportunity for the receiver to give instant feedback. A conversation between two people or a speech in which the speaker (sender) can sense the response of the receivers by their actions are examples.

"Walked" guest   A guest who arrives with a confirmed reservation but must stay elsewhere because the facility has no rooms available.

"Water fountain syndrome"   The ability of certain employees, generally in management, to maintain a low profile during critical periods of stress within the organization.

"ZAP"   "Zone of acceptable performance." The level of quality attainment that is acceptable to hospitality management. Surveys indicate that management views 85–90 percent compliance as acceptable. In quality assurance, anything short of 100 percent is unacceptable.

Zero defects   Operating totally without error.

Bibliography

Cohen, Allan R., et al. *Effective Behavior in Organizations*. Homewood, IL: Richard D. Irwin, Inc., 1988.

Crosby, Philip B. *Quality is Free*. New York: McGraw-Hill, 1979.

Desatnick, Robert L. *Managing to Keep the Customer*. San Francisco: Jossey-Bass Publications, 1988.

Finnis, John. *The Fundamentals of Ethics*. Washington, DC: Georgetown University Press, 1983.

Freudberg, David. *The Corporate Conscience*. New York: American Management Association, 1986.

Keirsey, David, and Bates, Marilyn. *Please Understand Me*. Delmar, CA: Prometheus Nemesis Books, 1978.

Lash, Linda M. *The Complete Guide to Customer Service*. New York: Wiley, 1989.

Ludenan, Kate, Ph.d. *The Worth Ethic*. New York: Dutton, 1989.

Mathis, Robert L., and Jackson, John H. *Personnel—Human Resource Management*. New York: West Publishing Company, 1985.

Peters, Thomas, J., and Waterman, Robert H., Jr. *In Search of Excellence*. Newark, NJ: Harper & Row, 1982.

Rogers, Everett M. *Diffusion of Innovations* (3rd Ed). New York: Free Press, 1983.

Solomon, Robert C., and Hanson, Kristine R. *It's Good Business*. New York: Atheneum, 1985.

Townsend, Patrick L. with Gebhardt, Joan E. *Commit to Quality*. New York: Wiley, 1986.

Zemke, Ron, and Schaaf, Dick. *The Service Edge*. Markham, Ontario: Penguin Books Canada, Ltd., 1989.

Index